Tax
Options
and
Strategies
for
People
with
Disabilities

Tax
Options
and
Strategies
for
People
with
Disabilities

S t e v e n B. M e n d e l s o h n

Demos

Demos Publications, 386 Park Avenue South, Suite 201, New York, NY
10016

Printed in Canada

ISBN : 0-939957-36-1 (soft)
       0-939957-55-8 (hard)

Library of Congress Cataloging-in-Publication Data
Mendelsohn, Steven B.
    Tax options and strategies for people with disabilities / Steven
   B. Mendelsohn.
        p.   cm.
    Includes bibliographical references and index.
    ISBN 0-939957-36-1 (soft: $19.95).—ISBN 0-939957-55-8 (hard:
$34.95)
        1. Income tax—United States—Deductions—Expenses.
    2. Handicapped—Taxation—Law and legislation—United States.
   I. Title.
   KF6394.M46 1993
   343.7304'0240816—dc20
   [347.30340240816]   93-20021
                                                            CIP

Contents

Preface

As a lawyer and public policy analyst, I have been personally and professionally involved in the disability rights field for a dozen years, first as the director of an innovative job placement program, then as a proponent of the use of enhanced technology. In this capacity, I wrote a book on financing adaptive technology that contained a fairly brief chapter on the tax system. It outlined some of the federal income and state sales tax benefits available to people who purchased equipment needed in employment, education, and independent living. Since the main focus of the book was sources of third-party funding, however, taxes were only lightly covered.

Following its publication, I had the privilege of speaking to many groups around the country about technology funding issues. Repeatedly, before audiences of all kinds, I was amazed by how many questions I was asked about tax benefits that might be available. By degrees it became clear that many people with disabilities and their family members needed a great deal more information on how the tax system could be used to reduce the economic costs of living with a disability.

I initially assumed that the appropriate information was available, and that all I needed was a better list of reference materials to offer in response to these questions. Much to my amazement, such information was not readily available. Yes, there were countless books, videos, and seminars providing tax education to the general public. The IRS itself publishes information for taxpayers with disabilities. Other specialized sources of information are available for tax preparation assistance. But none seemed to meet the need as expressed in the hundreds of questions I had been asked. Another book was clearly necessary.

I have tried to organize the contents of the book in a way that will make it as useful as possible to both average taxpayers and tax professionals. The text is fully footnoted, so that interested taxpayers, accountants, or attorneys can look up the cases, rulings, and statutory provisions, chapter and verse. These notes will not be needed by readers whose main goal is to obtain general information applicable to his or her tax situation, but may be brought to the attention of their tax preparers.

The first chapters provide a detailed yet readable overview of the tax system and its terminology and a discussion of how the tax law defines "disabled." This is followed by four chapters that discuss major areas in which taxes and disability interact: medical care, education, employment and business, and a variety of special situations. State and local taxes are then considered both separately and as they interact with our federal taxes. The last chapter sets out a program for systematically restructuring provisions relating to disability in the Internal Revenue Code that would make tax law as it relates to disability more consistent and rational in its approach.

However imaginatively the material is organized, a book on the subject of taxes cannot avoid being a little dense. Adoption of a narrative style, along with occasional attempts at humor, represent the best strategy I could think of for dealing with that problem. I hope that you will find it more readable than you might expect from a book about taxes.

Throughout the book, I observe that people with disabilities must often know more than those they deal with in order to obtain needed goods and services. No one is as interested in your tax bottom line as you are, and even if you do not become an expert from reading this book, you should be able to learn enough to represent your own best interests in planning and paying your taxes.

At every point in this book, I try to demonstrate the connection between the income tax system and the lives of Americans with disabilities. At bottom, this relationship is no different from the connection between the tax system and the lives of all Americans - only the details differ.

For precisely this reason, it is important to offer a word of caution. Although we know that the tax system can influence the economic and social conditions of life, its manipulation is no panacea, for people with disabilities or for society as a whole. However enlightened our tax policy may be, there are many people and many situations for which tax policy holds no great promise or meaningful solutions. If this book were used to justify further curtailment of direct governmental expenditure programs, or if it were used in support of the contention that self-help is the answer to our nation's pressing problems, this author would regret that a word of it had ever been written. The income tax system offers few meaningful solutions to those without income or resources. This basic truth must never be overlooked.

Yet it would be a mistake to begin only on this somber note. The power of tax law in shaping economic and social institutions is immense. Today the relationship among our diverse sources of public policy is coming to be recognized as never before. The claim for equality and opportunity by people with disabilities is an integral part of that process, not as special pleading, but as an indispensable element of any effort to revitalize long-term economic and social progress in our nation. Opportunities for unparalleled experimentation and change lie ahead.

For those who are inclined to ruminate or debate over public policy, or for those who simply want to save a few dollars, the tax system is a wonderful place to start.

Acknowledgments

No book, even if it bears a single author's name, is wholly the product of a single individual. First, I want to thank all those people whose questions and expressions of interest contributed to the conception and content of this book. Some specific individuals also need to be mentioned.

Without the help of my long-time friend and primary research assistant, Frank Cavallaro, and my other assistants, Sherri Walsh, Katy Sullivan, and Aaron Cuthbertson, the monumental data collection effort could never have proceeded. Without the invaluable input from Darien Ryan, whose technical mastery of tax law and practice combine so remarkably with a profound understanding of the human goals of this book, many of the options and strategies referred to in the title would never have come to light. Without the support and faith of my publisher, Dr. Diana M. Schneider, and the technical assistance of her associate, Joan Wolk, the book would never have reached this audience.

And most of all, without Judy Ann Wilkinson, my greatest supporter and most stalwart critic, the world's greatest editor who combines supreme attention to both form and substance (and who since midway in this process has been my wife): to you, Judy Ann, without whom my stamina and capacities would long since have proved unequal to the task, all my love and thanks.

Finally, to you, the readers, a word of thanks is also in order, for you will ultimately determine the meaning and value of this book. I hope it is worthy of you and offer my sincerest thanks for your time and attention. Good luck!

Steven B. Mendelsohn
New York, December, 1992

Tax
Options
and
Strategies
for
People
with
Disabilities

Introduction

Nothing is certain but death and taxes. Is there anyone who has not heard this cliche?

Like many old sayings, this one raises as many questions as it answers. For even if taxes arc inevitable, the questions of who pays and how much remain to be answered. These issues can be raised in several ways. From the standpoint of law and public policy, they can be addressed in statistical or broad philosophical terms. Among the variables policymakers consider are revenue needs of government, impact on the economy, political reactions, fairness, and distribution of wealth. However, to most of us these far-reaching issues of policy and equity are only a remote abstraction. The tax system is confronted in far more personal terms by the individual who sits down each April with a shoe box full of papers and a stack of forms.

With the possible exception of traffic regulations and motor vehicle licensing agencies, more Americans have direct contact with the tax system than with any other body of law or government agency. As people with disabilities enter or remain in the economic mainstream in ever-growing numbers, this annual ritual will increasingly become a part of their new equality.

People differ widely in their attitudes as taxpayers. For some, taxes represent the means by which government accomplishes its responsibilities to enhance the civility and quality of our lives. For others, they are a cruel confiscation, by which government takes away what is rightfully theirs. For many, taxes are a source of anxiety and frustration; for still others, a stimulating intellectual exercise and challenge. But whatever one's attitude or emotional reactions, the tax system affects our lives profoundly and pervasively.

Sometimes we recognize the impact of tax considerations on the economic and personal decisions we make in everyday life. For example, in the autumn of 1986 many people rushed to purchase automobiles or other "big-ticket" items because the federal tax law was about to change. State sales taxes, which had been allowable as an itemized deduction on federal income tax returns, would no longer be deductible after the end of 1986. In this instance, people were keenly aware of the tax consequences of their actions, and the making or the timing of personal decisions was heavily influenced by tax law.

However, many decisions we make in daily life are influenced by tax laws in ways that we do not recognize. How many of us stop to consider that the available supply and the comparative costs of renting versus owning our homes are influenced by the tax code? And how many of us realize that when the costs of getting from one city to another by train, plane, or bus differ, tax law is part of the reason why? Indeed, whether we buy our groceries at a suburban mall or in a downtown shopping district can also be traced, in significant part, to our tax laws.

Wherever we shop and however we get there, each of us is concerned with how much money is required for our purchases and how much we will have left when we finish. Within the limits of our needs, our resources, and our knowledge, each of us is concerned with how we can plan our activities to obtain and retain as much money as possible. If for no other reason than this, the workings and requirements of the tax system are worthy of our attention. And if you will give us a few pages to prove it, be assured, whatever your previous experience, these tax matters are well within your capacity to understand. With the technical jargon stripped away, even complex principles of tax law and policy can be made clear to anyone who is willing to devote some time to the effort.

In light of the complexity of the issues and the vast amounts of money at stake, it is not surprising that tax advice has become a major service industry. Attorneys, accountants, and professional preparers have emerged as an indispensable resource for many taxpayers, as have authors whose tax books grace bookstore shelves in abundance each year as the tax season comes upon us. These books vary in their scope, in their emphases, and even in their interpretations of various points of law, but they all impart valuable information to their readers. The Internal Revenue Service itself also publishes a wide array of booklets dealing with many subjects and written for people in many situations.[1.1] These include IRS Publication No. 907, "Tax Information for People with Handicaps or Disabilities." With so many worthwhile resources already available, it is eminently fair to ask why the world needs another book about taxes.

Congress estimates there are 43 million Americans with disabilities.[1.2] As participants in the tax system, they vary as much as any group of comparable size. They are income earners and dependents; they have large incomes in some cases, small ones in all too many; they derive their incomes from wages, business or governmental transfer payments; and their feelings about the role of taxation in their economic destinies run the normal gamut. But despite their diversity, certain generalizations are warranted.

First, because Americans with disabilities tend to be poorer than average,[1.3] they are likely to have more limited access to sophisticated tax advice than citizens of greater means commonly enjoy. Second, when persons with disabilities consult accountants or other tax preparers, they do not do so primarily as disabled persons. Tax advisers, therefore, may not know of a taxpayer's disability, or of the disability of a dependent or spouse. Even if made aware of the existence of a client's disability, the tax professional may have little experience or familiarity with those tax law provisions that could benefit the client. Third, even when the tax expert is fully aware of the existence of a disability and of the relevant provisions of law, substantial understanding of the disability itself may be necessary in order to appreciate fully how these legal provisions apply to the life situation, expenditure patterns, plans and needs of a particular client.

One more generalization may also be appropriate here. However much people with disabilities differ in their financial profiles and tax situations, a disability normally imposes economic costs. Whether for assistive technology devices, for the services of others as assistants, for the additional time that some tasks may take, or in other respects, people with disabilities know that, function for function, activity for activity, the dollar costs of living productively often exceed those that would otherwise be incurred.

The importance of comprehensive and understandable tax planning becomes all the more compelling once we recognize that many of the add-on costs incurred as a result of disability can be offset through the tax law, either by reason of their tax deductibility or by the application of other provisions. In the context of education, employment, and independent living, the tax deductibility of many disability-related costs is the equivalent of a governmental subsidy. To the degree that people with disabilities and their families can become adept in utilizing the opportunities that the law provides, the potential exists for them to retain substantial sums.

Indeed, it seems no exaggeration to suggest that what is at stake is a potential transfer of resources and wealth equal in scope to any service or benefit program that government could conceivably undertake. As a source of self-financing for needed goods and services, available but largely unutilized tax subsidies represent a resource of enormous magnitude for the disability community. And, for those who feel uncomfortable with the self-image or the label of being "disabled," what could be more self-affirming than the opportunity to share in the dignified and fully lawful national pastime of saving on taxes!

For those with small incomes and limited means, tax planning may appear to be a faintly ludicrous endeavor. However, the leveraging of even small sums can mean a great deal when relatively few dollars can make the difference between being able and not being able to afford something of importance.

It is not only through deductions that the Internal Revenue Code can give an economic boost to people with disabilities and their families. There are instances in which specific sources of income are exempt from taxation; cases in which the presence of a disability leads to the waiver of penalties or charges; situations in which advantageous methods of accounting can be adopted because a disability exists; and numerous other circumstances in which the existence and role of a disability make a significant difference. Taxpayers and tax practitioners need to be alerted to and informed about these provisions of the law to a far greater extent than currently seems the case.[1.4] Effective tax planning always requires a partnership between taxpayer and tax advisor. Taxpayers with disabilities and their families may find this especially true. Fair or not, in this realm as in so many others, it behooves taxpayers with disabilities to come to the tax planning process with as much knowledge as possible, often with more knowledge than would be expected of other taxpayers.

No one knows exactly how much more money people with disabilities would save for their own use if they and their tax preparers were fully aware of the legal provisions discussed in this book; we believe the sum is large. Of equal importance to the amount is the role played by money that people actively retain for their own use, a role that cannot be matched by funds expended or contributed by others, however wisely or well-intentioned.

Viewed against this backdrop, mastery of the tax law becomes an important dimension of the self-help and the consumer movements. For those willing and eager to take full responsibility for their own destinies, financial planning, of which tax planning is in turn a key component, is surely an appropriate place to start. Because fiscal constraints sharply limit the ability of government to address human needs through the expenditure of funds on new or reinvigorated social programs, the tax system represents an especially important, but as yet largely untapped, resource for persons with disabilities as they strive to finance education, obtain the training or technology needed for work, and live lives of dignity and independence when their working years are done.

Human services professionals may also benefit from the information and ideas contained in this book. The tax law offers many significant opportunities to leverage increasingly scarce public and charitable funds. Such leverage may often make the difference between success and failure in achieving educational, vocational, and personal goals. Health care, social services, and rehabilitation or counseling professionals may fear that venturing into these areas represents too great a departure from their training and experience. But if they do nothing more than simply keep in mind that a particular need or situation may have a tax dimension, they will already have accomplished a great deal for those they seek to assist. We hope that after reading this book they will recognize the existence of a tax dimension often enough to make a difference.

Taken together, people with disabilities, their families, their friends, their employers, and the service providers with whom they work, constitute a large proportion of our population. To all of you, we offer this book.

two

Overview of the Tax System

Like any other group of people, Americans with disabilities vary widely in their knowledge about taxation. They range from those who can find the tiniest loophole in the most complicated regulation to those who might find it difficult to distinguish an income adjustment from a chiropractic one.

This chapter should be particularly helpful to readers with little background in the tax area, including those who have been frustrated in previous attempts to take control of their own tax planning, or those who doubt their capacity to cut through all the legal and accounting jargon to any real level of under standing. No one has ever claimed that the tax system is simple. The variety and often contradictory nature of its objectives ensure that it is not. But the law need not remain forbidding for anyone of ordinary intelligence and average perseverance.

If we do our best to strip away the jargon and to present information clearly, and if you do your best to travel along with us patiently and attentively, you can be confident of coming away not as a tax expert, but at least with some information or insight that can help you, a friend, or a loved one next April 15th and on many April 15ths to come.

(a)

W here Does the Tax Law Come From?

Federal taxes are not the only taxes we pay, and income taxes are not the only kind of tax the federal government levies. Yet when people speak of taxes it is generally the federal income tax to which they refer.

The federal income tax law as embodied in the Internal Revenue Code (IRC) is set forth as Title 26 of the United States Code (USC). The U.S. Code is the official codification of the laws of the United States. Any tax law question begins with the IRC.

Because the statute cannot hope to cover every detail or anticipate every eventuality, implementation and interpretation of the Internal Revenue Code are delegated to the Internal Revenue Service (IRS), an agency under the jurisdiction of the Treasury Department. Most people are familiar with IRS as an enforcement and tax collection agency, but its role in interpreting the law is ultimately as important as its responsibility for enforcement. The IRS interprets and applies the law in a variety of settings, including regulations it issues in connection with various statutory provisions, instructions, or announcements to taxpayers and tax professionals, rulings on issues of widespread interest or importance, rulings provided to individual taxpayers to resolve specific questions about their own tax situations, and through a variety of other means. From time to time in this book, we will have occasion to cite regulations, revenue rulings, or private letter rulings, and other authorities which reflect this diversity of sources for tax law interpretation.

For many people, the most vivid illustration of IRS's role in interpreting and applying the law occurs in their personal dealings with the agency. When taxpayers and the government disagree over a question of fact or law, the court system also has an important role to play. The U.S. Tax Court, federal district courts, and appeals courts, including ultimately the Supreme Court, are available for, and frequently involved in, the interpretation and application of the Internal Revenue Code.

The family is considered a single economic unit for many purposes in our society. Thus, we speak of family income, family finances, or the like, and we make many economic decisions as a family unit. For the nuclear family of parents and children, and some-times also for more extended families, this is true under the tax code as well.

(b)

T he Individual As a Member of a Family

The family unit provides taxpayers with a means of pooling or distributing income. Equally important, the income tax code provides a mechanism by which family members with higher incomes can benefit from deductions available to, or incurred on behalf of, other family members who earn less. The personal exemption that taxpayers can claim for their depen-dents and the deductibility to parents of their chil-dren's medical expenses are the most obvious illus-trations of this opportunity.

The role of the family under the tax law can best be understood in connection with what is called *fil-ing status*. Four different filing statuses exist:

- single taxpayer (an unmarried individual with no dependents);
- head of household (unmarried individual, who maintains a household in which a relative lives, typically a single parent);
- married person filing jointly (includes married cou-ples filing a single combined return, or widowed individuals with children who qualify as surviving spouses);
- married person filing a separate return.[2.1]

Filing status determines where the boundaries between tax brackets are set. One need only look at the tax rates to know how much a difference filing status can make. In 1992, single taxpayers pay at the rate of 15 percent on their first $21,450 of taxable

income, whereas married couples filing jointly continue paying at the 15 percent rate until their taxable
income reaches $35,800; heads of households pay at
15 percent up to $28,750. Comparable spreads occur
at the higher income levels where the rates go from
28 percent to 31 percent. The precise taxable income
figure at which the rate (or bracket) for each filing status changes will vary from year to year, because these
tax brackets are indexed for inflation.[2.2]

Some people have no choice about which filing
status they use. For example, a single person who has
no dependents or children and who does not maintain a household for anyone but him/herself can use
only the single filing status. But when an individual
does have a choice of filing status, such as a married
person who can choose to file jointly or separately,
this decision can have important bottom-line implications. Married couples ordinarily file a joint return. It
usually seems the natural thing to do, and it is usually
the most advantageous approach. But there are times
when filing separate returns has advantages that
make it worth considering, even if it results in the forfeiture of certain options. If the incomes of the two
people are vastly different, and if the spouse with the
lower income incurred substantial medical care costs,
filing separately could result in a larger overall medical care deduction for the family than would be forthcoming from a joint return. If what you lose by filing
separately is outweighed by what you gain, it is the
better strategy. Then, too, there are situations in
which the law specifies what filing status must be
used in order to utilize a particular provision. For
instance, a taxpayer who is married as defined by the
law[2.3] cannot claim the child and dependent care
credit unless she/he files a joint return.

We encounter situations throughout the book in
which this choice and other choices matter. For the
moment, it is enough to remember that the choice of
filing status, like the decision whether to itemize,
which form to use, and many other choices, should
always be considered as an element of your overall
tax strategy.

Families have always looked for ways to divide
the income of their highest-earning members among
as many other lower-earning or non-earning members
as possible. This strategy can be useful for a person

with a disability, especially if his or her income is small. This does not mean that income can be assigned to family members who did not earn it. It does mean that family members with lower incomes benefit in a variety of ways from the law's treatment of the family as a single economic and taxpaying unit. The reverse is also true. Families seek to pool expenses in ways that allow those members with higher incomes to obtain tax benefits for deductible expenses attributable to the lower-earning or non-earning members.

In any subculture or specialized field, a knowledge of basic terminology is frequently the key to understanding. This is as true with the federal income tax system as it is with music or baseball.

(c)

B asic Terminology

Gross Income

Our starting point is gross income, from which we peel away certain specified items to get to adjusted gross income; next strip away certain additional elements to get down to taxable income, the amount on which our taxes are actually computed. Each layer plays an important part in the process of determining how much we owe, and each step bears heavily on the others. Taxable income is, of course, important because it is the amount on which our taxes are actually paid. Adjusted gross income matters because many itemized deductions, including medical care, are computed on the basis of a percentage of this figure. Without gross income none of these subsequent computations can be definitive.

Gross income (GI, as it is called in the shorthand of the tax world) is the total of everything you earn or receive except items or revenues that the law defines as "excludable" from income.[2.4] Items that are excludable or exempt from GI include many fringe benefits of employment, the portion of scholarships used for tuition, or other specified expenses, or the interest on state and municipal bonds. Other revenue items are partially excludable, and still others are sometimes excludable and other times includable, depending on the size of our income or other factors. For example, Social Security benefits are exempt if income is low enough, but they become includable when income rises above a certain level.[2.5]

With gross income we encounter our first possibility for confusion if we are not careful. Obviously, the money we receive that is excludable from gross income is still *income* to us. The compensatory damages award from a personal injury lawsuit or a monthly Social Security check can be put into our bank accounts or our wallets. If anyone asked what our income was, we would not ignore these sums, but although they represent *income* for accounting purposes, and even for purposes of common sense, they are not considered *income* for federal tax purposes.

In this way, something can be *income* but also not be *income,* depending on the context in which we use this term. We can usually avoid misunderstandings if we remember that many words used in the context of the tax law have both technical and ordinary meanings. Another fertile area for the introduction of such confusion might be over the term *earned income.* In various settings the tax law makes distinctions between *earned* and *unearned* income, particularly in the taxation of children.[2.6] Again, if someone asked how much we earned last year, we would include all our income. The technical distinctions the law makes have little to do with how we talk and think in ordinary life. It is always important, therefore, to remember that even the simplest terms may have technical connotations that have little to do with common usage.

The law is very inclusive in its definition of gross income. The Internal Revenue Code and the regulations published by the Internal Revenue Service to interpret it explain: "Gross income means all income from whatever source derived unless excluded by law. Gross income includes income realized in any form whether in money, property or services."[2.7]

Here the reader may be forgiven for wondering how the term *gross income* can be so comprehensive in its scope if there are exclusions such as those noted previously, not to mention a long list of other exempt items. The answer lies in the phrase "unless excluded by law."

In fact, so many categories of income are excludable that many economists believe our tax base is too narrow. Some go so far as to argue that what we have in this country is a wage tax, not a real income tax at all. Whatever the merit of such claims, many taxpayers devote a good deal of effort to making sure that as much of their income as possible is excludable. This may or may not always be wise. I have known a number of people who put the bulk of their savings into tax-exempt bonds, thinking they would avoid taxes. But the bonds they bought paid so much less than other investments they could have made that they ended up worse off than if they had paid taxes on the higher-yielding investments. I have even met a few people who did this despite having incomes so low that they would have owed no taxes even if they had kept their money in fully taxable investments.

One situation in which it is actually possible and beneficial to opt for excludable over includable income occurs in relation to fringe benefits of employment, as discussed in Chapter 6(j). For workers with disabilities or for workers with disabled spouses or dependents, the choice of what fringe benefits to take, where such a choice exists, may be a very important one.

A number of revenue items encountered by people with disabilities are ordinarily excludable. These include the proceeds of accident or health insurance policies,[2.8] government payments based on need [2.9] (such as Supplemental Security income), and the value of vocational rehabilitation or special education services provided by state or local agencies.

The language of the statute on gross income presents a good opportunity to make a point about how to read law, a point that goes far beyond the question of what GI means, and one that will apply to almost any provision of law you ever have occasion to read or need to understand. The statute is inclusive in its definition of GI, yet there are many exceptions. These need not be listed or even necessarily referred to in the section of the Code defining GI. The lesson to be learned is that it is dangerous to take a single provision or section of the law out of context. A particular section of the code may appear clear and unambiguous and may use language that leaves little doubt as to whether the answer to your question is yes or no; but it would be premature to draw any final conclusion until you have determined that no other provision of law modifies yours. Until one has done the research, it is unwise to conclude that even a seemingly clear statement represents all that the law has to say about a subject.

When we speak of *context* we mean not only the entire Internal Revenue Code, but also the federal regulations interpreting it, and several other layers of administrative rulings and court decisions. (Consult the index to this book for a brief description of these authorities and for an explanation of the abbreviations and citation formats used to refer to them in the notes.)

When you first begin to think about your taxes, it is best to assume that every penny you have received or will receive is includable in GI, even the fair market value of goods and services you received free or for less than their normal cost. You should probably start this way even if you already know that certain items are excludable. By beginning from such a pessimistic premise, you can never be disappointed and the only way you can be surprised is pleasantly! Also remember that a number of excludable items may have to be shown on your income tax return. Reporting an item is not the same as paying tax on it. Filing and reporting requirements are one thing; payment obligations are quite another. The clearest example of this is a fairly grim one. If your gross income is less than the minimum amount on which taxes are due ($5,900 for the average single individual in 1992), you will not be liable for the payment of any federal income tax on that income. Yet there are situations in which the law requires you to file an informational return, and situations in which, though not required to file, it is in your interest to file a return reporting that income, such as when you are entitled to a refund of taxes withheld during the year. (Even when there is no economic reason or legal requirement that you file a return, it would probably be a good idea to do so if you are planning to run for public office at some future date so that you will be able to release all your prior tax returns to the press!)

Deductions

No sooner has GI been determined than our task shifts to whittling it down, which we do by taking all the deductions to which we are entitled. For various reasons of public policy, the law has been written to allow us to deduct from income those amounts which we have spent in specified ways that the law favors, wishes to subsidize, or seeks to encourage. For instance, the law grants a deduction for charitable contributions because it wants to encourage charity; it allows the deduction of our medical care expenses above certain levels to offset some of the economic loss that these entail; and it confers deductibility on other types of expenditures for other policy, political, or historical reasons. A deduction is in some ways similar to an exclusion, except that whereas the excludable item is removed from our income at the start—usually by reason of its source—the deductible item is removed from our income at a later point—usually because of the way we spent it.

Business expenses represent by far the largest category of expenses to which deductibility is accorded. The reasoning here is that since only the profits derived from business can be considered as income, amounts expended in producing that income should be broadly deductible.

To the degree that we incur and can substantiate a deductible expense, we are permitted to subtract all or part of it from our income. In some cases that amount, called the allowable amount, will be equal to the entire amount we spent in the specified way; at other times it will be a portion of the amount, determined on the basis of some percentage or formula.

The law concerning deductions is strict, no less so than with the definition of income. But whereas we are obliged to treat everything as income unless the law tells us it is not, we are barred from claiming something as deductible unless the law says it is.[2.10]

By saying that deductions are strictly construed, we do not suggest that there is no room for argument or interpretation about their meaning and scope. A substantial proportion of the tax law cases litigated and decided each year revolve around just such questions. For this reason, it is important to stress again the indispensability of thorough research to determine how a particular deduction is defined and interpreted. Consider also that the IRS, the tax court, or even the Supreme Court may be changing its interpretation of the provision even if the statutory wording has not been altered in a number of years. At any given time, the trend of the law may be toward the broadening or the narrowing of a particular deduction. This can be said of any other element of the tax law as well, and indeed it is a truth applicable to all law. Law is not a single voice; it is a conversation.

In general, the Tax Reform Act of 1986 [2.11] (which is the most recent major revision of the Internal Revenue Code and the largest revision since 1954) reduced the number of deductions available to people on their personal income tax returns. But contrary to this general trend, that landmark legislation also created and clarified a number of deductions for persons with disabilities, among which *impairment-related work expenses* are the most far-reaching. This is discussed in Chapter 6(a).

Different deductions are taken at different points in the computational process. The fact that something is deductible does not tell us where or when on the return it may be claimed. Let's examine what the options are.

Businesses and individuals use different approaches. Businesses report only their profit (or net earnings) as income. For example, self-employed individuals total up their revenues and expenses from the conduct of trade or business on Schedule C, which yields a net figure representing their profit from these activities. It is this figure, carried over to their individual tax returns, that is included in their GI. Thus, self-employed individuals will frequently file with their form 1040 a Schedule C, which enumerates their expenses from business, as well as a Schedule A, which lists their itemized deductions.

Adjusted Gross Income (AGI)

Deductions are taken in two different ways and at two distinct points in the computational process. Here the term *adjusted gross income* becomes crucial. Some of our deductions such as business expenses are taken directly from gross income. Not until we have taken these deductions can we determine what our AGI is; without taking them our AGI would appear larger than it needs to be.

The majority of our personal deductions, however, are taken as itemized deductions only after we have determined our AGI. These itemized deductions (or the standard deduction if we do not itemize) represent the means by which we move from AGI to taxable income, with the allowable amount of many of these itemized deductions being based on the size of AGI. For the bridge players among us, the concept of "above-the-line" versus "below-the-line" should be a fairly straightforward way of introducing AGI. For the rest of us, the distinctions it entails may initially be a little harder to grasp. Adjusted gross income is the line. Deductions that get you to AGI from GI are said to be above-the-line deductions; those that come into play after AGI has been determined are characterized as below-the-line deductions.

Because the term *deductions* is used in this twofold way, some degree of confusion is possible. To simplify the matter, we should try to use the term *adjustments* rather than *deductions* to identify the above-the-line group. After all, since these deductions get us to adjusted gross income, they really are adjustments to income. Unfortunately, although the term *adjustments* is sometimes used in this way, it is also technically correct to use the term *deductions* to describe both types. Faced with such dual usage, another way to avoid confusion is to refer to the below-the-line deductions as *itemized* deductions.

If the timing and location of a particular deduction did not matter, we would not have to be so concerned about terminology. Regrettably, they matter a great deal for at least two reasons. First, above-the-line deductions can be taken regardless of their amount, whether or not we itemize. Second, as noted previously, the size of many itemized deductions is determined on the basis of percentages of AGI, so that a lower AGI will yield larger itemized deductions for things like health and employee business expenses. The medical expense deduction, for example, is available to the extent that health care expenses exceed 7.5 percent of AGI. This means that the lower your AGI, the earlier deductibility kicks in and the sooner the threshold for deductibility will be reached. Such thresholds or floors also apply to a number of other key deductions, as we shall learn later.

Given a choice, most people prefer their deductions to be of the above-the-line variety, because then they do not have to worry about having enough deductions to allow itemization, and they do not have to worry about thresholds attaching to some of the deductions. Moreover, if more of their deductions are concentrated above-the-line, as adjustments, a smaller AGI applies to those that remain. Unfortunately, very few deductions are available as adjustments to income above-the-line. Most of the deductions that can be claimed by individuals are of the itemized, or below-the-line, type. Some adjustments the law allows include alimony payments, employee business expenses of actors and other performing artists, contributions to tax deferred retirement plans, and reimbursed employee business expenses.[2.12]

When considering activity engaged in for money, three distinct types must be borne in mind. These three categories are the conduct of a trade or business, [2.13] activities engaged in for the production of income, [2.14] and employee business expenses. [2.15] As noted in our discussion of gross income, expenses of a trade or business are removed from income before the individual taxpayer's GI is even determined. As this relates to the decision of whether to itemize on the owner's personal return, it yields the same practical result as if the trade or business expenses were treated as income adjustments. The deduction for business expenses will be available whether or not we itemize.

By contrast, expenses incurred "in the production of income" are deductible only as itemized deductions. Although engaged in for profit, such activities do not constitute being in business. The expenses attributable to them must be claimed as miscellaneous itemized deductions.

The third group of deductions are those for employee business expenses. Strictly speaking, the term *employee business expenses* is a fiction, since the concept of business expenses technically applies only to those activities entered into for profit, not for wages. We create the concept of employee business expenses by characterizing people who work for wages as being engaged in the business of being employees. But their unreimbursed employee business expenses are deductible, for the most part, only below-the-line as miscellaneous itemized deductions. This means that employee business expenses are deductible only if one itemizes one's deductions and only to the extent that miscellaneous itemized deductions exceed two percent of AGI.

One might well ask why this discrepancy exists. Since we characterize expenses incurred in working for wages as a type of business expense, why shouldn't such expenses be available as income adjustments on the same basis as costs incurred in working for profit? Isn't our net income from wages after work expenses are subtracted our "profit" from employment? If so, why should our employee business expenses be deductible only when we itemize, and only to the extent that they exceed two percent of our AGI?

Arguments have been made to justify the distinction, including the contention that if the expense were bona fide the employer would pay it, especially if large, and the contention that small employee business expenses would pose difficulties for tax administration. Yet, expenses incurred for profit are not disallowed when they involve small amounts. In the end, there lies beneath the answer to our question another important generalization that you can use in interpreting the tax law or other statutes: while there are theoretical arguments to justify the disparate treatment of the two types of business expenses, the real reason they are treated differently is because the law says so! The law isn't always fair; the law isn't always consistent or logical.

Whether someone is in business or is an employee may not always be clear. This distinction can be important for people who do consulting work or perform various kinds of contract work, and for the many people with disabilities who work at home. Because it bears on what is deductible, when taxes must be paid, what forms must be filed and by whom, the question of whether someone is an employee or an independent contractor is far from academic. Among other things, the self-employed individual is liable for the payment on a regular basis throughout the year of self-employment tax (which is the self-employed person's equivalent of the Social Security and Medicare taxes withheld from the wages of employees).

Basically, one's status is a question of fact, generally resolved under the "direction and control" test. The status of the relationship as either a contractual or an employment relationship is not determined by what the parties say it is, not even by what they intend it to be. If I offer you a certain amount of money to do something for me, but tell you where, when, and how to do it, there comes a point at which, whatever we intended, the law says you are my employee.

An important point is thus illustrated. There are times when the tax status of our activities is determined by our intentions and times when it is determined by other facts. When I visit a doctor to seek treatment for some pain, that intention determines the potential tax deductibility of the fee I pay. On the other hand, if I visit the doctor with the intention of asking his or her opinion about the effectiveness of the Food and Drug Administration, the fee I pay is not deductible as a medical expense. In that case, intention largely controls.

In other cases, intention plays a lesser role. Whether something qualifies for the medical care deduction will be a question of fact. My intention in buying vitamin C supplements may be self-treatment of an ailment; there may be good evidence in the medical research literature to support my strategy, and my doctor may have endorsed the strategy, but the law says that my costs for this or other nonprescription products are generally not deductible. Here my intentions do not matter very much. As often as not, when we ask what the law is, we are really asking what range and combination of facts, states of mind, definitions of words and concepts, and what types of evidence and documentation are relevant to the issue we need to decide. In every situation, the trick is to know what elements matter.

In some situations the trick is to know whether you're being taxed at all. For example, banks or other financial institutions impose penalties on the premature withdrawal of certificates of deposit (CDs). Such premature withdrawal penalties should not be confused with the penalty imposed by the tax law for early withdrawal of retirement funds. The bank penalty, since it is not imposed by or collected on behalf of the government, is not a tax. With banks or anyone else, you never know how to deal with a charge or other short-fall until you know why and on whose behalf the money was withheld from you. If the bank took it pursuant to its contract with you, your claim for waiver or refund is with the bank. If the bank withheld it as tax, your claim for refund is with the Internal Revenue Service. In any case the premature withdrawal penalty that the bank charges can be claimed as an above-the-line adjustment to income, [2.16] whether or not we are also liable for a tax penalty on the early withdrawal.

As indicated earlier, for most of us there are few, if any, income adjustments to implement. Accordingly, the journey from gross income to adjusted gross income is a fairly uneventful one, but AGI (Line 32 of Form 1040 or Line 17 of Form 1040A) is an important point of departure, from which there are many roads we can take.

After determining AGI, every taxpayer must make the critical decision to take the standard deduction or to itemize. All else being equal, and except in those comparatively rare cases in which the law mandates one or the other course, taxpayers obviously choose whichever method yields a larger deduction. In order to make this decision intelligently, we have to do three things: calculate the total amount of our expenses that meet the conditions for treatment as itemized deductions; determine how much of that total is allowable as a deduction; and compare this amount to the standard deduction that applies to our filing status. The decisions made at this point affect our bottom line as much as any other computations or choices.

Standard and Itemized Deductions

With a few exceptions, most taxpayers are permitted to use the standard deduction. The law simply allows everyone to deduct the amount that applies to their filing status. The amount of the standard deduction is fixed by law, and since 1986 has been indexed to inflation. For 1992, the standard deduction amount for a single individual is $3,600; for a married couple filing jointly, $6,000 ($3,000 for a married person filing a separate return); and for someone filing as a head of household, the standard deduction is $5,250. People who are blind get an additional standard deduction [2.17] for 1992 of $900 if they are single or head of household filers, and $700 if they file a joint return. The additional standard deduction is discussed further in Chapter 7(d). Taxpayers over the age of 65 also qualify for the additional standard deduction.

Thus if you are blind and over the age of 65, you get one additional standard deduction for each category, meaning that a single taxpayer both over the age of 65 and blind is entitled to a standard deduction of $5,400 ($3,600 basic standard deduction available to a nonitemizer, plus $900 additional standard deduction for blindness, plus $900 additional standard deduction for age).

The large majority of taxpayers choose to take the standard deduction. If you have itemized deductions worth more than your standard deduction amount, you would usually elect to itemize in order to lower your tax liability. We say *usually* because there are cases in which this is not the best strategy, as we shall learn later. Some people choose not to be bothered with itemization even if they lose a little money by opting for simplicity. If this choice is made with full knowledge, the preference for simplicity or for saving time cannot be faulted, but for most people the choice is based on the numbers. Because the standard deduction amount is indexed to inflation, these numbers will change slightly each year. Of course, you may not know which method is better for you until you have calculated your itemized deductions, so this calculation is worth making even if you end up choosing the standard deduction.

Computing itemized deductions involves two steps (and now, for upper-income taxpayers who may be subject to what are called phaseout provisions or to the alternative minimum tax, several additional steps as well). After first identifying the deductible expense categories, we must calculate what proportion of each deduction category is allowable: that is, how much of our health care expenses, how much of our miscellaneous itemized deductions or other categories of expenses we can actually claim. This second step is dictated by the fact that a number of itemized deductions are determined with reference to AGI, based on percentage-of-AGI floors or thresholds. Remember that we can not deduct our entire health care expenses, only the amount that exceeds 7.5 percent of AGI. Similarly, we can only deduct the amount of miscellaneous itemized deductions exceeding two percent of AGI. The amount we are finally able to deduct is called the allowable amount.

An important point to note here is that impairment-related work expenses [2.18] are not subject to the two percent threshold.[2.19] They can be deducted, however small their amount, but if you don't have enough itemized deductions to exceed the standard deduction amount, this exception to the threshold yields no benefit. (See Chapter 6 sections (a) and (b).)

To be sure, the majority of itemized deductions are not subject to percentage-of-AGI floors. For those that are, it is important to remember that the size of one's allowable deduction, indeed even the allowability of any deduction at all, changes as AGI changes. If your AGI were $10,000, allowable health care expenses would be anything over the first $750 that you spent, but if your AGI is reduced to $9,000, the 7.5 percent threshold goes down to $675. This is part of the reason everyone wants the lowest possible AGI.

We mentioned previously that there are several provisions applicable to higher income taxpayers. One of these is the "phaseout" provisions introduced into the law several years ago, which are currently scheduled to expire in 1996. Once adjusted gross income exceeds a threshold amount (for 1992, $105,250 for a single taxpayer, $157,900 for a married couple filing jointly, $131,550 for a head of household), itemized deductions are reduced as income rises. They are reduced at the rate of three percent of the amount by which AGI exceeds the threshold up to a maximum phaseout of 80 percent of their value. Not all itemized deductions are subject to this phaseout. Among those not phased out, medical care expenses are the most important.[2.20] Impairment-related work expenses are subject to this phaseout.[2.21] On the assumption that people with incomes high enough to trigger phaseout have access to tax advice, we will not deal with it further.

Taxpayers who choose to itemize do so by filing Schedule A to the Form 1040 (the so-called long form) individual tax return. Schedule A is one major example of the seemingly infinite number of forms or schedules, designated with letters or numbers, that taxpayers may need to append to their returns. These forms and schedules provide the details and the computation procedures pertinent to the particular provision you want to invoke. Schedule A details one's itemized deductions.

Taxpayers who choose to take the standard deduction do not need to file Schedule A, and in many instances do not even have to use Form 1040. They can use the so-called short form 1040A, or in many cases even the shorter Form 1040EZ.

This gives rise to an important general point. Choice of the correct forms and the proper schedules is imperative for effectively implementing any tax strategy. No matter the merit of your claim, its consideration and success will be impeded, perhaps even prevented, if the right forms are not filed.

Personal Exemptions

The distance between adjusted gross income and taxable income is traveled mainly in the company of our deductions, but they are not the only companions we meet along the way. Beyond the standard or itemized deductions, our income is further reduced by the personal exemptions we claim. Every person (unless claimed as an exemption on someone else's return) is entitled to a personal exemption. Spouses filing jointly get two exemptions, and taxpayers are generally allowed one exemption for each dependent, such as a child, whom they claim. Indexed to inflation like the standard deduction, the personal exemption amount for 1992 is $2,300, up from $2,150 for tax year 1991. The figure for 1993 (that is, for use in your tax planning for 1993 and for use on the 1993 return, which must be filed by April 15, 1994) will be announced in December 1992. At that same time the standard deduction amount for 1993 will also be specified by the Treasury Department.

Personal exemptions have nothing to do with deductions or with which form a taxpayer uses. One does not even really need to perform any calculations or make any decisions beyond knowing the number of dependents to be claimed. If the appropriate boxes and lines (for example, the items under Line 6 of Form 1040) are checked and filled in, the tax tables and rate schedules automatically reflect the tax saving involved. The personal exemption does become an element of tax strategy when deciding whether to claim someone as a dependent. We are not required to claim someone as a dependent just because we are entitled to, and situations exist in which foregoing the exemption claim could be advantageous.

There are five tests that must be met in order for a taxpayer to claim someone as a dependent.[2.22] One of these, the income test, can prove of special importance to people with disabilities. Generally, a person cannot deduct medical care costs they pay on behalf of another person unless that person is a spouse or dependent. But there is an important exception to this general rule which will be discussed in Chapter 4(k) that comes into play when the other person meets all the tests for dependency except the income test. Additionally, it is easier to claim someone as a dependent if their income is derived from employment at a sheltered workshop than if their earnings come from other sources. This will be discussed in Chapter 7(g).

Like itemized deductions, our personal exemptions are now subject to phaseout.[2.23] This phaseout kicks in at the same income levels as the phaseout for itemized deductions, but the method of computation is different. Here we lose two percent of the value of our exemptions for every $2,500 or fraction thereof by which AGI exceeds the threshold amount. Moreover, our personal exemption can be totally phased out if income goes high enough.

Taxable Income (TI)

With our deductions (standard or itemized) and our exemptions, we have pretty much arrived at the proverbial bottom line: net income, or taxable income as it is technically called. Our taxes are computed as a percentage of this figure, with the tax tables or tax rate schedules provided by the IRS specifying exactly how much we owe for the year. We are entitled to a refund if the tax withheld during the year exceeds our total tax liability, exactly even if the two are equal, and obliged to pay the difference if our tax liability exceeds the amount withheld.

Ours is a progressive tax system, meaning that those with higher incomes pay at higher rates. At one time, the law included a larger number of tax brackets (or rates), which were much more steeply graduated than today's, at times ranging to over 90 percent for the highest bracket. At present, three basic tax rates exist for individuals: 15, 28, and 31 percent.

In computing our tax obligation for the year, we should not confuse our income tax with our Social Security/Medicare tax. Our tax return is the place where we settle both accounts, so they may seem to blend together, but the two computations are separate. Our tax deductions and personal exemptions have nothing to do with our Social Security obligations. A person can owe no federal income tax in a particular year but still be obliged to pay Social Security tax on wages or earnings from self-employment that fall below the threshold for income taxability. If our withholding or estimated tax payments during the year resulted in our having paid more than we owe in income taxes and less than we owe in Social Security tax, or vice versa, the tax return provides a means for making the necessary adjustments.

Looking up the tax due on our taxable income may not be the end of the journey. Once we know our tax liability for the year, it is time to consider any tax credits that may be available to us.

Tax Credits

Tax credits differ from tax deductions in several important respects. Deductions reduce our taxable income, so that we have less on which to pay taxes, whereas credits are deducted directly from the amount of tax we owe. Therefore, dollar for dollar, tax credits are generally superior to tax deductions. A $100 tax credit lowers our tax bill by $100. A $100 tax deduction reduces our tax by only $15, $28, or $31, depending on our tax bracket (or marginal rate, as that bracket is also called). For people who pay state income taxes, the real value of a deduction may of course be greater because your real tax rate is the sum of both the federal and state percentages. In high tax states, the true value of a deduction can reach near 40 cents on the dollar for people in the 28 percent federal bracket.

Credits can be of a business or personal nature. Two business credits of particular interest to people with disabilities are the targeted jobs credit[2.24] and the disabled access credit,[2.25] discussed in Chapter 6 sections (f) and (g) and Chapter 7(c). Personal credits of particular interest to people with disabilities include the child and dependent care credit[2.26] and the credit for the elderly and the permanently and totally disabled,[2.27] which are also discussed in Chapter 6 (i) and Chapter 7(b).

The second major difference between deductions

and credits is that you can claim your credits whether you itemize your deductions or not. Thus from a technical standpoint, deductions and credits have no connection, but this does not mean that credits and deductions have nothing to do with each other. On the level of your tax planning they may be closely linked.

From the standpoint of your tax strategy, they can sometimes be used in complementary ways, while at other times we may have to choose between them. Assume, for example, that you have attendant services costs for a spouse with a severe disability, and that you incur these costs in order to be gainfully employed. Typically, this care would qualify for the dependent care credit. If the nature of the care amounts to nursing services or their equivalent, these costs would also qualify for the medical care deduction. Which method you should choose depends on the circumstances. As we have occasion to repeat throughout this book, there is no substitute for running the numbers.

Another important distinction is between refundable and nonrefundable credits. Most credits are nonrefundable. This means that the maximum credit available to you cannot exceed the amount that would reduce your tax obligation for the year to zero. For example, the maximum size of the child and dependent care credit is $1,440, but even if you met all the conditions for claiming it, you would neither get nor need the entire amount if a lesser sum reduces your tax for the year to zero anyway. So if your tax for the year was $1,300 without the credit, that $1,300 credit is all you could get. Any credit over that amount is useless, unless you could carry it backward or forward to other taxable years. With business credits such as the disability access credit or the targeted jobs credit, carryover is potentially available,[2.28] but for personal credits it is not.

By contrast, the earned income credit is a refundable personal credit.[2.29] This means you can get a refund of the amount to which you are entitled, even if that amount is more than would be required to zero out your taxes. So, if you were entitled to a $1,000 earned income credit, but your tax for the year was zero prior to application of the credit, you would still get a check, much like a refund check, for that $1,000. Or, if your tax obligation was $400 prior to computation of the credit, you would get a refund of

$600. The refundable credit is the closest thing to a negative income tax that we have. The earned income credit is important to all low-income taxpayers with children, but it can be especially important to families with children who have disabilities because such children can continue to qualify for the credit even after reaching the upper age limit that normally applies. The earned income credit will be discussed in Chapter 6(i).

Other Concepts and Terms

Terms such as *modified adjusted gross income, net regular tax liability,* or *alternative minimum tax* may strike a vaguely familiar or slightly ominous chord in some readers. These terms and dozens of others we could easily list represent exceptions, additions, or alterations to the tax computation process we have described. A few words about several of these concepts should prove useful.

Modified AGI

We have already seen that adjusted gross income (AGI) plays important roles in the computation of our taxes, from determining the floors for certain itemized deductions to triggering the application of phaseout rules, among others. In other cases, AGI is used to determine whether certain money received is includable in or excludable from our income. When AGI is used in this way, it is sometimes defined a little differently than usual. Hence, the term *modified AGI.* For example, if you receive Social Security or certain Railroad Retirement benefits, you may owe tax on these otherwise excludable items if your "modified" AGI exceeds $25,000 ($32,000 in the case of a married couple filing jointly). The modification in question consists of adding certain otherwise excludable items, such as the Social Security payments themselves and municipal bond interest, back into AGI.[2.30]

Net Regular Tax Liability and Alternative Minimum Tax

All the computations described so far relate to figuring out our regular (or our section 26, as it is technically called) tax. Not everyone ends up paying tax in this way, though. Some people must instead pay the alternative minimum tax (AMT).[2.31] The AMT represents efforts to limit the benefits that wealthy taxpayers can derive from what are called tax preference items. The AMT is subject to a $30,000 exclusion, meaning that taxpayers will not be liable for it unless they have at least $30,000 in tax preference items. Accordingly, though some people of moderate means may have tax preference items in their tax picture, the people to whom this provision primarily applies are generally those with access to skilled tax advice. Nor would any lay person be wise to attempt to deal with the AMT on his or her own. For this reason, and because they have no particular connection with the disability-related provisions of the tax law, the alternative minimum tax and similar topics of limited applicability are not dealt with in this book.

Terms such as the ones just noted apply to limited numbers of people. They make the taxpaying and filing processes more complex than we would like, but once our labors have brought us to the point where it is time to deal with them, the overwhelming probability is that the worst is over.

(d)

T ax Planning

Without using the term *tax planning,* we have already talked a good deal about this subject. In the previous section, we demonstrated a form of tax planning each time we discussed a choice or an option. In a very real sense, every tax conscious decision we make is an example of tax planning, even if only negative planning, such as when we decide to disregard the tax consequences of our activities in favor of other criteria.

Although every tax conscious decision we make exemplifies tax planning, certain decisions lie at the core of the planning concept. For the average person, timing (that is decisions about when we do what we do) constitutes the most common and useful form of tax planning at our disposal.

Timing

People do not always have control over when income is received or expenses are incurred. A new job or a medical emergency can hardly be foreseen, let alone controlled. Even when one does exercise a measure of control over the timing of events, accounting principles and legal precepts may dictate when they are deemed to have occurred for tax purposes. For example, if one receives weekly paychecks, taxation of income cannot normally be delayed a year by waiting until January 2 to deposit a paycheck received on December 31; the date of the check is the date the income is realized for tax purposes, and the income on your W-2 form undoubtedly shows the money as paid in Year One. Nevertheless, in many situations we do have the discretion to determine the timing of major financial events or the option to choose when these events are "recognized" for tax purposes.

For example, given a choice between doing a job and being paid for it either in December of Year One or in January of Year Two, many taxpayers would elect to defer the income to the second year by not doing the job until January. Delaying the receipt of the income by one month (perhaps in fact by only a few days) effectively postpones its taxation for a full year.

Many tangible benefits, apart from simple delay, can result from a decision to defer income. An individual might anticipate being in a lower income tax bracket in year two. For a worker who becomes disabled, a temporary reduction in income frequently takes place. If deferring the income from the higher-earning Year One to the lower-income Year Two results in its taxation at 15 percent instead of 28 percent, the taxpayer succeeds in keeping 13 cents more of each dollar. In effect, the taxation of that money has not only been delayed by potentially as much as a year, but the rate of tax has been cut nearly in half.

Even if one expects to have exactly the same income in both years, one's anticipated deductions could be a factor in favor of postponement. For instance, if you expect very large deductions in Year Two, such as expenses for substantial purchases of assistive technology (defined in chapter 4 (a)), you might wish to defer as much income as possible to offset these deductions. It can also work the other way, making acceleration rather than deferral of the income the wiser course.

From the standpoint of timing, the opposite of income deferral is deduction acceleration. If you take the standard deduction in some years and itemize in others, you want to concentrate as many of your deductible expenses as possible in the years you itemize. One way of doing this is to accelerate the following year's deductions as much as possible. A good example of this strategy relates to charitable contributions. Until 1986, you could take a deduction for some charitable contributions, whether or not you itemized; since then, itemization has been required. Many non-profit organizations feared that this change would result in a fall in their revenues. To counteract this possibility, some charitable organizations urge their contributors to donate two years' worth of contributions every other year. The theory is that by concentrating their charitable deductions in alternate years, taxpayers will be more likely to generate sufficient deductions to warrant itemization. Say that your annual charitable contributions average $3,500. By itself that is less than the standard deduction amount, so unless you have other itemized deductions, you will get no tax benefit from your contributions. By waiting and contributing $7,000 to charity in year two, you assure yourself the opportunity to itemize. This same logic applies to all itemized deduction categories.

With deductions, no less than with income, the logic can go either way. Though we normally want to defer income, there are cases in which we prefer to accelerate it. Also, whereas we ordinarily prefer to accelerate deductions, instances inevitably arise when their deferral is in our financial best interest. Such a case occurs when you already owe no taxes in Year One. Once your taxable income falls below the level at which any taxes are due, additional deductions gain you nothing. Deductions and credits benefit us only if there is taxable income for them to offset. Of course, one guaranteed way to avoid tax problems is to have no income, but this is not a strategy we endorse.

Deductions or credits that reduce your income below zero present one intriguing wrinkle. Many accountants believe that showing negative taxable income on a return is a good idea, reasoning that this gives taxpayers a cushion in the event their returns are audited. Thus, if your return shows a $1,000 negative taxable income, the government would have to disallow $1,001 in deductions or exclusion claims before you would owe any money.

Even if timing decisions regarding income or expenses do not change the rate or amount of our taxes, other good reasons exist to take timing seriously, perhaps the most important being "the time value of money." This is an economic concept, not a legal one. The sooner we can obtain money and the longer we can keep it, the better off we are economically. If I can delay the payment of tax on money for a year, I can use, hold, invest, or otherwise benefit from that money for this period of time. Similarly, if we can hasten deductions, we get their value that much sooner.

As suggested previously, tax rules sometimes dictate when income must be "realized" and "recognized," and these rules can deprive us of desirable timing options. The law often decides when money has been received, and this date can occur before or after the date on which it actually comes into our possession. Various legal principles and accounting conventions surround the determination of when income is *received*. One of these is the doctrine of "constructive receipt," which treats income as received when the recipient has a right to it, even if that right is not exercised. Understanding timing rules is an important adjunct to tax planning.

The same issues arise with deductions. All else being equal, the year we paid the expense is the year in which we claim the deduction. But all else is not always equal, so there are some key exceptions to this rule. Two major exceptions should be discussed: one that allows you to claim a deduction before the money is actually paid, and one that requires you to wait several years after paying in order to claim your deduction.

The first exception involves credit card purchases. When you make a purchase with a bank credit card, the law ordinarily treats the money as paid at the time the charge is made.[2.32] Although you may actually pay off the credit card bill over a period of several years, the expense is deemed fully paid at the time you make the purchase.

The second exception to the principle of deductibility in the year money is spent involves cases where we must spread the deduction over a period of several years, even if we pay the entire cost up front. This occurs when we incur what are termed *capital expenses.* Capital costs are expenditures for items expected to remain in use for more than one year— machines, equipment, buildings, and the like. The law requires that the deduction for a capital expense be spread out over the *useful life* of the item or over some other period of time specified by law. When we allocate the cost of a capital expenditure over the property's useful life or over some other recovery period, we are "depreciating" the item. Depreciation is of importance primarily in the context of business. With business expenses, the key distinction is between *capital expenses* (which must be depreciated unless they qualify for one of the exceptions to depreciation) and *ordinary expenses* (which can be deducted in the year paid, and sometimes carried backward or forward to other years).

For persons with disabilities, the distinction between capital and ordinary expenses comes up in three settings. Because this distinction is mainly a business-related issue, it arises in relation to impairment-related work expenses that involve the acquisition of capital equipment. See Chapter 6(d). The distinction also arises in connection with architectural barrier removal, where the law allows certain expenses to be converted from capital to ordinary expenses. See Chapter 6(h) and Chapter 7(c). Outside of business, the capital expense concept can also become a factor in determining our allowable deduction when the health care deduction is used to offset the cost of modifications to a home necessitated by a disability. See Chapter 7(e).

This matter about the number of years over which something may need to be deducted raises the question of what is a "year?" Believe it or not, a year is not always a year. For most of us, the year begins on January 1 and ends on December 31, but the calendar year and the taxable year are not necessarily the same.

For accounting and taxpaying purposes, a few individuals and many businesses elect to adopt a fiscal year that does not correspond to the calendar year. The U.S. Government, for example, operates on a fiscal year that runs from October 1 to September 30. When a private business seeks to use a fiscal year that differs from the calendar year, it must show a good reason for doing so. Many individuals have attempted to use changes in the starting and ending dates of their taxable year as a tax planning strategy, particularly as a technique for deferring income from business. Because of severe restrictions on when and how this can be done, few individuals have occasion to seriously consider using this approach. Since the vast majority of our readers use the calendar year, we always use the word *year* in that sense.

There are a number of other practical limitations on our ability to control the timing of our income and expenses. For one thing, most individuals are what are called cash basis taxpayers. Other accounting methods such as the accrual basis method also exist, but the accounting method we use often determines when financial events or transactions will be deemed to have occurred. This book assumes that its readers are cash basis taxpayers.

Another important practical limitation on our control over the timing of income and expenses is that we do not really have a year to pay tax on the money earned in January of year two. We are required to pay taxes on our income as it is earned, either through withholding or through the payment of estimated taxes. If we owe too large a proportion of our overall tax when we file our annual return, this underpayment can result in penalties. For those who file quarterly estimated tax returns, penalties can even be assessed if payments are shifted to an excessive degree into the later quarters.

The concept of tax planning extends to what we do, as well as to when we do it, but too much of anything, especially too much of a good thing, can be dangerous. As in the case of the retirees we discussed earlier, some people subordinate everything to tax avoidance. They organize their economic lives around tax planning to such an extent that their efforts become counterproductive. What is the point of saving on your taxes if the income you give up is greater than the taxes you save?

The point to remember is that taxes are only one dimension of overall financial planning. Focusing on only this one element of a transaction or situation can lead to poor results. Taxes are an important consideration in every financial setting, but they are seldom the sole consideration.

Expenditures do not always fit neatly into the categories prescribed by the tax law. A particular expenditure is often either deductible or nondeductible, but sometimes our expenditures can be partly deductible and partly not, or partly attributable to one deduction category and partly to another. This duality brings up the need to allocate expenses between their deductible and nondeductible components. As an example, consider an individual who hires someone to provide nursing services and also to perform general housekeeping duties. Certainly at least the wages attributable to the nursing services portion of the work should qualify for deduction. The wages paid for the housekeeping probably won't. In that case, an allocation between the deductible and nondeductible portions of your expense is necessary. This allocation extends to the costs of food eaten by the employee, utilities, and any other incidental costs associated with hiring the worker.

Making such allocations is tricky, both because they depend on the facts and because the types of documentation we typically give or receive are not designed with this kind of record-keeping in mind. In our hypothetical case, the basis for the allocation is the percentage of time devoted to each category of service. However, our records do not reflect this breakdown unless we make it a point to track the two components separately. The government does not alert us to the need to allocate. The tax returns we file as employers and the W-2s or 1099s we furnish to the worker at the end of the year make no distinctions based on whether we have paid the employee for performing deductible or nondeductible tasks.

A classic occasion for allocation occurs when we pay college tuition. Educational expenses such as tuition are not tax deductible, but if any portion of the tuition is for health insurance, then that portion is deductible as a medical expense. If the tuition bill does not separately state its components, the taxpayer should request such a breakdown so that an allocation between medical and nonmedical expenses can be made. This issue is discussed in Chapter 4(i).

The payroll or other employment taxes we pay on behalf of our household employees are deductible as taxes.[2.33] In some allocation cases, the portion of

Allocation

employment taxes attributable to the medical care can also be deducted under the medical expense category.[2.34] As these examples suggest, anticipating our documentary needs is itself a key element of tax planning. What is the role of documentation, and how do we go about proving the soundness of our claims?

(e)

T ruth Versus Proof

One of the most elusive concepts that strains our ability to cope with all bureaucracies revolves around the distinction between fact and law. A former Chief Justice of the United States once commented that he didn't care who had the power to decide the law so long as he had the power to find the facts. What concerns us here is not the opposition of fact and law, but the interplay between them, particularly when the key facts in the lives of persons with disabilities may be unfamiliar to tax advisers and to tax compliance officials.

With regard to the tax system, this interplay between fact and law can best be understood in terms of the relationship between truth and proof. The facts of a situation may be utterly beyond dispute, and the truthfulness of a taxpayer's contentions may be utterly unassailable, but even the most upright and honorable citizen can lose if the documentation and evidence the law requires are lacking.

There are two basic types of substantiation. Proof may take the form of documents, papers, receipts, prescriptions, W-2 or 1099 forms, contracts, check stubs, or other similar materials. Beyond these is another level of evidence. This second level of proof consists principally in demonstrating the rationale for your expenditures and in the arguments supporting the tax treatment you seek for them. Such proof may or may not be written and in certain cases may be in the form of a statement attached to your tax return.

Unfortunately, many cases are on record in which taxpayers were unsuccessful in their claims, not because they were untruthful about how they spent their funds or because they were unable to furnish receipts, but because they failed to adequately apply their facts to the governing law. Different kinds of documentary evidence are required, depending on the tax provisions in question.

The Form W-2, provided by the employer and included with the individual's tax return, is presumptive evidence of the amount of wages paid. A canceled check or a receipt usually serves to demonstrate that a particular expense was incurred and shows the date and to whom the expense was paid. But more may be required when the issue goes to the purpose and rationale for the expense. We do not mean to suggest that taxpayers should ever forego legitimate deductions or well-founded claims. We do mean that, for many persons with disabilities, more than average thought may need to be devoted to the question of proof. Marshalling such proof usually poses no problem for justifiable expenditures, but the taxpayer with a disability may be obliged to educate as much as to prove.

For instance, for an individual who is prevented by a physical disability from driving to work or using mass transit, the costs of a driver or taxi should arguably be deductible as impairment-related work expenses. As obvious as the need may be and however appropriate the method adopted for meeting that need, it may prove surprisingly difficult to convince a tax official unfamiliar with the disability that personal preference or the desire for a chauffeur is not the true motive for our commuting practices.

Far from deterring us in using the law to maximum advantage, the need to anticipate how we prove our claims should be a source of encouragement. The better able we are to explain and justify what we have done and why, the greater the prospect that our decisions are sound ones. That a course of action is based on solid tax ground is no guarantee of its wisdom for our lives, but thinking through the tax implications of a proposed expenditure can certainly contribute to clear analysis of its merits on other levels.

Some readers may wonder about audits or other challenges to their returns. People raise this question against the backdrop of their varying temperaments. Some people fearlessly claim all they believe they are entitled to; others claim nothing in the hope of escaping notice. Whether you are timid or bold, a small proportion of tax returns are routinely examined, audited, or followed up by demands from the government for more money. Beyond random reviews, experts believe that some returns are selected for audit based on criteria not publicized by the IRS. Suffice it to say that tax returns can also be challenged for many reasons that are publicly known. Such challenges can reflect arithmetical error or some other mistake in filling out the tax return; can result from failure to include some required schedule, subsidiary form, or supporting documentation; or can, of course, be precipitated by the contention that a particular strategy adopted on the tax return is invalid or incorrect. The taxpayer with a disability who takes maximum advantage of what the law allows should feel at no greater risk than anyone else.

It is not within the scope of this book to discuss the details of tax administration, since many readily available tax books deal with this subject in considerable depth, and since the subject does not impact any differently on taxpayers with disabilities than on anyone else. To this last assurance, one caveat must be added, however. Many of the tax strategies that people with disabilities need to adopt are initially unfamiliar to both tax advisers and tax enforcement officials. Realistically, if only because of this initial unfamiliarity and misunderstanding, it is wise to assume that once in a while questions will be raised.

If your analysis of the law is sound, your statement of facts truthful, and your application of the facts to the law well thought out, you should be able to proceed with total confidence. In doing so, it may also be useful to remember that the Internal Revenue Service is not the final arbiter of the law. Like any government agency, the IRS understandably interprets the law in the manner most favorable to itself, but when good faith differences of opinion or interpretation exist, ultimate responsibility for their resolution lies not with the IRS but with the courts, including the federal courts and the U.S. Tax Court, to which taxpayers have a right of appeal when faced with demands for more taxes.

If you use the services of an accountant, lawyer, or other tax adviser or preparer in the planning and formulation of your return, you certainly have the right to expect the assistance and support of that individual or firm in responding to any challenge from the government. What cannot be overemphasized is that for their initial participation or subsequent advocacy to be effective, it is critical that the tax professional be adequately educated regarding the disability issues involved with the return. Therefore, when we say it makes sense to be prepared in advance to respond to any questions that may arise, we mean that the planning, preparation, and possible defense of a tax claim are all parts of a single process. You can not effectively do any one of these without doing all of them!

Fairly or unfairly, the person with a disability often bears the greater burden of needing to know more than other people. When seeking employment, many have had the experience of taking the lead in apprising prospective employers of technology that would enable them to do the job. So, too, must people have knowledge of the law. And with tax law, this is likely to remain the prevailing reality for some time to come.

Having spoken about some generic tax planning concepts and having suggested some special issues surrounding their application to taxpayers with disabilities, it is now appropriate to ask: Who is disabled? We turn to this question next.

three

Who Is Disabled?

Who is disabled and how many Americans with disabilities there are depends on the definition we use. One leading demographer has recently offered this definition:

> For convenience, let us adopt a working definition of disability as a limitation on the performance of actions and/or activities resulting from some physical and/or mental difference. Let us call such physical and mental differences impairments.[3.1]

Surprising as it may seem, the Internal Revenue Code employs no uniform definition of disability. In fact, when referring to people with disabilities, the Code uses a number of different terms, including *disability, handicap,* and *impairment*.

41

The use of divergent, sometimes inconsistent terminology is explained in part by the fact that each provision has its own purpose and target group. But beyond differences arising from the complexity and variety of tax policy objectives, this pattern has other causes. This diversity of language reflects the ambiguity surrounding society's notions of disability. The terminology that has been inserted into the Internal Revenue Code over a period of fifty years mirrors the history of our public policy and social assumptions over two generations.

To understand the different ways our tax law treats disability, it will be helpful to survey how other major federal laws and programs approach disability. As this brief review will show, our laws deal with disability as a basis for entitlement to services and financial assistance, as a basis for conferring civil rights, and as a legal status. Faced with this multiplicity of objectives, and in light of the complexity of our underlying attitudes, the lack of definitional uniformity becomes easier to understand.

The most important definition of disability contained in present law is the one set forth in the Americans with Disabilities Act of 1990:[3.2] "The term 'disability' means . . . a physical or mental impairment that substantially limits one or more of the major life activities of such individual."[3.3]

The ADA is a civil rights statute aimed at protecting people with disabilities from discrimination in employment, transportation, public services, and public accommodations. For that reason, it goes on to define disability to include persons who have "a record of such an impairment" or who are "regarded" as having such an impairment.[3.4]

In contrast to this functional approach, definitions differ when dealing with entitlement to public services or public funds. For instance, in defining who is disabled for purposes of Social Security Disability Insurance (SSDI) eligibility, the Social Security Act defines disability to mean:

> inability to engage in any substantial gainful activity by reason of any medically determinable physical or mental impairment which can be expected to result in death or which has lasted or can be expected to last for a continuous period of not less than twelve

months; or in the case of an individual who has attained the age of 55 and is blind . . . inability to engage in substantial gainful activity requiring skills or abilities comparable to those of any gainful activity in which he has previously engaged with some regularity and over a substantial period of time. . . . An individual shall not be considered to be under a disability unless he furnishes such medical and other evidence of the existence thereof as the Secretary may require.[3.5]

As befits its very different purpose, this definition of disability differs significantly from that in the ADA. These differences chiefly relate to the severity or degree of impairment that is required and to the means by which the existence of a disability is proved. The definition demands that a disability be sufficiently severe to preclude gainful work. By contrast, the ADA is predicated upon the conviction that people with disabilities can work. So far as proof is concerned, the Social Security definition mandates the involvement of the medical profession, since an individual can not qualify for SSDI unless the nature of the disabling condition can be medically determined and certified.

Another variation on the definitional theme is provided by the Federal Rehabilitation Act. Title V of the Rehabilitation Act, dealing with civil rights, uses essentially the same definition as the ADA.[3.6] But in defining eligibility for vocational rehabilitation (VR) services, Title I of the Act specifies:

> . . . "Individual with handicaps" means any individual who has a physical or mental disability which for such individual constitutes or results in a substantial handicap to employment and can reasonably be expected to benefit in terms of employability from vocational rehabilitation services . . .[3.7]

Thus, under the Rehabilitation Act an individual will not qualify for VR services unless deemed to have the potential to benefit from the services the rehabilitation system offers. Therefore, people regarded as too severely disabled to benefit from VR services are not considered *disabled* within the meaning of Title I. Incongruous as it may seem, cases actually exist in which people have been denied VR services because they are considered too severely disabled to benefit, but have been found ineligible for SSDI benefits because they are deemed capable of at least some gainful employment, i.e., because they are not disabled enough!

For our final illustrative definition of disability from the general body of federal law, we turn to the Technology-Related Assistance for Individuals with Disabilities Act of 1988.[3.8] This legislation was designed to make assistive technology available to disabled persons, and defines an individual with disability as:

> any individual who is considered to have a disability or handicap for the purposes of any federal law . . . or for the purposes of the law of the state in which the individual resides; and who is or would be enabled by assistive technology devices or assistive technology services to maintain a level of functioning or to achieve a greater level of functioning in any major life activity.[3.9]

This approach to defining eligibility for services is more inclusive than the Rehabilitation Act's. It confers eligibility on a much larger number of people, which seems appropriate, given that many more people could benefit from specific applications of technology than from extensive VR services. Moreover, an individual qualifies for technology services under any federal or state law that defines him or her as having a disability. This differs from VR, where the state agency makes its own evaluation of both the existence of a disability and capacity to benefit from services.

In this connection, compare the Tech Act with the Social Security Act. Under the former, the finding of disability can be made by any federal or state agency, whether or not their criteria are medical, whereas with Social Security Disability, such a finding is permissible only upon the furnishing of highly structured medical evidence, no matter how palpable the existence of the disability.

These varying definitions of who is disabled may seem inconsistent, even contradictory. How is it that the same person could be insufficiently disabled to qualify for services in one government office, too disabled to be helped by the program in the next building, but just right for the folks a block away? The answer is that none of these definitions was intended to be universal. Each definition was crafted for a specific and different purpose. Each public policy goal in the definitions just surveyed is also present in our tax laws. Thus the Internal Revenue Code is a microcosm of society's attitudes and agendas about disability.

Like the broader body of law, the Internal Revenue Code does not utilize uniform definitions in its approach to people with disabilities and to the status of being disabled. Whether someone is considered disabled and the tax consequences of that status depend on the particular code provision at issue. The following examples drawn from the Internal Revenue Code illustrate this point.

(a)

Disability As Incapacity for Self-Care

This is the definition used in connection with the dependent care credit (see Chapter 6(i)), which is available for expenses for the care of a disabled dependent incurred by a taxpayer in order to earn income. The individual receiving care need not be *permanently and totally* disabled or be disabled on a long-term basis. Nor must the taxpayer furnish any diagnosis or medical certification of the extent of the incapacitation.[3.10]

While the absence of these formal requirements reduces the practical burdens of qualifying for the credit, the incapacity for self-care test is nevertheless a rigorous one, connoting both inability to care for oneself and inability to earn a living.

(b)

Inability to Engage in Substantial Gainful Activity

Compare the standard of disability for the dependent care credit with the approach under the credit for the permanently and totally disabled. Here the qualifying individual who can claim the credit must be "permanently and totally" disabled and incapable of engaging in "substantial gainful activity." Specific medical certifications are required to claim this credit.[3.11] This credit provides an excellent illustration of the medical model of disability, which is the test predominantly used throughout the tax code. The definition of disability applicable to this credit[3.12] is the same as the one just quoted from the Social Security Act.

Another example of this medical model of disability can be found in the little-known provision bearing on premature withdrawl of retirement funds. Early withdrawals from most retirement plans ordinarily entail a 10 percent "additional tax," but this penalty is waived if the worker or account holder makes the premature withdrawal because of a disability. The definition reads:

> For purposes of this section an individual shall be considered disabled if he is unable to engage in any substantial gainful activity by reason of any medically determinable physical or mental impairment which can be expected to result in death or to be of long-continued and indefinite duration. An individual shall not be considered. . . disabled unless he furnishes proof of the existence thereof...as the secretary may require.[3.13]

For further discussion of this penalty exception, see Chapter 7(a).

At this point a paradox must be noted. With eligibility for SSDI benefits, with qualification for the permanent and total disability credit, and with many other provisions defining disability as inability to work, a person who actually performs gainful work will cease to be deemed disabled. Medical evidence is necessary to qualify, but no amount of medical evidence can preserve the disability status if the vocational facts refute it. Were ability to work solely or simply a medical question, competent and truthful medical assessment ought to be conclusive. Even apart from the need to catch cheaters, it is evident, even to those who know little of assistive technology or of the evolution of our attitudes about disability, that medical diagnosis and prognosis never provide a definitive answer to the question whether a particular individual is able to work.

In its implementation of this awareness, the law falls short. While it is not unreasonable to try to identify people who are prevented for medical reasons from working, the law's reliance on only two mutually exclusive categories may create more problems than it solves. From the standpoint of these laws, people are either disabled (in which case they qualify for the benefit in question) or they are not (in which case they get no permanent and total disability credit, no SSDI, and no help under a variety of other programs).

In some areas, the law has taken steps to mitigate the harshness of its own dichotomies. For example, under the SSDI program minimal earnings will
not result in a finding that the beneficiary is *able* to
perform substantial gainful activity (SGA).[3.14] Nor will
people who earn over the SGA amount (between
$6,000 and $9,200 per year, depending on whether
the beneficiary is classified as "disabled" or "blind")
be denied benefits until they have worked for a sufficient period (usually 9–12 months as a trial work
period) to demonstrate their capacity to do so.[3.15]
Moreover, even if people can earn more than the SGA
amount for extended periods, they will still not lose
their benefits if their impairment-related work
expenses leave them with net monthly incomes that
fall below the SGA amount.[3.16]

No comparable softening is evident in the Internal Revenue Code provisions defining disability, however. Where the Social Security Act has introduced
incentives for returning to work, the tax law remains
concerned only with rigidly distinguishing those who
can work from those who cannot. In our discussion
of the permanent and total disability credit (Chapter
7(b)), we will examine how this frustrates the objectives of rehabilitation and full participation, and how
it could be remedied without risk to either the
integrity of tax administration or the achievement of
relevant policy and revenue goals.

Our three examples so far of how the Internal
Revenue Code defines disability have two common
elements: the existence of a medically provable
health problem and the consequent inability to work
or otherwise participate in economic activity. As such,
these definitions make disability synonymous with illness, helplessness, and a variety of other fundamental
incapacities. As we know, elsewhere in our law the
term *disability* refers to mental or physical factors that
limit one or more major life activities. When the Internal Revenue Code uses the term, *working* is the life
activity with which it is principally concerned.

There are other settings in which people with
disabilities are acknowledged by the tax code. In
1990, the ADA's definition of disability was incorpo-
rated into the new disability access tax credit.[3.17] In
other places as well, the code recognizes the ability of
people with disabilities to contribute to society, but in

these cases, the term *disability* is not used; other terms such as *impairment* or *handicap* are used instead. Let us examine two illustrations of the use of these alternative jurisdictional terms.

The law provides a tax deduction to businesses for the removal of architectural or transportation barriers to the use of their facilities by the elderly and "handicapped."[3.18] The term *handicapped* is defined in terms of a "physical or mental disability" which "constitutes or results in a functional limitation to employment" or which "substantially limits one or more major life activities."

Any function can be involved: seeing, hearing, walking, lifting, learning, and so on. There is no requirement of medical proof. Indeed, there could be no such requirement since the law does not require the business removing the barriers to identify in advance the specific handicapped or elderly individuals who will benefit from these environmental modifications.

In the area of employment, the law provides a deduction for impairment-related work expenses.[3.19] Here, the term *impairment* is not defined, but the deduction is made applicable to handicapped persons as defined in the architectural barrier removal provision. This use of the term *impairment-related work expenses* in the Internal Revenue Code should not be confused with the Social Security Act's use of the term. They have different meanings in these two settings.

This brief survey of alternative definitions of disability serves to illustrate a key point. Even within a single statute such as the Internal Revenue Code, disability means different things in different contexts. Over the course of a lifetime, an individual with a disability may satisfy different definitions at different times. Which definition a taxpayer needs to satisfy and which factors need to be emphasized depend on what provision of the law you are attempting to invoke.

Given the purposes for which the Code uses the word *disability,* the requirements for a high level of medical involvement and for medical findings are not unreasonable. Certainly, when a tax law provision is intended to mitigate economic hardships associated with inability to work, the government can not be faulted for wanting proof that only those intended to be targeted by the provision in fact benefit from it.

Nevertheless, definitions that approach disability in terms of functional impairment or environmental and social barriers are preferable to those equating disability with illness and nonparticipation. Foremost among the advantages of a functionally-based definition of disability is that it underscores the realization that any characteristic or status is "disabling" only insofar as it limits major life activities. As things stand now, the tax law definition of *disability,* while laudable in seeking to mitigate economic hardship, gives comparatively little recognition or encouragement to the millions of people with major activity limitations who do work, and the millions more who would like to.

A tax law provision that encourages measures aimed at achieving functional goals in the economic sphere serves both to focus and to reinforce this simple truth. A tax code that encourages strategies for achieving full economic and social participation has merit from both a philosophical and an economic perspective. To the extent that independence and participation are encouraged, the demand for public funds to support dependency is commensurately reduced. Moreover, whether one looks at tax policy from the standpoint of promoting economic activity or from that of limiting "tax expenditure" (that is, costs to the treasury resulting from the tax breaks that the law provides), an approach that encourages the achievement and enhancement of functioning, in the economic and the personal realms, makes considerable and consistent good sense.

Failure to appreciate the distinction between functional and medical issues contributes to the confusion of disability with illness. Doubtless, a majority of disabilities are caused by illness or injury, but the practical problems to which they give rise are not medical ones. Some would go further, arguing that the most significant barrier people with disabilities face is the attitudes of others toward them, not any limitations inherent in the disability. The ADA reflects this awareness by including within its definition of disabled persons those individuals who are erroneously regarded as having a disability.

Our society cannot be faulted for attempting to use the tax code to offset the income loss and other hardships associated with inability to work. If anything, the thrust of criticism in this connection is that these efforts have been too limited to have a material effect. Nor can we expect the tax code, any more than other large and complicated bodies of laws, to change as quickly as we like in response to our evolving sensibilities. Where disappointment is warranted, however, is in the code's widespread failure to recognize disability in any but these negative and compensatory terms. In Chapter 9 we discuss policy initiatives and structural reforms that could help to remedy this imbalance. The tax law does a creditable job of recognizing the misfortune and loss that is sometimes associated with disability. It can and should be bolstered to do an equal job in encouraging the potential for productive work and full life that always exists.

Pending the incorporation of our emerging consciousness into the tax laws of our nation, people with disabilities must take maximum advantage of the current law. In that regard, the following chapters show that considerable opportunities exist for tax subsidy of many of the costs of living with a disability. Sadly, they also show that in availing ourselves of these opportunities we must often accept terminology, assumptions, and stereotypes that are needless from the standpoint both of tax administration and individual dignity.

At present, the health care deduction offers the greatest degree of flexibility for obtaining the subsidies the law allows. Accordingly, we turn first to this monumentally important, but often awkward and unwieldy, deduction category.

four

Medical Expenses

(a)

Background

There are two basic types of income tax deductions: those available to businesses and those provided to individuals. While personal expenses are generally not deductible,[4.1] several expense categories incurred by individuals in nonbusiness settings are not considered personal expenses. Among these, medical and dental care is one of the most important.

People get their notions of health and their definitions of health care from many sources. Insurance companies tell us what constitutes medical care by what they include in their coverage and by what services, procedures, and devices they do and do not agree to pay for. Doctors tell us what constitutes health care by the range of subjects on which they give advice and by when they do and do not offer treatment. The government tells us what health care is in a variety of ways, including through the scope of the medical care deduction in the Internal Revenue Code. None of the definitions that come from outside the tax law are adequate or sufficient to tell if and when a particular expense qualifies for the deduction. The tax law is a world of its own as far as this is concerned.

For routine health care costs—treatment by a physician, prescription pharmaceuticals, dental work, or hospitalization—it makes little tax or practical difference whether the recipient of the care is disabled or not. A disability may influence the nature or the amount of these costs, but it has no impact on their tax status. The scope and intricacies of the tax code's definition of medical expenses take center stage when we deal with the distinctive expenses that people with disabilities incur.

The presence or absence of a disability has no bearing on the procedures we use to compute our deduction. Medical care expenses that exceed 7.5 percent of adjusted gross income (AGI) are deductible as itemized deductions on our tax returns. In order to itemize, the total deductions from all categories, including medical care, must exceed the amount of the standard deduction. Thus, even when an expense qualifies as medical care, its actual deductibility depends on meeting two conditions: Do we have enough itemized deductions from this and other sources to itemize; and do we have enough medical care expenses to get over the 7.5 percent of AGI deductibility threshold? These two questions are linked because in assessing our total itemized deductions, only those health care costs exceeding the 7.5 percent are included in the calculation.

Generally speaking, whether or not an expense qualifies as medical care depends on its nature and purpose. Numerous factors play a role in determining what expenses qualify as medical care. Many people assume that in order to qualify for deductibility, a health care expense must involve something done or ordered by a physician or dentist. Or they assume that the expense must be for the treatment of a specific disease or illness. At the other extreme, some people believe that the intention to improve their health and well-being is sufficient to justify the deduction. Neither of these views is correct.

People with disabilities incur many costs that others do not. They may need to purchase assistive technology devices, or rehabilitation, personal assistance, or other services. They may pay heightened costs for transportation; they may need to modify their homes to make them accessible; or they may incur any number of other costs that result from the interplay between the disability and their attempts to reduce its impact on their lives.

Because some readers may be initially unfamiliar with the range and scope of these expenses, let us put assistive technology into the context of better-known devices. In the area of technology, such devices as oxygen tents, hospital beds, or home dialysis machines are known in insurance and governmental parlance as durable medical equipment. Other devices, ranging from pacemakers to artificial eyes, generally fall under the rubric of prosthetic devices. *Assistive technology devices* are those that aim to enhance the functioning of people with disabilities in the various spheres of their personal, economic, and social life. Also called by such names as adaptive technology, sensory, communications, or mobility aids, assistive technology devices are defined by the Technology-Related Assistance for Individuals with Disabilities Act of 1988 as, "any item, piece of equipment, or product system, whether acquired commercially off the shelf, modified, or customized, that is used to increase, maintain, or improve the functional capabilities of individuals with disabilities."[4.2]

What is crucial for people with disabilities and their families to remember is that many of these costs are tax deductible under the medical care rationale. Unfortunately, individuals and families also need to remember that although enhanced dignity and independence may be the objective of a given expenditure, the law can accommodate these goals only through the prism of care, treatment, or mitigation.

(b)

L egal Basis for Deductibility

The deduction for "Medical, Dental, etc. Expenses" is set forth in Section 213 of the Internal Revenue Code. Subsection (d) provides the definition of medical care. It includes amounts paid "for the diagnosis, cure, mitigation, treatment or prevention of disease or for the purpose of affecting any structure or function of the body."

For people with disabilities, the key words in this definition are *mitigation* and *for the purpose of affecting any structure or function of the body.* What do these words mean, and why are they so important?

On one level, their meaning is fairly obvious. If we obtain an artificial limb, we affect a structure of the body by replacing an arm or a leg. If we wear corrective lenses or a hearing aid, we are affecting a function of the body by improving our sight or hearing. No one would be surprised to learn that such items as artificial limbs, contact lenses, or hearing aids are deductible.[4.3] However, the implications of the "structure or function" language, particularly for assistive technology, are more profound than may be immediately apparent.

To understand these implications, we must think about the nature and purposes of disability-related costs. The majority of disability-related costs that people incur do not result from attempts to cure or treat illness. People with disabilities are no more or no less ill than anyone else. What disability-related costs more typically involve is the effort to cope with the functional consequences of the impairment; the effort to find alternative strategies for performing various activities and tasks, and to achieve a level of function that minimizes the effects of the disability on the quality and opportunities of life. In common parlance, many, if not most, of the disability-related costs that people incur represent the attempt to compensate for the effects of the functional impairment.

For these expenses, *mitigation* is the key word in the law. Many people concentrate their efforts on seeking a cure, but for growing numbers of people, getting on with the day-to-day business of living represents their central and overriding concern. It is in connection with these aspirations that the unexpected scope of the medical care deduction may prove a revelation.

When the statute speaks of mitigation, it does

not refer only to medical improvement, although those are the terms in which many people still instinctively respond. It connotes something broader: mitigation of the functional consequences of the disease or, in this case, of the impairment. We mitigate the impairment of one or another function or structure of the body when we:

- obtain a guide dog or a van lift to facilitate our mobility;
- purchase a closed-caption decoder to facilitate access to the audio portion of TV broadcasts;
- obtain an environmental control system to operate devices and appliances we can not reach or manipulate manually;
- pay for the training and technical support necessary to utilize any of these resources.

Mitigation of functional impairments is the legal logic underlying the characterization of these and similar costs as health care expenses. Each of these measures affects a function or structure of the body. This is the hook on which their deductibility is hung.

The scope of this mitigation concept becomes clear if we reflect upon a few of our common pleasures. We naturally enjoy strolling through a scenic park, gazing at the faces of our loved ones, or immersing ourselves in the sounds of beautiful music. Such activities all have aesthetic values for which there is no literal substitute, but to a large degree walking, seeing, and hearing are not ends in themselves but means to an end. Walking is the means of getting somewhere; seeing and hearing are the vehicles for communicating and acquiring information. Mitigating the effects of a disability by providing alternative methods of function achieves the same practical result as restoration of the function by traditional medical means. Obviously a wheelchair does not restore the use of our legs, but it does engender mobility, which is the purpose of walking. An optical character reader does not restore sight, but it does make the material on the printed page accessible, facilitating the functional goal of reading.

Ultimately, this confusion between restoration of the organ system or body part on the one hand, and utilization of alternative means for achieving its functions on the other, lies at the heart of most disputes over the medical deductibility of assistive or rehabilitative technology. This confusion derives from our culture, from the role played by the medical model, and from emotion; not a confusion inherent in the law.

The people who write, interpret, enforce, and advise us on the law are typically not thinking of mitigation in the way contemporary experience defines it. For the most part, disabilities are still thought of as medical conditions, and mitigation is identified with therapeutic intervention.

Our advancing technology has created new opportunities for mitigation and new ways for affecting the functions of the body. In the wake of these changes, it is not always clear how the standards of proof and the conventional terminology of tax law can be adapted to meet the rapidly evolving new realities that technology and social change are creating. If we are to obtain all the tax advantages to which we are entitled, our task is to translate these new realities into the day-to-day language of tax consultation and administration.

Particularly in the area of information processing impairments (which some people call cognitive or perceptual impairments, and which include learning disabilities), we repeatedly face the problem that techniques for mitigation have expanded far beyond the expectations of those who drafted and now implement our laws. Imagine what is involved in demonstrating to those with little or no notion of information processing disabilities why a computer program that combines spoken with visual output may be therapeutic for an individual with a reading disability?

This example gives rise to an important illustration of how the law can mean what it says while not always being taken literally. Since the statute refers to structures or functions of the *body,* it is natural to wonder if the *mind* is excluded. Such fears are groundless. Mental and emotional illness, their treatment, and mitigation are covered in much the same way as sensory, motor, or physical disabilities. To the degree that mental, emotional, or information processing disabilities are recognized objects of diagnosis, treatment, or mitigation, deductibility is available for medical expenses attributable to them.

Our medical care expenditures may be divided into two categories: goods (tangible things that we buy) and services (the time, expertise, skills, or actions of others). The medical care deduction embraces both types.

The deductibility of goods and services interact in several ways. Sometimes goods will only be deductible if recommended by a physician or other credentialed health care provider. Pharmaceuticals are the best illustration of this category of goods. Since drugs are deductible only when prescribed, a physician's services will be indispensable to their deductibility. Other times, the health professional's diagnosis or recommendations, while not a legal prerequisite to deductibility, constitute powerful evidence of the nature and purpose of the expense. With goods and services alike, their source, nature, and purposes form the continuum along which deductibility is determined.

People with disabilities purchase many of the same items that anyone else uses. Tax issues arise when the cost is for a disability-related item. What are disability-related expenditures? Disability-related items may be divided into three groups: items designed or modified specifically for use by an individual with a disability; items in common use that acquire their significance through some unique functional capacity they confer on the user with a disability; and items that combine common use and specially-designed components.

A hearing aid illustrates the first type, since no one would wear one in the absence of a hearing impairment. A magic marker is a simple example of the second type, since its thick and heavy lines may be the only technique available for making handwriting legible to a person with a visual impairment. For the individual who finds this use for it, the felt-tipped pen becomes an item of assistive technology by reason of the circumstances surrounding its selection and use.

The third category of goods is composed of devices or supplies that are partly specialized and partly mainstream. Consider a standard automobile equipped with hand controls. The automobile itself is standard, but the add-on hand controls are designed for use by a person with a physical disability. Among

(c)

Assistive Technology Devices and Other Goods

categories of this *mixed-type technology,* computer systems that include standard hardware plus specially-designed peripherals or software, such as a computer equipped with a speech synthesizer for use by a blind person, are becoming increasingly common.

No standard tax nomenclature yet exists to describe or distinguish these three categories of devices. We will refer to dedicated devices, that is devices designed specifically for use by people with disabilities, as *special* items. Equipment not ordinarily used in any disability-related way we will call *ordinary* or *personal use* items. Devices or systems comprised of both special and ordinary components we shall term *mixed type* or *mixed systems.* This terminology comes as close as possible to the relevant tax law language.

In claiming deductions, taxpayers have the simplest task with special items. If the nature and features of such devices are sufficiently explained, no one would seriously contend that their purpose was other than mitigation of the impact of a disability or that they did not affect a structure or function of the body. On this basis, deductibility has been accorded to such purchases as:

- guide dogs and hearing dogs and other service animals;[4.4]
- telecommunications devices for the deaf (TDDs);[4.5]
- closed-caption TV decoders;[4.6]
- equipment to facilitate reading and writing by a person losing sight;[4.7] and
- hand controls and lift equipment for motor vehicle operation and access.[4.8]

The list of special items that have been accorded deductibility may seem short. Although a vast array of devices meet the definition of special items, only a tiny fraction of these have been the subject of court decisions or administrative rulings. This could mean either that people are not seeking deductions for such goods or that the IRS is granting deductions when claimed. Based on anecdotal evidence from many taxpayers with disabilities, we believe it means a little of both.

Even if litigation over special items were common, the law could never keep pace with the rapid proliferation of such new technology. Thus, taxpayers must always extrapolate from what has already been decided to the facts of their own cases. If tax advisers take the need for precedent too literally, they run the risk of failing to look beyond the specifics of a given decision to its reasoning and potential applicability. To illustrate this point, the IRS has issued specific rulings holding that guide dogs and hearing dogs used by people who are blind or deaf qualify as deductible medical expenses. Yet in a later case, a specially trained and registered cat used by a person with a hearing impairment was allowed because the animal was trained and functioned to alert the individual to the ringing of the doorbell and other sounds.[4.9] Nothing in the law at the time of the cat ruling referred to the deductibility of other animals than dogs, but the logic of these previous decisions extended to the cat trained and functioning in this way.

Since these decisions were rendered, the use of *service animals* has greatly increased, including the use by people with physical disabilities other than deafness or blindness of dogs, monkeys, and potentially other animals to provide them with needed services and assistance. In the wake of such decisions, and on the basis of the legislative history of the 1988 tax amendments, at least one major publisher of tax information and commentary has concluded that all service animals now qualify for the deduction.[4.10] Yet nothing in the Internal Revenue Code or its implementing regulations expressly grants deductibility, either to people with disabilities other than hearing or vision, or to animals other than dogs. Nevertheless, common sense and the trend of the law clearly indicate that they do.

In the absence of regulations or further clarification of the statute, we may not find out for sure until some taxpayer who was initially refused a deduction for a service animal appeals that decision. If the scope of the service animal deduction is expanding, taxpayers will need to anticipate additional issues of proof. Taxpayers will probably need to show that their animals meet applicable training or certification requirements of state law, or meet the requirements for antidiscrimination protection under the ADA.

The IRS recognizes equipment under the heading "special items and equipment," which are reported on Line 1 of Schedule A to Form 1040. The entire cost of special items usually qualifies for deduction. However, an allocation is typically required for mixed-type systems and configurations, with the total cost of the equipment divided between its specialized and ordinary components. A vehicle equipped with a wheelchair lift, for example, is not totally deductible. Only the cost of the lift (or the amount by which the lift increases the price of the vehicle if it is built in) is deductible under the health care rationale.

Also typical of allocation cases in this area is one in which the IRS allowed as a health care deduction the cost of braille books purchased for a blind child, but limited the deduction to the amount by which the cost of the braille editions exceeded the price of their print equivalents.[4.11] We will return to the subject of allocation later in this chapter. In the meantime, our discussion of allocation or partial deductibility should not be taken to imply that mixed-type systems are never fully deductible. There are times when they may be, but more complex problems of proof are presented.

In contrast with special items, litigation on the deductibility of ordinary goods is voluminous. This reflects the far more perplexing issues of justification and substantiation such items raise. With ordinary or personal use items, the problem is that they only become disability-related by virtue of the context of their use (how and by whom they are used). Put graphically, proving that a felt-tipped pen affects a structure or function of the body, thereby making it something other than a personal use item, is no easy task.

Deductibility of equipment hinges on three things: its role in mitigating a functional impairment by affecting a structure or function of the body; such mitigation as the motive for its acquisition; and actual use consistent with this purpose. In practice, these dimensions overlap and blur into each other. The design and function of special items tend to prove all three points. With ordinary items recommended by a physician, proving purpose and actual use may or may not present problems. For instance, a wig was held deductible when recommended by a physician to prevent psychological damage resulting from chemotherapy-induced baldness.[4.12] Under these circumstances, the taxpayer's motive for and use of the

wig raised no questions. Of course, peculiar circumstances could always arise to turn them into issues
again. Possibly the taxpayer was the world's most
ardent wig collector prior to receiving medical treatment, in which case some question of motive might
be raised. Similarly with use, it is possible that someone somewhere uses a wig as a table ornament. Such
bizarre scenarios are not the reality of tax law however. In the absence of very unusual facts, no one is
going to question the motivation for purchase of the
wig, nor does the taxpayer need to prove the wig was
worn for a certain number of hours each day or on a
certain proportion of occasions when the taxpayer
went out in public. After all, what else is a person
going to do with a wig than wear it?

    With other ordinary items, the situation is often
less simple. Although the pitfalls confronted in trying
to deduct standard items are many, the law furnishes
numerous examples of cases in which taxpayers were
able to sustain the necessary burden of proof. When
we speak of ordinary items, we are talking about
what the law typically characterizes as *personal use*
items. Although furniture, air conditioners, swimming
pools, and the like have qualified for the medical
expense deduction, their status as personal use items
places a heavy burden of proof on the taxpayer.
Because items intended for personal or family use are
not deductible, the taxpayer who would qualify such
items as medical must show that they are being used
in a fashion that transforms their status from personal
to medical items.

    Let us consider four cases that span the range of
possible outcomes. Case One involved the purchase
of a reclining chair by a cardiac patient. There was
nothing special about the chair—nothing to distinguish it from the kind of chair that anyone might
choose to have in their living room—but the taxpayer
was able to show that the chair had been recommended for specific therapeutic reasons by his heart
specialist, and that it was not used for recreation or as
a general item of furniture by either him or his family.
Thus a health care deduction was allowed for the cost
of the chair.[4.13]

    In Case Two, another cardiac patient installed a
car phone in order to contact his doctor or summon
help in the event of another heart attack. The tax-

payer had listed his car phone number in the telephone directory. By doing this, the taxpayer demonstrated his intention that the phone be used for other purposes, since if his motive had been solely what he claimed, there would have been no reason to publish the telephone number. Accordingly, the deduction for the cost of the phone was denied.[4.14]

Case Three concerns a family who purchased a clarinet and clarinet lessons for their child. Both the instrument and the lessons were deductible because the family was able to prove that they had been recommended by their orthodontist for treatment of a severe malocclusion of the teeth.[4.15]

Case Four introduces us to taxpayers who claimed a medical deduction for the cost of snow plows. They contended that physical disabilities prevented them from shoveling snow and that they needed this equipment to avoid further injury. Unfortunately for this creative effort, they lived in a region of the country where heavy winter snows were the norm and where most people owned snow plows, and their land required plowing when it snowed. Since there was no evidence or likelihood that they would have refrained from using plows if they did not have back problems, their claim was denied.[4.16]

What these four cases have in common is that their outcomes hinge on the facts. In none of them does there appear to have been any basic dispute between the taxpayer and the government about the underlying law. All four involve the effort to characterize as medical what would normally be considered personal use items. While we do not know all the arguments that were made in each case, we can speculate about what factual differences might have changed the outcomes in Cases Two and Four.

In Case Two, the key distinction seems obvious. If the taxpayer had not listed his car phone number in the directory, the deduction might have been allowed, since the IRS probably would not have gotten the impression that he wanted people to call him. Of course, the taxpayer may have had a good medical reason for putting the number in the book, which he should have explained! In all likelihood, the existence of a medical reason for installing the phone was not doubted. The trouble was that the medical purpose was not believed to be his sole motivation. Put in our frame of reference, while the taxpayer arguably had a medical justification for the car phone, he failed to prove his motives and perhaps his use of the device.

In Case Four, it is harder to guess what these taxpayers might have needed to prove in order to prevail. We can speculate that their chances of success would have been better if, instead of general assertions about back trouble, they had submitted detailed statements from their physicians indicating exactly what harm could result from shoveling snow. They did show that after receiving medical advice they purchased new tractor snow plows to replace the ones they already had. If they could have demonstrated that their selection of equipment model or design was dictated by the nature of their disabilities, they might at least have won a deduction for the amount by which the expense of modifying their equipment exceeded the cost of ordinary snow plows. Unfortunately, they failed to show that any such selection criteria were involved. Again in our terms, the government apparently doubted the existence of a medical justification, and hence disbelieved the purpose and use of the equipment.

People attempting to claim what are normally considered personal use items should, therefore, be prepared to provide proof on several levels. First, they must be able to document the expense: how much, to whom was it paid, for what, and when. They should also be prepared to show how the item mitigates a disability or what structure or function of the body it affects. What functions does it make possible that would otherwise be unattainable? What life activities does it make easier or safer?

Having thought through how the purchase meets these requirements, the taxpayer is only halfway to success because the equipment has to do more than just be capable of mitigating the disability; the taxpayer must also demonstrate that the equipment was purchased and is used for this mitigating purpose. With personal use items, these purpose-and-use layers represent the point at which problems most frequently arise. The ordinary home computer is probably the best example of a personal use item that becomes disability-related because of how it is used. Mixed-system cases which frequently involve the personal computer as their ordinary component present the most vexing problems here. All the issues of proof that we have discussed are involved in securing its deductibility. Since a computer can be used for many purposes by any member of the household, how can you prove that it was purchased and used to meet a disability-related need? Moreover, what is the nature of such a need? Under what circumstances does a computer mitigate a functional disability, and what medical or other evidence would document this role?

Depending on the circumstances, there may be several ways to assemble and prove the key facts. Perhaps the purchase of a computer was recommended by a rehabilitation services agency, by an assistive technology service provider, or even by a physician. Perhaps the particular model chosen was dictated by its interface capabilities with specialized peripherals or adaptive software. Maybe the computer was bought as part of a turnkey system along with the adaptive components. Possibly the family already had a computer that the individual with the disability was unable to use. Maybe features that nondisabled users would need were removed or omitted, such as the monitor in the case of a computer bought by a blind user. Perhaps only specialized software was purchased for use with the machine, making its use awkward or impossible for a person without the disability.

When you stop to analyze them, the possibilities are virtually limitless. If you purchased the computer to compensate for a disability, some facts that will help prove it are bound to exist!

What is the disability-related need that gives rise to the purchase of a computer? In mixed-system situations, this is often the major hurdle. The difficulties associated with showing such a need are illustrated in the law's treatment of the automobile. Although the specialized hand controls for driving it and the wheelchair lift for entering and leaving it are now routinely includable under the definition of medical expenses, the car itself is not deductible. This is because the disability does not give rise to the need for the car; in most places in this country, a car is a practical necessity whether one is disabled or not. From the tax law standpoint, the hand controls or wheelchair lift qualify as medical care expenses precisely because they permit access to and use of the motor vehicle.

The same logic applies to specialized hardware peripherals or software used by people with various disabilities to access and use the home computer. After all, it is not the computer that mitigates the disability, but the specialized access tools that do so by giving us access to and use of it. For the vehicle or computer to be deductible, something more needs to be shown. In their attempts to show this *something more,* taxpayers have adopted various approaches. Under the current state of the law, none is entirely satisfactory for showing the necessary connection between the personal use item in question and its role in overcoming a disability.

Relying on the fact that the items in question had certainly been bought for use in overcoming a functional limitation, some taxpayers have simply claimed the deduction, hoping they would not be challenged. This strategy has sometimes worked for them, but it can neither be recommended to individuals nor offered to the disability community as a solution to the underlying problem. Confronting the problem more directly, other taxpayers have argued that the special and ordinary components were so interrelated as to make distinction between them meaningless. As it relates to the motor vehicle, this argument runs as follows: true, the lift makes the automobile accessible, but the vehicle would not have been bought without the existence and availability of the lift. Likewise, the lift has no practical utility in the absence of an automobile.

Where this logic falls short is in its failure to demonstrate a sufficient connection between the automobile and the disability. Disabled or not, you still use an automobile for moving about. Hence, you did not purchase the car because of the disability. Yet what if you could prove that prior to becoming disabled, you had lived long and happily without an automobile, walking or taking mass transit until prevented by disability from doing so? In that event, the automobile becomes the only means by which you have any mobility now that there is no other way for you to get around. In such a case, you would want medical evidence of why you could not travel by your previous method or by any other method, and indeed, evidence as to how alternative mobility strategies would expose you to further health risk. The law being what it is, it also would not hurt to show that inability to travel would deprive you of needed medical care, though this is likely harder to prove.

Or if, like most people, you drove a car before the onset of your disability but abandoned it in favor of a different model that accommodates the necessary add-ons, the argument that your vehicle costs are directly attributable to and incurred to overcome the disability is also credible. Regrettably, we cannot say that such an argument is likely to succeed, but such arguments are worthwhile both in the hope of prevailing in your own claim and for the sake of making new law from the ground up.

Along similar lines, other taxpayers have confronted the problem by maintaining that the standard item mitigates the functional impairment. A person with a visual disability might argue that the computer facilitates reading, writing, and other tasks normally performed with vision. In this situation, more perhaps than in the case of the automobile, the computer is used in a fundamentally different way than it would be by a person without a disability.

The problem with this reasoning is that blind people have written and read quite well with readers, magnifiers, braille, tapes, and other methods, long before the advent of the computer. Even if the computer makes these activities easier, cheaper, or more effective, one is hard pressed to claim that the computer makes these things possible. A computer makes possible the reading of disks or electronic bulletin boards, but it does that for people with and without vision. Having chosen to use a computer, your needs in accessing it will be subsidized, just as the needs of getting into and out of a car or of watching television with a decoder will be subsidized. But your underlying decision to use the computer remains a personal choice, not a medical one. Again, in terms of our three levels of proof, you have not shown that your motive in purchasing the computer was to overcome the impairment, since even without a visual limitation, you might well have purchased the identical computer. If you can show that the demands of the access technology obliged you to select a more expensive computer than you otherwise would have bought, you can at least claim a deduction for this difference in price. But even here, proof may not be easy since it is difficult to prove what computer you would have bought under different circumstances. To be sure, if someone already owned a computer but then had to upgrade it with additional memory, interface ports, or other features in order to accommodate an access system, the issue would no longer be proving what you would have spent. In this case, you know the amount by which access increased the cost of your standard computer.

The case for the computer as an assistive device in its own right can be made with greater cogency by persons with learning disabilities for whom the computer represents not merely a preferred means, but perhaps the only viable method for reading printed material. For example, some people need simultaneous or interchangeable visual and auditory output in order to read. In that context, the computer with its dual output modes becomes the only realistic means for presenting the material. The argument for treating the ordinary computer and its special output capabilities as a single entity also has considerable force when made by a person with a vocal communication impairment who uses the computer to drive an alternative communication device that embodies the only means by which the individual can communicate orally.

One way of summarizing these approaches to deducting the personal use components of mixed systems is what can best be called a "but for" argument. This does not mean that "but for the disability" you would not have bought the item. Rather, the formulation of this argument is "but for the disability" this item or method would not have been necessary to achieve the function in question. Had there been no limitation of function, this purchase would not have been needed.

Still another variation (about which we have received no anecdotal reports) involves the use of analogy between the devices in question and services. Under this approach, the question is posed: what services does the technology replace or make unnecessary? If the services would have been deductible, then the technology that replaces them should be as well. The weakness with this argument is the difficulty of proving what deductible service costs would have been incurred, or what their exact amount would have been in the absence of the technology. On the other hand, this argument for deductibility becomes stronger for someone who has been regularly receiving and paying for deductible services over a long enough period to establish a record of their amounts, and where it is therefore possible to demonstrate that without the substitution of technology, these expenses would have continued at comparable levels.

The most compelling case for the deductibility of mainstream equipment is presented by an individual who uses a standard computer to drive an environmental control unit (ECU) to turn on lights, open and close doors, access the telephone, or activate kitchen and other appliances. The ECU, which functions with a computer at its core, is the only means by which these functions can be independently performed, the only source of control over one's physical environment. Use of the ECU system is not a matter of marginal preference or relative convenience; it makes the difference between being able and unable to perform a number of basic life functions.

As we have repeatedly noted, a physician's recommendation is a key factor in the outcome of many personal-use-item cases. The precise role of the physician depends on the type of items or supplies under consideration, and on the rationale for the recommendation. For example, the role of the physician has been decisive in cases involving the need for air conditioning [4.17] and in cases involving the need for modified household items such as a mattress of a particular thickness.[4.18] Like other personal use items, air conditioners are deductible only if they meet a medical need. In order for the air conditioners and mattresses to be deductible in these cases, the IRS had to be persuaded of the existence of such a medical justification and satisfied that the purpose and use of the items was consistent with this need.

The elements of proof that need to be assembled in the case of the air conditioner differ somewhat from those required to justify the reclining chair or the clarinet. While the role of physician recommendation is the same in each case, the question of use comes up in very different ways. Anybody could sit in the chair or theoretically play the clarinet. Accordingly, the families must be ready to prove that the items were used only for the benefit of the "sick person." But with the air conditioner, everyone else in the house obviously breathes the air. There would be no practical way to prevent that! Or would there? The legal issue in this air conditioner case actually revolved around whether central air conditioning or only a room air conditioner could be deducted. It was held that central air conditioning was allowable, but only on the basis of medical evidence indicating that restriction of the child to her own room, cut off from family activities, would result in psychological damage.

Although the recommendations and reasoning of physicians are a necessary prerequisite to deductibility in cases such as these, a physician's involvement will not by itself guarantee a deduction. In addition to cases in which the IRS doubts the real motive or actual use of the items in question, medical recommendations will also not be decisive when the physician's expertise or reasoning are not deemed relevant to the asserted need. When a physician recommends a specific chair for a patient with a heart condition or air conditioning to alleviate the breathing difficulties of a child with a pulmonary disorder, the bases for these recommendations are easily tested and understood. But with much of the personal use technology that becomes *assistive* for people with disabilities, a physician's recommendation will often be marginal.

This greatly complicates our task. On the one hand, we need medical justification in order to win deduction for our computers, but on the other hand, doctors have little interest or knowledge about assistive technology and may not be taken very seriously by the IRS even when they do recommend it. Here then lies the crux of our dilemma. The tax law has entrusted doctors with the role of gatekeepers over the deductibility of our expenses, but doctors have not expanded their own definitions of treatment and mitigation in ways that are responsive to the growing disparity between medical and functional criteria. At bottom, many of the measures which yield the greatest potential for contributing to the performance of major life activities have no medical dimensions, in the view of most doctors.

From the doctor's perspective, an assistive listening system or an optical character reader, let alone a computer, do not fall within the domain of medical practice because they do not improve hearing or vision. Until we solve the separation that assigns walking, seeing, hearing, and other basic life activities to the jurisdiction of medicine, while vesting responsibility in other disciplines for the specific functions which these sensory and physical capacities permit, significant progress in the evaluation of ordinary items under the current tax law is unlikely.

To the degree that some medical specialties such as low-vision ophthalmologists, physiatrists, and rehabilitation medicine specialists have begun to take an interest in technology, their recommendations and reasoning are likely to carry greater weight with the IRS than those of physicians who know less about the subject or who are merely accommodating a patient by signing a letter drafted by someone else. For the most part, the professional impetus for recommending, publicizing, and supporting assistive technology has come from nonmedical disciplines such as physical and occupational therapy, audiology, speech pathology, rehabilitation counseling, and rehabilitation engineering. These professionals should play an increasingly important role in providing the medical justification for assistive technology. Sadly though, in our society, none of these practitioners has the authority (the clout) of the medical doctor, even though their pertinent knowledge and experience may greatly exceed the physician's.

Psychology is another discipline some people have looked to for medical justification. They have attempted to secure deductibility for their technology by arguing, with appropriate diagnostic support, that inability to perform functions of daily living would adversely affect their mental or emotional well-being. The role of psychiatrists and psychologists has thus far proved most important in connection with the deductibility of special education expenses, as we shall learn in Chapter 5 (a).

Because of the historical separation between medical and social care, mitigation used to be defined much more narrowly than we have now come to understand this term. At one time the IRS and the tax court tended to look not only at whether the items in question helped to overcome the effects of a disability, but also at what structure or function of the body the taxpayer intended to affect. Using this line of reasoning, a deduction was sometimes denied because an item was used to meet a personal rather than a medical need, because it was acquired for the convenience rather than the treatment of the taxpayer, or because the life activities and bodily functions to which the item contributed were not basic or important enough. Fortunately, those days seem long behind us. As one court put it, the functions to be ameliorated need not be limited to eating, sleeping, and going to the bathroom.[4.19]

Thus it is now clear that efforts to mitigate functional limitations can qualify for the medical expense deduction, whatever function or structure of the body is involved. This has been made especially clear in home modification cases. For example, deduction has been allowed for enclosing the passageway between garage and house so a taxpayer with a serious mobility impairment would not be exposed to the difficulty and potential danger walking on ice entailed.[4.20] Similarly, another tax payer with a serious disability was granted a deduction for equipment to facilitate his movement from one part to the other of his split-level property.[4.21] Obviously, going between house and car or between levels of one's property are not major life activities, but the mobility that underlies one's capacity to do them is.

However clear the law may be, its implementation still depends on human beings. All too many people still think of mitigation only in traditional medical terms. To them, devices for accessing or operating a computer, such as a mouthstick, a one-handed keyboard, or an eyegaze system, would not represent mitigation because the underlying motor impairment has not been addressed. Such narrowness results from several misconceptions. It may reflect an unduly restrictive notion of what a *function* of the body is, involving a distinction, conscious or unconscious, such as that between use of the hands and the activities we use hands for. This narrowness may also reflect anachronistic views including the idea that medical equipment can only be provided or recom-

mended by doctors, or the belief that assistive technology represents some form of nondeductible self-
treatment.

Whatever the explanation, people who should
know better sometimes display maddening obtuse-
ness. Several health care providers and bureaucrats
have adamantly insisted to this writer that a computer
can never be a medical care device. These same people who do not understand the role of a computer in
operating an augmentative communications aid readily acknowledge the medical nature of an artificial lar-
ynx. Yet aren't both designed to achieve the same
functional goal: restoration of communicative capacity? Might their opinions be different if the microchip
were surgically implanted in the throat rather than
housed on a lapboard? This is not so far-fetched as it
may seem, since attachment to the body (which is an
element in the definition of prosthetic devices) is
often the key variable in determining insurance or
other third-party reimbursibility, state sales tax exemption, or other statuses. Happily, our income tax law
seems to have gone beyond such arcane distinctions.

Precisely because of the dramatic and immediate
impact of assistive technology devices, demonstra-
tions of what they can mean to their users are often
quite vivid and persuasive. Many a government fund-
er or private insurer has preferred to yield discreetly
on a point of principle or law rather than witness a
display of technology's benefits on behalf of a sym-
pathetic plaintiff before a jury and the press. With the
tax system, such opportunities for direct personal
demonstration of what technology can do rarely present themselves. Taxpayers have to approach the task
of proof in a more cerebral and technical way.

For people faced with in-person tax audits, some
accountants advocate use of the technology to the
maximum feasible extent. Other accountants regard
such techniques as manipulative and potentially
counterproductive. As always, the answer to such a
question of strategy depends on the facts and circumstances of each case.

Ideally, the law will evolve to the point of
according deductibility to all items and devices that
meet the definition of assistive technology set forth in
the Technology-Related Assistance for Individuals
with Disabilities Act. Until that time, taxpayers should

remember that items which normally would fall into the personal use category can be converted to medical status when their nature, purpose, and actual use prove that they mitigate a functional impairment by affecting a structure or function of the body.

Like goods, services can generally be divided into those that are explicitly of a medical nature and those that are not. The services of physicians, dentists, and other licensed health care providers are the most straightforward example of deductible medical services. With a few exceptions, such as ear piercing, plastic surgery for cosmetic reasons, or illegal procedures, the services of these professionals for diagnosis, treatment, cure, or mitigation are routinely deductible. The deductibility of the services of non-health care professionals, practitioners in disciplines without certification or licensing requirements, or persons who have no specialized training at all depends on the nature and purpose of the services provided. Services provided by nonprofessional persons have been granted deduction on innumerable occasions.

For example, one famous case concerns a family who was allowed to deduct the costs of "patterning exercises" recommended and administered by a lay therapist to improve the functioning of their mentally retarded child.[4.22] Particularly in such areas as retardation and learning disabilities, a number of lay people have developed and popularized treatment approaches, which have sometimes been accorded deductibility.

Analysis of what services we may deduct as health care costs involves much the same approach as with goods: who provided the service, for what purpose, and what was its nature? Broadly speaking, there are two major differences, however. First, with services, the question of actual use does not come up in the same way as when dealing with goods. No one is obliged to accept a physician's diagnosis or recommendations in order to deduct the consulting fees, lab tests, and other expenses involved in securing them. Second, the status of the service provider is often more important than that of the purveyor of goods, since professional status is often the key element in establishing the nature of the services as medical.

(d)

Personal Attendant and Other Services

Just as with equipment and supplies, people with disabilities need to purchase many services that others do not. People with visual impairments may need the services of readers; those with hearing impairments may need the services of sign language interpreters; and people with various physical impairments may need assistance with personal care or household management tasks. Most people with disabilities will have occasion to utilize rehabilitation services of some kind at some point in their lives. These may be for vocational rehabilitation, for training in activities of daily living (ADL), and, increasingly, in the realm of assistive technology.

Rehabilitation and other specialized services are not typically provided by physicians, although some medical screening or treatment may be involved. These services are usually provided by persons with professional training in a variety of disciplines that may or may not involve state licensure, professional certification, or academic qualifications. When a service is provided as part of an agency-based rehabilitation or adjustment program, its deductibility usually should not be hard to establish. Deductibility should be apparent if the service involves training that is rehabilitative in nature, is designed to teach compensatory skills or alternative strategies, or if the training focuses on any of the adjustment issues associated with the onset or mitigation of disability.

A rehabilitation agency setting does not guarantee the deductibility of fees that one may pay, however. As community facilities, many rehabilitation and social services agencies host or sponsor a wide variety of programs. Sports, recreation, social activities, self-assertiveness training, or other nonrehabilitative activities or services do not necessarily qualify for deductibility, even when specifically targeted to people with a disability. As rehabilitation and social agencies look for new funding sources, means testing and cost sharing with clients are likely to become more common. People with disabilities who need services are therefore increasingly likely to incur costs over the coming years.

The range of professional disciplines from which people with disabilities can obtain relevant services is greater than ever before. Because of the varying assumptions and terminology these disciplines employ, the task of rationalizing and translating what they do into terms that the tax system understands has become both more challenging and more important. Moreover, the premium now placed on interdisciplinary or team services contributes to the difficulty of describing exactly what services one has received from whom, and for exactly what deductible purpose. Nowhere is this challenge more acute than in the area of *independent living* services.

Independent living approaches disability with a distinctive vocabulary utilizing concepts of consumer empowerment and individual choice, instead of reliance on expert prescription or satisfactory adjustment. It believes that peers, as role models and sharers of a common experience, can and often should supplant medical and other professional experts.

From the tax standpoint, this philosophy means that an individual who wishes to deduct fees paid to independent living organizations may have to devote extra effort to adequately describing what services have been received. For example, in order to help consumers select the technology that best meets their needs, many independent living centers offer unstructured exposure to various assistive devices and provide opportunities for hands-on comparisons among them. No formal evaluation, rigorous training, or qualified experts need be involved. The consumer makes her or his own choice.

If analyzed only in these terms, identifying exactly what service has been obtained may be difficult. The consumer has undoubtedly received something of potentially great value in embarking on a new life, but a deduction for any fees paid may be hard to justify. Although different from traditional services, we paid for and received something very tangible, something that enabled us to take mitigating action, something that would not have been needed in the absence of a disability, and something that in many cases results in the acquisition and effective use of equipment that is in all likelihood deductible. Yet in many cases, the experience of learning about and selecting technology in this way does not rise to the level of a deductible service as defined in the tax law. From the tax standpoint, this is equivalent to claiming a deduction for medical services when all the physician did was allow you to browse among the medical books on her shelf.

Faced with such a situation, the recipient of independent living services must be as specific and technical as possible about what services were received, about what functional impairment(s) they were intended to mitigate and how, and about the unique ability of the independent living center to provide them. In short, the recipient must show that these services could not have been obtained in the local electronics store. When specific services are involved, they should be relatively easy to document. If one received training in the use of specific devices, set-up or troubleshooting assistance in their operation and maintenance, or other readily identifiable services, no problem of vagueness should exist.

One of the goals of independent living is to promote heightened personal autonomy through the use of attendant services. Issues surrounding the use of personal services in the home have given rise to some of the most voluminous litigation in the annals of tax law. These cases consistently distinguish between medical and other types of services, using such terms as *personal services, domestic services, household services companionship services,* or even *custodial services* to distinguish the nonmedical services denied deductibility. In this area, as with other services, the nature of the service, not the credentials of the provider, is the deciding factor.

For individuals who employ attendants, deductibility of their costs depends on what the workers do. No question should arise with traditional medical services rendered directly to an individual, such as administering medication, changing bandages, catheterization, or preparing food to conform with medical requirements. Because such services are the equivalent of nursing services, they are deductible, regardless of the professional qualifications of the person providing them.[4.23] At the other end of the service spectrum, the Internal Revenue Service generally refuses to accord deductibility to household services, even when medical reasons are advanced for their justification, and even when the individual is unable to perform the household tasks.

Along this continuum, where does the law place attendant services of the kind that people with disabilities need in order to live in their own homes? To answer this question, we must examine the distinctions embodied in two lines of tax law cases. The first line of cases concerns baby nurses whose services are deductible if the child needs care because of illness but are nondeductible if the care is routine, even though the content of the services may be indistinguishable.[4.24]

The second line of cases involves nursing homes. Because our nation's laws and budgetary priorities favor institutionalization over home-based care, one might suppose our tax laws would reinforce this preference by granting deductibility for nursing home care. However, this is not generally the case. If the motive for being in the nursing home is treatment of illness, the costs will qualify for the medical deduction. But if the motive is one of preference, family convenience, or the infirmity associated with advanced age, the costs represent personal rather than medical expenses.[4.25]

When people enter nursing homes, they are often motivated by the inability to maintain lives of independence, dignity, or safety at home. Would such motives be sufficient to qualify the nursing home costs as medical expenses? While we have uncovered no rulings squarely answering this question, it seems likely that such motives do not establish the medical nature of the need. If the nursing home cannot be justified on medical grounds, what about the arguably comparable care expenses of people who manage to remain in their own homes by availing themselves of the services of attendants?

People with disabilities need personal attendants to assist them in such tasks as dressing, grooming, personal hygiene, cooking, eating, elimination, or similarly basic functions of daily living. In order for these attendant services to be deductible, we must convince the IRS that they are the equivalent of nursing services rather than a form of personal, household, or domestic service. The IRS already accepts that bathing and grooming constitute nursing services, but many other services attendants perform are not so obviously medical in nature. By all accounts, the outcome can go either way. A number of taxpayers and several accountants report success in audits or on appeal in their attendant services cases. What arguments should taxpayers make and what points should be emphasized?

Several arguments are worth raising. The most

powerful and direct of these is that, taken altogether, the services attendants provide to people with severe disabilities do amount to the equivalent of nursing services. The force of this argument ultimately depends on exactly what services the individual needs, but how can anyone reasonably deny that a matrix of services such as those listed above—dressing, bathing, etc.—constitute the *equivalent* of nursing care? In this connection, a number of cases, listed and summarized in note 4.26, have granted a deduction for various combinations of services that fall within this group.[4.26] These include cases where the services included just such assistance as helping people in and out of bed, insuring that they would not fall while walking, helping them with eating, dressing, bathing, toileting, and other basic functions. A key point, though, is that none of these cases uses terms like *attendant services* or *attendant care*. A taxpayer who would use only such general terms would be virtually certain to lose. What the taxpayer must do is provide details and specifics about the range of services needed and performed. Very frankly, the more graphic the better.

A number of supporting or subsidiary arguments can be made to strengthen one's attendant services claim. For example, where applicable, taxpayers should be prepared to show (preferably with appropriate medical support) that even if the services do not technically qualify as medical, failure to receive them would result in adverse medical consequences. In almost every attendant services context, this risk does exist to a greater or lesser degree. So, while the motive for getting up in the morning may be mundane and personal, the medical consequences of being unable to get up on a daily basis could include skin breakdown, pneumonia, muscle atrophy, depression, or any number of other distinctly deductible conditions.

In buttressing attendant services claims, it is always useful to highlight applicable distinctions between attendant and domestic services. One of the criteria for any medical service is that it be provided directly to the "sick" person. With cooking, cleaning, and other conventional household tasks, the services can be performed whether or not the occupant or beneficiary is present. Hence, they are far less direct than the services performed by an attendant.

Another more subtle distinction relates to the fact patterns that have dominated previous home-care cases. If we look at the nursing home and home-care cases decided over the years, most of them involve either infants or elderly people. For the very young or the very old, the need for care is not so much a function of illness or disability as it is an incident of the normal life process. Although no decisions have directly said so, this factor must surely be an element in the law's resistance to home services. But when the need for assistance is precipitated by a disability rather than by the exigencies of the life cycle, a stronger argument exists for the contention that such assistance is medical rather than personal. This distinction has more profound implications than may at first appear, for if it is true that the taxpayers claiming attendant services deductions today differ demographically from those receiving them in the past, it is also true that the very independence they seek ironically works to undercut their contentions.

Many people utilize attendant services in order to work and lead fully active and productive lives. All the cases that can be relied on as precedents for the argument for attendant services involve extremely ill people who were largely helpless. The reaction of tax officials and judges to the attendant services claims of the energetic and productive is likely to be a good deal more ambiguous. Our underlying challenge in these cases, though no statute or decision will ever say so, is how to make credible the seemingly contradictory dimensions of significant need in some areas and self-sufficiency in others. In one respect, the Internal Revenue Code recognizes this paradox by including "attendant care services" within its definition of impairment-related work expenses. See Chapter 6(a).

A final source of support for the deductibility of attendant services is found in the ways various federal and state laws have characterized these services. Over the last several years, a number of federal programs have given some recognition and support to various means for keeping in their own homes people who are at risk of institutionalization. In particular, a number of states have established their own attendant services programs. Such state initiatives, along with provisions of a number of federal programs, can fairly be characterized as reflecting public policy that defines attendant services as a health or medical service.[4.27]

While the IRS is not bound by the definitions other agencies or levels of government give to health care, in many instances it does defer to local law. Accordingly, if, in any one of the literally dozens of ways available for doing so, your state has defined either personal attendant services per se or home health care generally as a medical service or as a medical issue, the argument for characterizing attendant services as a medical expense for purposes of the tax law should be considerably strengthened.

Beneath the technical issues, taxpayers also need to confront an undercurrent of suspicion about attendant services. Many people unfamiliar with what attendants do may fail to understand why employing them is not a matter of personal preference. Such misconceptions are especially likely if the variety of tasks the attendant performs include some that anyone, with or without a disability, would choose to pay someone to do for them. Few people would choose to have someone else dress them or lift them out of bed in the morning if they could do it independently; but how many people would not like to have their houses cleaned, their meals cooked, or their cars driven for them by someone else if they could afford it? If services are not clearly medical in nature, great care must be taken to prove that they are necessitated by functional limitations resulting from the disability, not by preference.

The following case, though not involving attendant services, well illustrates the skepticism with which home services claims may be met. A taxpayer claimed that he was obliged for medical reasons to hire someone to mow his lawn and claimed the sums paid as a health care deduction.[4.28] The taxpayer lost his case because he failed to show that he would not have hired someone to mow his lawn anyway, even if he were not disabled. The outcome does not necessarily indicate disbelief of his medical claims, but is based on the premise that few people enjoy mowing their own lawns and that almost everyone who could hire a neighborhood teenager to do it would do so. If the taxpayer had hired someone to do it in the past, or could be expected to hire someone to do it now, whether he had a disability or not, what difference did his disability make?

Is there any way this taxpayer's lawn care expenses could have qualified for the deduction? Maybe, and maybe not. What if he suffered from allergies that made an unmowed lawn injurious to his health, or what if he had a walking disability that made long grass a serious impediment to his mobility or safety? We cannot be certain that any of these facts would result in a favorable outcome, but the key point to remember is that even when a service is not of an ostensibly medical nature, its purpose can still suffice to make it deductible. To return to a previous illustration, clarinet lessons are hardly a medical service, but became deductible when their purpose was the treatment of orthodontic disease. Nevertheless, if this taxpayer had an environmental illness or a mobility impairment that made grass dangerous to his health or safety, he would probably have been better advised to replace his lawn with a rock garden.

The disbelief problem as it relates to the purpose of the expenditure is also illustrated by the case of a taxpayer who sought a medical deduction for the cost of her daughter's dancing lessons on the ground that the lessons were therapy for a spinal abnormality. Although the lessons may have had therapeutic value, she lost her case because the child had shown aptitude for and interest in dancing independent of her spinal condition.[4.29] Although an understanding of the role of preference is helpful in distinguishing attendant from other domestic services cases, the presence or absence of this element is only one of several key distinctions. While the absence of preference strengthens our attendant services claims, some of the other distinctions tend to weaken them.

In the lawn mowing and dancing lesson cases, the services in question would have resulted in some fairly conventional forms of medical improvement. If the IRS had been inclined to credit the motives of the taxpayers in these cases, the medical benefits that were anticipated and achieved could have been demonstrated. However, with attendant services, this is not necessarily true, except insofar as additional medical problems are forestalled. But there is no measurable abatement of symptoms or improvement of spinal x-rays. At bottom, attendant services are a quality of life issue, one that for the present we must squeeze and torture into a medical mold.

As a practical matter, when we employ one or more personal assistants to provide a wide range of services, we typically end up with an *allocation* problem. Some of our expenses are probably deductible; the rest may not be. Consequently, many attendant services cases turn on allocation, meaning the issue is less about whether a deduction is allowed than about how large it should be.

If allocation of wages paid is necessary, the taxpayer should keep records in a way that facilitates these distinctions. Any number of methods are available to maintain appropriate records. You might give the employee separate paychecks, use time sheets that show how the work hours were divided, or keep notes indicating the particular needs that accounted for when and how long the assistant worked. Allocation of wages between deductible and nondeductible services is based on the amount of time devoted to each.

Allocation issues also come up when the costs of attendant or other services are shared between the recipient and a governmental or other third-party payer. To the degree that the third-party payment is based on need, represents the proceeds of health or accident insurance, or is provided under a governmental program to promote the general welfare, the value of these payments will be excludable from GI. The residual tax issue will relate to the deductibility of the service recipient's out-of-pocket costs. Where a taxpayer has any discretion in the matter, her/his contributions should be targeted and tracked to those components of the service or care with the highest potential for deductibility.

As noted earlier, no particular professional training is prescribed for the work of a personal assistant or attendant. If the taxpayer chooses to hire a trained nurse, this should be a medical decision. The tax law does not demand that people pay more than necessary (which they would often be required to do if obliged to hire a nurse) in order to claim a deduction. By the same token, hiring a nurse does not guarantee the deduction, since the services performed still determine deductibility. Even the services of a nurse can be denied deductibility if companionship is deemed the motivation for the hire.

Complications arise when the right to perform or provide a particular service is restricted by law or when the service or procedure is illegal.[4.30] If the service can be lawfully provided only by someone licensed to do so, a deduction will be much harder to claim for its provision by an unlicensed practitioner. The right to perform surgery is limited to licensed physicians, for example. Hence, you could not ordinarily deduct the cost of a fee you paid to a helpful neighbor who removed your inflamed appendix, even if no physician were available.

The illegal services issue returns us to the impact of state law. To the extent that state law determines who is married, when a given medical procedure is legal, or who can lawfully perform a certain service, federal tax outcomes often hinge on where we live. Perhaps the most well-known example of this is the ability of people who live in states that recognize common-law marriage to file joint returns.[4.31] State law will play an increasing role in the licensing of service providers as well.

For people with disabilities, this issue of licensure can come up in the area of assistive technology services. State licensing laws usually govern who can fit or sell hearing aids or eyeglasses. Outside of these and other more traditional medical devices, laws do not usually specify who can recommend or evaluate assistive devices. In the absence of qualifications for who can be a technology services provider, the nature of the services becomes an even more important issue.

Professionalism and quality control are emerging as key concerns in the assistive technology field. A number of professional organizations such as RESNA are developing standards for credentialing assistive technology services providers. Coupled with this trend, the desire of the assistive technology community for greater access to health insurance reimbursement is likely to lead to the formulation of state certification criteria for some or all technology service providers. For those in established disciplines such as occupational or physical therapy, prosthetics, or orthotics, this will make little difference, since they are already licensed. However, for practitioners in newly emerging fields such as rehabilitation engineering, computer access, or job analysis, where few professional standards or legal qualifications yet exist, such a trend bodes important changes. For tax-oriented consumers, these developments will be both good and bad: good because professionalism tends to equate to a higher and more uniform standard of service, and because the increased professional status of providers will add weight to the claim for deductibility; bad because certification will both drive up costs for technology services and weaken the claim for deductibility when provided by a noncredentialed person or organization.

Bearing in mind that the nature of a service determines its deductibility, failure to use a licensed practitioner will not necessarily result in the loss of an otherwise valid deduction. Even if rehabilitation engineers, medical equipment suppliers, or others do become subject to strict state licensing requirements, no law is foreseeable that would require people to obtain assistive technology services only from members of specified disciplines.

Professional certification or state licensure will complicate the choice of service provider in several ways, however. On the one hand, choice of an unlicensed service provider or of a provider from a discipline that has not come under regulation may make deduction claims harder to substantiate when there is a question about the deductibility of the service. For example, mainstream computer training is not a deductible medical service, but if the training is intended to facilitate use of assistive technology, a deduction claim is credible. Such a claim would be materially strengthened by certification of the training's provider as someone specially trained or skilled in this field, to work with people with disabilities.

As we mentioned in connection with attendant services, another factor in the deductibility of services is *directness*. That is, a service can usually be deductible only if it is received directly by the person for whom it is purchased. If the service is not sufficiently direct, it may be deemed too remote to qualify for the deduction. This issue of directness comes up in another way, too. Some services, though not medical in their own right, are necessary in order to obtain medical services. The law has had occasion to consider the deductibility of a number of indirect services. As usual, the facts of each case determine the outcome.

The best example of an indirect cost that qualifies for deduction is transportation. We can deduct as medical expenses the costs of getting to and from medical care. Obviously, the services of a bus driver or the price of gas do not represent medical care, but without transportation, there would be no way to get it, so the transportation expenses that are "essential to" medical care become deductible.

One of the strangest examples of indirect expenses being deductible is lawyer's fees. Lawyer's fees do not constitute medical expenses, but what happens when they are incurred in order to obtain medical care? Such fees have been deductible when incurred to gain legal guardianship over a person so that he could be institutionalized for treatment of a serious mental illness.[4.32] The individual had apparently refused to seek care, making compulsory commitment the only way to obtain it, and making a guardianship proceeding the only means to gain the requisite legal custody over him. By contrast, the legal fees associated with gaining control over the incompetent person's property were not deductible, since obtaining control of the property was not essential to securing psychiatric care. We may well ask whether the lawyer's fees for gaining guardianship over the property might also have been deductible if the property had been needed to pay for the care.

Regrettably, we have not found any rulings or cases dealing with the deductibility of legal costs associated with getting out of an institution. In the most dramatic cases, people need to bring *habeas corpus* or other legal proceedings to secure their release from institutional confinement. More commonly, the issues surrounding deinstitutionalization for people with disabilities revolve around the availability of appropriate support services in the community. One would hope that people with disabilities who incur legal costs in order to secure the support services necessary to live independently in the community would be granted a medical expense deduction for these deinstitutionalization expenses as well.

Even when seeking services from public agencies under various entitlement programs, people must on occasion rely on legal assistance or other advocacy resources to establish both their right to such services and the level of services to be provided. Sometimes, as in the case of special education, the statute creating the entitlement program provides for the reimbursement of attorney's fees if the case is won. (See Chapter 5(a).) However, this is not necessarily the case in other programs that might be relevant to living outside the hospital or nursing home, such as rehabilitation, Medicaid, or state-sponsored attendant services.

When reimbursement is available, tax deductibility becomes a moot point. But when reimbursement is not forthcoming, tax considerations once again become important. From the tax standpoint, the problem is that efforts to obtain release from an institution may give the impression of being incurred to avoid medical care. To avoid this misimpression, such efforts should be coupled with parallel efforts to obtain necessary post-release services in the community.

Relying on such precedents as the guardianship cases, it seems safe to hypothesize that legal costs incurred to secure deductible goods or services would themselves qualify for deduction. Generally, if legal costs are incurred to secure goods and services that meet the definition of medical care, such costs should be deductible. It makes no difference that the services would be free, that they are provided by government, or that one is legally entitled to them. What matters is that you incurred legal costs in order to obtain services that would qualify as medical expenses if you had paid for them yourself. Assistive technology under rehabilitation or Medicaid would be among the best examples, although until the issue is litigated, we cannot be certain.

In some situations, there might be other theories under which such legal fees could be deducted. Depending on the exact service involved, they may qualify as costs for the production of income, for the securing of an interest in property, or as job-seeking expenses. Such strategies are beyond the scope of our discussion, but should be borne in mind for legal fees and for other nonmedical expert or consulting fees as well.

When an expense is deductible, certain related costs are also likely to be deductible. If a device or appliance is deductible, the costs of its upkeep and maintenance are also deductible. This comes into play with service contracts on equipment and with other maintenance and repair costs. Supplies necessary to operate a deductible device, such as batteries, paper, and the like, also qualify for deduction. However, follow-up costs are deductible only as long as the need for the equipment continues. Maintenance costs for the equipment would no longer be deductible if the disability ceased.

The word *need* should not be misconstrued here. People stop using technology for any number of reasons. They may no longer need the equipment because their functional capabilities have changed, or they may no longer need it because they have moved on to other devices. This lack of need for the device is different from and should not be confused with the lack of need resulting from cessation of the disability. The law does not require you to follow a doctor's instructions as a condition for deducting the costs of obtaining that advice. Nor does it require you to continue using equipment that no longer meets your needs.

Our ability to deduct operating and upkeep costs and supplies for assistive devices also does not depend on our actually having claimed the deduction for the device when we obtained it. Perhaps we did not itemize in the year we obtained the equipment, or perhaps we incurred no cost in getting it. Provided it qualifies as a medical device in the year we incur the follow-up costs, those costs are deductible.

The purchase of deductible health care services frequently gives rise to some interesting incidental costs, such as withholding, Social Security, or other employment taxes we pay on behalf of those who work for us. While these taxes are deductible as medical expenses in the same proportion as the wages on which they were paid, taxes also constitute medical expenses in their own right.[4.33] Similarly, if the employee is fed by us, lives in our home, and uses our utilities, these costs should also be deductible according to the appropriate allocation. Taxpayers' increases in rent are even deductible when the increases result

(e)

F ollow-up and Consequential Expenses

from moving to a larger apartment in order to make room for a live-in caregiver.[4.34] Whether the moving costs to the new apartment are also deductible is an interesting question. To the degree that the move is motivated solely by the need for medical care, they might well be.

Another interesting application of follow-up expenses occurs in connection with long-distance telephone calls. In one case, a drug rehabilitation patient who called her therapist long-distance after the therapist moved out of the area was allowed to deduct the cost of these calls.[4.35] The treatment had begun while the therapist resided in the patient's area, and the calls represented its continuation after the therapist relocated. If the patient had chosen to initiate treatment with a practitioner in a distant city, the telephone calls would have been deductible only if the taxpayer could show a reason why a far-away practitioner was chosen. The government is very suspicious, especially regarding travel, that people will use medical care as an excuse for trips or for telephone calls that actually have another motivation.

For people with disabilities, these telephone cases make an important point. In the area of assistive technology, expert resources remain thinly spread. It may be necessary to do a lot of phoning around the country to identify the configuration that will best meet one's needs, to get advice on its installation, to do troubleshooting when problems arise, or for similar purposes. As long as such objectives are the true and substantially sole purpose for the calls, and provided one can show that the necessary expertise was not available locally, the costs of such calls should come within the medical expense deduction.

(f)

Medical Travel and Transportation

Of all the indirect costs that people incur in order to obtain medical services, few are more important than travel. These costs are addressed specifically in the law; they probably represent the largest amount of money involved in any of the indirect cost areas; and they have engendered a remarkably large volume of litigation. Travel costs are especially important to understand since the goods and services needed by people with disabilities are frequently unavailable locally.

Travel expenses are deductible when the travel is "primarily for and essential to" obtaining medical care.[4.36] For local travel, such as trips to and from the doctor's office, a standard mileage rate of $0.09 per mile plus tolls, parking, and similar costs can be claimed. For taxpayers who do not drive or who do drive but choose not to claim the standard mileage rate, actual costs can always be used. The advantage of the standard mileage rate is that it makes life easier because all you need to remember and document is how far you drove. The standard mileage rate for medical travel should not be confused with the standard rate for business use of an automobile, which is $0.28 a mile for 1992.

Before examining the medical travel deduction, some terminology that could cause confusion should be explained. When the law speaks of *travel,* it means travel away from home overnight. Local travel is referred to as *transportation.* The rules surrounding medical travel away from home are complex. To add to the possibilities for confusion, in the world of taxes *travel* does not mean what you think it does. Travel here includes *transportation* and *meals and lodgings* while away from home. Under the travel rubric, different standards and different restrictions apply to the *meals and lodgings* components than to the *transportation* portion of your travel expenses. Still further complexity arises from the fact that the kind of facility or institution where you receive the medical care influences how much of your travel costs can be deducted.

Basically, the Internal Revenue Code looks on medical travel suspiciously. For people with disabilities who must travel for assistive technology or other rehabilitative services, a number of issues need to be anticipated. The underlying difficulty arises from the tax code's preference that medical services away from home be provided in hospitals or other equivalent medical settings, and that such services be provided by or under the supervision of physicians. Although medical screening is often required, ongoing medical supervision is not necessarily a part of the rehabilitation or other services people with disabilities may need. As a result, travel claims may face a number of barriers and may require various kinds of proof in order to prevail.

The first concern is justification of one's transportation costs. The key to their deductibility hinges on the deductibility of the services that occasioned the travel. If the services are deductible, if the transportation costs were incurred in order to obtain them, and if obtaining them was the purpose of the trip, then the transportation costs qualify for the medical deduction. As with local service providers, a variety of factors can be marshalled to demonstrate the deductibility of the services. In addition to their basic nature, these include the facility's accreditation, the academic and professional credentials of its staff, the specialized nature of the services received, and the unavailability of the services in your locality. A physician's recommendation of the facility also helps, both by reinforcing the medical justification and by explaining the choice of provider. Justifying one's choice presents different issues here than it does with local service providers. Our choice becomes an issue due to the second obstacle facing deductibility of medical travel.

Even if we can demonstrate the receipt of deductible medical services, our travel costs will not qualify for deduction if the choice of service provider was motivated by any significant element of vacation, recreation, or personal preference. People are free to select their medical care providers, but when deducting their transportation costs, the choice of a provider in a location away from one's home may become an issue, as it relates to the true motivation for the trip. Be prepared to show why a distant location was selected. This would typically be because the needed resources were unavailable in your local community.

Common sense dictates that travel during high season to a facility near a glamorous resort makes one's motives more suspect than travel to a facility in a nondescript place. If someone who lives in northern Maine goes to Hawaii in mid-winter for assistive technology training, the burden of proof is understandably higher. *Personal* is the key word here. You certainly have the right to choose one service provider over another, to entertain a preference based on who will best meet your needs; such a personal preference is within your right. But whatever criteria you use for selecting a service provider, obtaining medical services must be your motive.

There is one other special concern raised by the

transportation component of medical travel expenses. For those who are unfamiliar with the kinds of services that people with disabilities may seek, rehabilitation and convalescence can easily be confused. Travel for convalescence is not deductible, because convalescence is not treatment. Confusion arises when a person with a disability goes to a non-medical facility for rehabilitation services, particularly if the rehabilitation commences shortly after hospitalization or other medical care for an underlying injury or illness.

When it comes to the meals and lodgings aspect of travel expenses, additional problems are encountered.[4.37] If the institution or facility provides room and board, these costs are deductible provided the services are. An individual who chooses to stay outside the facility cannot claim a travel deduction for the cost of outpatient lodgings unless some good medical reason exists for doing so. Many of the facilities and centers where people with disabilities obtain technology, vocational rehabilitation, activities of daily living, or other training and services do not offer room and board, in which case the recipient has no choice but to take lodgings outside. These off-premises lodgings may be deductible, but limitations on the scope of their deductibility pose some problems.

The deduction for lodgings is limited to $50 a night per person, and the accommodations must not be "lavish or extravagant." Nightly rates of $50 or less are advertised in most vicinities, but people with accessibility needs that restrict the supply of suitable rooms may frequently have to pay more or travel farther for accommodations. Until the hospitality industry completes the process of complying with the ADA, Congress should provide an exception to the $50 limit for lodging costs attributable to accessibility needs.

The second major restriction on the deductibility of lodgings is far more significant. The law specifies that such lodging qualifies as medical travel only if the medical service to which it relates is, "provided by a physician in a licensed hospital or in a medical facility which is related to or the equivalent of a licensed hospital."[4.38] For the large proportion of people who get their services at accredited facilities that are not hospitals, from credentialed health care and other personnel who are not doctors, this restriction imperils deductibility for their lodging costs.

The problem is with the definition of *hospital.* Clearly, since many such settings do not meet the definition of hospital, the key question becomes whether they qualify as "related to" hospitals, or as "equivalent" to licensed hospitals. In its regulations, the Internal Revenue Service indicates that the definition of hospitals does not include institutions whose "primary purpose" is to "train handicapped people to pursue a vocation."[4.39] This definition appears to exclude many rehabilitation facilities,[4.40] but it gives little guidance as to their coverage under the equivalency category.

A number of facilities and institutions can probably show sufficient relationship to licensed hospitals to qualify under that part of the test. Any number of legal, staff, or other relationships, reciprocal agreements, facility-sharing, or the like, should warrant making the claim. But for free-standing centers, the scope of the equivalency test remains to be determined by future rulings.

The argument for equivalence of assistive technology services or rehabilitation programs can best be made along lines such as these. When Congress allowed outpatient lodgings as part of the medical travel deduction, it must have understood that outpatient services are often provided in facilities that would neither qualify nor represent themselves as hospitals. Knowing that specialized clinics, in-office surgery, and other developments in medical services offer an enormous range of modalities and venues, Congress had every right and every reason to restrict the deduction for lodgings. Congress was under no obligation to tie the deductibility of the lodgings to the deductibility of the services.

That said, is there any basis for believing that Congress meant to place a flat ban on deductibility of lodging expenses incurred by people with disabilities when away from home in order to obtain necessary services that could not be found in their own communities, that almost certainly qualify for deduction, and that involve no element of vacation or recreation? While many of the facilities in question are not hospitals, most are accredited according to standards that should suffice to respond to the real underlying concern and to the law's broadening definition of the meaning of medical care.

The underlying problem here is the tax law's suspicion that all medical travel is a pretext for vacation!

The purpose of this restriction in favor of hospitals is to prevent abuse, such as by people who go to a warm climate for the winter and then seek to deduct the costs of their winter quarters on casual medical grounds by obtaining outpatient treatment in the area. Such abuse is clearly not a risk here. We can only hope that the law will change to reflect an awareness that hospitals and comparable facilities are not the only appropriate venue for medical services away from home.

So far, we have been talking about the travel expenses of the individual receiving the medical services. What about the expenses of an accompanying family member, friend, or employee? With a companion, no distinction is made between the transportation and housing components of their travel costs. That is, if the companion's transportation expenses qualify for deductibility, the costs of their lodgings (up to the $50 per night maximum) will be deductible as well. The test is whether the companion's presence is *necessary* in order for the patient or service recipient to obtain the medical care.

Basically, necessity can be defined and proved in one of two ways. The first justification for the travel expenses of a companion is that person's role in actually providing medical care. A case in which someone needed bandages changed, temperature checked periodically, or other hard-core nursing services would be a typical example. Second, the transportation (and hence the lodgings) of a companion have been held deductible when the care recipient would have been unable to get to and from the treatment location without the assistance of another.[4.41] This rationale also justifies the accompaniment of children by a parent, since the tax law does not demand that children travel or reside alone. The presence of a parent or spouse would also be justifiable if, for any reason, the patient were unable to give informed consent to medical treatment or decisions.

People with disabilities may need assistance away from home that is either of the same nature or different from the assistance they regularly utilize. Whatever kind of assistance may be involved, if it is necessary as a practical matter for the individual to receive the medical services, then that need for assistance suffices to justify deduction for the companion's travel expenses. Whether the assistance qualifies as a medical deduction to you has nothing to do with whether or not the assistant's travel expenses qualify for deduction. Although the wages we pay to an assistant to facilitate our medical travel away from home will often qualify for deductibility in their own right, their tax status and the tax status of the assistant's travel expenses should never be confused.

With meals, deductibility is available only when they are provided as part of inpatient care. Neither people receiving outpatient services nor their companions can deduct the cost of food while away from home for medical reasons. Even if a companion stayed in the medical facility, the cost of his or her in-house meals would not qualify for deduction.

One possible exception exists to the nondeductibility of meals. If they would have been deductible at home, as in the case of an individual who paid to have salt-free foods specially prepared pursuant to medical instructions,[4.42] it should make no difference that comparable expenses are incurred away from home. Be warned though that this salt-free food case is an old one, long predating the widespread availability of low-sodium menus. Some other special food preparation costs or some unusual food selection requirements would probably be necessary today for a deduction to be granted in the first place.

(g)

Level of Costs

The tax law does not limit people to the least expensive goods and services available. People are accorded wide latitude in their selection of treatment modalities and service providers, but there are instances in which limits do exist, and in every case the taxpayer must be prepared to prove that costs were actually incurred for the health-related goods and services claimed.

In practice, even though you have a right to select the most expensive services you can afford, cost is always relevant to deductibility. If the cost of something seems high, questions are more likely to be raised, not about your right to deduct those costs, but about the truthfulness of your claims. It is only common sense to take extra care in assembling the documentation necessary to justify large expenses, but the point must be stressed that the nature and purposes of an expense, not its size, determine its deductibility.

If the costs are for assistive technology, which often involves expensive items, questions may likewise be triggered by the size of the cost. However, the government has no role in telling people that they should have chosen a different technological solution. An individual who chooses a braille-output computer terminal in preference to the far less expensive synthetic speech-output need not fear having his or her choice second-guessed.

One major exception exists to the principle of deductibility for our actual costs. This occurs in connection with home modifications. The medical expense deduction includes home modifications to make residential property more accessible to its occupants. Normally, such modifications are capital expenses, because they involve alterations to property. Capital expenses are not deductible in the year paid, but instead are added to the basis of property for recovery over a period of years or for reducing the amount of profit realized when the property is sold. When a capital expense also meets the standard for medical expenses, the law grants an exception, allowing it to be treated as a deduction. Although the law allows these costs to be treated as medical expenses, it limits the size of the deduction to the amount by which the cost of the modification exceeds the increase in the value of the property. This aspect of the medical expense deduction will be discussed further in Chapter 7(e).

(b)

T iming

In Chapter 2(d) we talked about timing as an element of tax strategy. In that connection, the timing of our medical care expenses can have a dramatic effect on our bottom line.

Medical care expenses often include capital equipment (devices or equipment expected to remain in use for more than one year). Many assistive technology devices qualify as capital assets under this definition. While capital goods are generally deductible over several years, medical expenses are deductible entirely in the year in which they are paid. As a result, when we purchase capital equipment as a medical expense, it is fully and only deductible in the year in which we buy it. In other settings such as in business, taxpayers may have a choice between handling the deduction this way or spreading it over several years. No such option is granted for the medical care deduction, however.

With major assistive technology purchases, and in many cases with the purchase of services, we may have some control over when our expenditures are incurred or paid. Tax considerations can and probably should never be the sole criterion for the timing of our expenditures, but timing can influence our net costs. Deciding when to buy may be a complicated assessment, may involve planning and cooperation among the entire family, and may depend on predictions about future income and expenses. Nevertheless, to the degree that timing does influence our real costs, we should take it into consideration whenever possible.

Ideally, we can make our major assistive technology purchases in a year when the entire deduction is available to us. For this to happen, three conditions must be met. First, our other medical expenses need to exceed 7.5 percent of AGI so that none of the deduction for the technology is lost in reaching that threshold. In addition, we want to make the purchase in a year when we plan to itemize. Finally (and this may seem paradoxical), we want to make the purchase in a year when our income is large enough to absorb the entire deduction. Of course, these ideal conditions will not always exist. Often our need for the technology will be greatest precisely when income is low. The deduction could be wholly or partially lost if savings, loans, or gifts from family or friends have to be substituted for income to pay for the technology.

It would be extremely valuable to people with disabilities if the rules concerning medical expense deductions were modified. Specifically, these deductions, or at least a limited group of assistive technology expenses, should be converted from itemized deductions to income adjustments described in Chapter 2(c). In this way, taxpayers could claim the deduction for them whether or not they itemized and whether or not their medical expenses exceeded any threshold. In addition to this, some form of *carryover* should be applied to these expenses to enable them to be carried backward or forward into other years when income is large enough to absorb them. These proposals are discussed in Chapter 9.

One additional important point about timing concerns when the law deems our expenses to have been *paid.* In most cases, this is straightforward. The day on which we write the check or hand over the cash is the date of payment. But if you make a purchase with a bank credit card, the law treats the expense as having been paid when the charge is made.[4.43] The credit card bill may be payable over several years (and if you pay only the monthly minimum on the card, the debt might not be paid for many years), yet the tax law regards the expense as having been paid entirely on the date the goods or services were charged. This means that you can get the benefit of the deduction in advance of actually paying the expense.

Interesting possibilities surround this exception to the deductible-when-paid principle. These possibilities relate to the definition of a *bank* credit card. Today, a growing number of industrial, communications, and other nonbanking companies issue credit cards. While the names of these companies do not suggest that the Visa or MasterCards they issue are bank cards, the firm for which the card is named usually issues it through a banking subsidiary or affiliate. In such cases, the bank is technically the issuer, so the card should qualify as a bank card, yielding a highly accelerated deduction.

With time-purchase agreements, revolving charge accounts, or installment contracts directly between buyer and seller, payments are applicable to the year in which they are made. If the term of the contract extends over two or more years, the deduction will be available proportionally to your payments in each of those years. Because medical deductions must be claimed in the year when paid, the only way to divide a deduction over several years is by actually making your payments that way. With multicomponent equipment systems, another way to divide the deduction over time is to purchase some components each year.

(i)

I nsurance

The premiums we pay for health insurance coverage for ourselves, our spouses, and our dependents qualify for the medical expense deduction. Sometimes we purchase umbrella insurance policies including health insurance along with other kinds of insurance, in which case we may not know the proportion of our premium attributable to medical care. At other times, we may pay fees, such as school student activity fees, which include a health insurance component, perhaps without our even knowing it. In both these situations, our ability to claim a deduction depends on finding out how much of our payment or fee is applicable to health insurance. If such a breakdown is not provided in your contract, you will need to ask for an itemized statement.

The problems faced by people with disabilities in purchasing health insurance are notorious. If coverage is available at all, it may be only at extremely high prices. For that reason, it is important to note that the actual cost of the health insurance is all that matters. The IRS cannot refuse to allow the deduction because the insurance was grossly expensive. However, there is one exception that comes up in connection with insurance policies that combine coverage for medical and other risks. If the IRS believes that the proportion of total premiums attributable to health insurance is excessive, it can deny part or all of the deduction.

Expense reimbursement is another area in which health insurance has tax implications. When we speak of the deductibility of medical expenses, remember this refers only to net expenses, that is, to whatever we spent after insurance payments or other third-party reimbursement has been taken into account. Health insurance reimbursement often takes considerable time after claims are submitted. For that reason, it is not uncommon for claims submitted in one year not to be paid until the next. Since people do not know whether or exactly how much they will receive in insurance reimbursement, the sensible course is ordinarily to claim a deduction for your unreimbursed Year One medical expenses. If reimbursement is thereafter received in Year Two, some or all of it may need to be reported as income. In accordance with what is called the tax benefit rule, you must treat as income in Year Two the amount of reimbursement that equals the tax you saved by claiming the deduction in Year One. If you claimed no deduction for the unreimbursed expenses in Year One, then there is no need to report any of the reimbursement as income in Year Two.

It should be noted that failure to claim available insurance reimbursement may render the expenses nondeductible.[4.44] The reason for this is that your economic loss is deemed to result not from medical expenses, but from your failure to seek reimbursement. This risk does not apply if the taxpayer was unaware of the availability of such reimbursement.[4.45] People with disabilities who buy items they know insurance companies refuse to cover do not need to go through the motions of filing futile reimbursement claims. Nevertheless, good reasons may exist for doing so, even when the outcome is a foregone conclusion. Over time, claims for assistive technology have an educational value and then, too, it is always possible that the insurance company might pay your claim by mistake or review it after the office party on Christmas Eve.

In today's health insurance environment, policyholders have an additional worry. I have encountered a significant number of people who have refrained from filing insurance claims for fear of premium increases, curtailment or even cancellation of coverage. For people who would find alternative coverage difficult or impossible to obtain because of pre-existing condition limitations, this creates a stark and serious problem, a problem made still more vexing if they are denied deductibility for their medical expenses because of failure to file a claim.

If a taxpayer is threatened with denial of a deduction because of such a failure to seek reimbursement, the person might well argue that, given the alternative, failure to claim insurance represents a sound economic decision and should be treated as an exception to the generally applicable rule. We know of no precedents for such a strategy in the health insurance area, but an analogous approach has been used to defend against denial of business or casualty loss deductions for failure to file claims under liability or other insurance policies.

(j)
S ubstantiation and Evidence

Throughout this chapter we have talked about what people who claim medical deductions should be able to show or prove. The key to all tax planning is record-keeping. In many cases, the records we need to keep are obvious: receipts, prescriptions, labels, and the like. Basically, we should be able to substantiate every material element of the expenses we claim by showing their amount, date, to whom paid, on whose behalf, and for what purpose. However, in some cases the nature of the records we should keep is not as self-evident.

When the deductibility of an expense hinges on what somebody did, said, or thought, contemporaneous documentation of those elements becomes a crucial step. We should write down our own assumptions and intentions; we should keep careful records of what people tell us about the goods and services we purchase; and when professionals make recommendations that are not embodied in formal prescriptions or reports, they should put those recommendations in writing. When the recommendations are included in formal reports, we should try to get a copy, which may not be so easy, as anyone who has ever been a client well knows. The problem is that the physician or other professional who made the assessment or recommendation may not be available, may not remember, or may not want to be bothered if a question comes up later. In one case, a taxpayer lost his deduction because the physician died before the needed documentation could be obtained.[4.46]

Our records should be timely, meaning they should be made at the same time or as close as possible to the time of the events they document. In the course of even a year, our own memories may fade, and in addition to accuracy, timely records have greater credibility than later reconstructions. If our records—not merely of what we spent but of exactly why we spent it—do nothing but spur our memories, the time and effort invested in maintaining them will pay handsome returns.

We need to know and recall what information and expectations led to our purchases. If we bought an item of technology to mitigate a functional limitation, we need to understand how it does so or how we came to believe that it would. Assuming that we were fortunate enough to have hands-on experience with the equipment (as we should always have before we plunk down our money or request anyone else's), our experience should suffice to provide much of this information. Inevitably, we must always rely to some degree on the assurances or expertise of others. One occasion when we should never rely on the word of others is when someone assures us that a purchase is tax deductible, especially if the person offering the assurance wants to sell us the reputedly tax-favored item.[4.47] Since not even the IRS is legally bound by the oral statements of its own employees, one can hardly expect to get a tax deduction because of good faith reliance on the word of a third party.

Our emphasis throughout this chapter on the relevance, accuracy, and detail of records should not be interpreted to mean that one can never succeed in getting deductions without them. Just as with the dog that ate the homework, there are times when records will be lost or destroyed. The IRS is always free to believe us, and the Tax Court, under the famous Cohan rule,[4.48] frequently makes its own determinations, based on whatever credible evidence does exist. In one case, a taxpayer could produce no records to justify his claim to a deduction for dental care received by his late wife. The apparent reason for this inability to produce records was the fact that he was in prison for her murder. Nevertheless, the Tax Court was persuaded by the highly detailed nature of his recollection and by the reasonableness of his contentions that he had indeed incurred the claimed expenses.[4.49] So our task is to amass whatever plausible and persuasive evidence we can. The government is not legally obligated to disbelieve us.

Because the family is a single taxpaying unit, we can deduct the medical care expenses paid for our spouse and dependents. On the other hand, we cannot ordinarily deduct the medical expenses of those who do not qualify as our dependents. However, in certain situations, medical expenses we incur on behalf of people who do not meet the test for dependency can still be available to us as deductions.

As discussed in Chapter 2(b), a fivefold test is used to determine whether one person can claim another as a dependent. One of these tests is called

(k)

Other
People's Needs

the *income test*.[4.50] The taxpayer's child under the age of 19, or under 24 if a full-time student, automatically meets this test. Older children, parents, or certain other relatives of the taxpayer who have income that exceeds the personal exemption amount ($2,300 for 1992) do not meet the income test and, therefore, do not qualify to be claimed as dependents. But if all the other tests of dependency are met, the payer of the medical expenses will still be able to claim a deduction for those costs, even though not entitled to an exemption. For people with disabilities, this provision is worth keeping in mind, especially for major expenditures such as expensive technology that may require financial assistance from family members.

This chapter has introduced us to some of the ways in which the medical expense deduction can assist people with disabilities and their families in obtaining the goods and services they need, but the health care rationale has implications far beyond what we have discussed so far, including its role in our efforts to offset the costs of special education. It is to this matter, and other tax dimensions of educational financing that we turn next.

five

Education

Education is critical in the life of our nation. With the continuing decline of low-skilled jobs in our national economy, a good education is more crucial than ever before. People with or without disabilities face many of the same issues in seeking a quality education: the adequacy of local schools, the high costs of college, and the need to upgrade or retrain skills during the working years. For those with disabilities, such universal concerns are often compounded by a host of additional issues, including the range and quality of special education resources available in their communities, the amounts by which technology and other special needs increase the cost of higher education, and the demands placed on their labor force competitiveness by the rapidly changing interfaces between assistive and mainstream technology in the workplace.

The tax system does not provide answers to our pressing questions about where to find the funding or expert resources needed to obtain a quality education. Nor does it offer many opportunities to deduct educational expenses. Once resources are found, however, it does offer a degree of subsidization to students with disabilities and their families.

(a)

S pecial Education

Many of the additional expenses that students with disabilities incur can be summarized under the heading special education. Since the passage of the Education of the Handicapped Act of 1975[5.1] (now the Individuals with Disabilities Education Act of 1990),[5.2] all children with disabilities are entitled to a "free and appropriate" public education in the "least restrictive environment" possible. Determinations of what these concepts mean in terms of school placement and services are made on the basis of individualized assessment of each eligible student. These assessments are embodied in the child's Individualized Education Plan (IEP), which becomes, in effect, an annual contract between the family and the school.

The federal special education law does not mandate that pupils with disabilities receive all the special education services needed for an optimal education; it requires only that they receive the services that will ensure an "adequate" education. Thus, even in situations where a school system is reasonably cooperative in regard to special education and assistive technology, families may feel that additional measures to maximize the quality of their child's education can and should be taken. If the expense can be shown to have a sufficient connection to overcoming the consequences of disability, the attempt to deduct it is well worth making.

Special education services and the related services that the law mandates are diverse. When such services are provided, federal law requires that they be made available at no cost to the student's family. Hence, there is no tax issue. As with routine public education services, the value of such special education services is not includable in family gross income. With no includable income and no expenses to be recouped, an effective special education process has no tax implications for the family.

The special education relationship does not always proceed smoothly, however, and a variety of issues can arise when the relationship breaks down. When this happens, the tax and educational dimensions become closely intertwined. To meet their children's special education needs, families may incur costs that the school district (or local education agency, as it is technically called) refuses to fund, or costs that will be reimbursed only later, if at all. In either case, the ability and willingness of families to incur the cost of needed goods and services can be affected by the role of the tax law in reducing net outlays.

Reimbursement by school districts for out-of-pocket special education costs or for attorney's fees incurred in establishing a child's special education rights are not taxable unless a deduction was previously taken for these expenses.

Broadly speaking, special education can be defined as any service that is needed by a student with a disability to achieve basic educational goals. Specifically, the term is defined as "specially-designed instruction at no cost to parents or guardians to meet the unique needs of a child with a disability, including instruction conducted in the classroom, in the home, in hospital, and institutions, and in other settings. . . . "[5.3] Specialized instruction is the best example of such a service.

In addition to special education services, *related services* include those resources a student with a disability may need in order to attend school. The law defines these as "transportation, and such developmental, corrective, and other support services (including speech pathology and audiology, psychological services, physical and occupational therapy, recreation . . . social work services, counseling services . . . and medical services, except that such medical services shall be for diagnostic and evaluation purposes only) as may be required to assist a child with a disability to benefit from special education, and includes the early identification and assessment of disabling conditions in children."[5.4]

Assistive technology is a key special education service that schools must by law provide, when appropriate, to meet a student's needs.[5.5] Assistive technology has become a frequent point of contention in the IEP process, with students and their families arguing that such technology is needed to meet their educational goals and school officials often contending that it is not. No means exist under current law for the school to acknowledge a student's need for technology, or any other special education service, without thereby obliging itself to provide it. Since schools are not permitted to refuse to provide services deemed educationally necessary, they take refuge in denial of the educational need. Ideally, the issues of educational necessity and school district finances should not be fused. As long as they remain linked, parents who undertake to finance their children's special education needs face two vexing problems:

1. They must find the services or the needed technology on their own; and
2. Deprived of any endorsement from the educational system, they must be prepared to support their claims for tax deduction with evidence derived from other sources.

In confronting the costs of self-funded special education services for their children, parents need to understand that educational expenses are not generally tax deductible. The tax law offers little help to those seeking to obtain a good education. Many proposals to change this are currently circulating, but at present there are only a few, fairly narrow exceptions. Special education costs for students with disabilities represent one of the most important of these exceptions.

It is not by virtue of their educational value that special education expenses are deductible, however. Special education costs must also qualify as medical care expenses in order to be deductible. As such, they are subject to the same thresholds and practical problems as other costs discussed in Chapter 4. To the extent that special education costs can be characterized as therapeutic, that is as treatment for or mitigation of a disability, they can qualify for the medical deduction.

Historically, before public policy favored the mainstreaming of students with disabilities in local public schools, tax cases on education dealt largely with tuition and other expenses in institutionalized, typically residential, settings. These cases generally reached the conclusion that tuition would be deductible if the student was sent to the special school or institution for *medical* reasons, but would not be deductible if the motives for the placement were primarily educational.[5.6] Such associated costs as room, board, or travel to and from the school would also be deductible when the tuition qualified for deduction. In order for tuition to be deductible, the curriculum or related program of school services had to include a significant element of something that could be classified as treatment. The presence of specialized treatment personnel on the school staff, the school's admissions criteria, and other factors were used as evidence in various cases to show that the school met these requirements.[5.7]

Thus, the costs of a school specializing in sign language and other training for deaf students were deductible, whereas the costs of college preparatory education for a blind student were not, since that training was primarily educational in nature and included no specialized services.[5.8] Using the same logic, the costs of sending a child to a school where the curriculum included therapy for psychological and emotional problems were deductible; the costs of a military school, whose therapeutic curriculum consisted principally of discipline, were not, since military-style discipline could not be classified as medical treatment.[5.9]

Beyond its availability, treatment had to be the primary reason for sending the child to the school. In this connection, medical recommendations, often those of psychiatrists, played an important role. The fact that placement was made pursuant to such recommendations tended to prove that the motive was to obtain therapy. However, physician recommendation was not enough to ensure deductibility because, as in the military school cases, the IRS has a right to make an independent determination of whether the school's curriculum and services are therapeutic in nature. Physician recommendation would also not guarantee success if the IRS believed that it was based on nonmedical considerations.

In these special school cases, you would have been allowed to deduct either all of the tuition or none of it. No provision was made for an allocation between the percentage of your motives (and payments) connected to education and the percentage related to therapy, or between the number of hours in the school day devoted to education and the number dedicated to treatment. As indicated earlier, this all-or-nothing outcome generally extended to incidental costs as well. If the tuition was deductible, so were the room and board, transportation to the school, and other associated costs; if the tuition was not deductible, there would be no basis for deducting these other costs either.

When no tuition was at issue, deduction was sometimes allowed for discrete and identifiable therapeutic or treatment services provided within the framework of an educational environment or curriculum. Such isolated or additional costs could be deductible in cases where they were purchased in an otherwise free educational environment, or when tuition expenses were supplemented by charges for special services.[5.10]

Although there have been a surprisingly small number of cases in this area, such expenses as braille or sign language instruction have long been considered deductible under the health care rationale. So have services that represented treatment for emotional, psychiatric, neurological, or other disorders, even when their purpose was to render the child capable of benefiting from education in the future.[5.11] Though provided in an educational rather than a therapeutic setting, the object of these services was to mitigate the consequences of a disability. Based on a similar theory, the costs of assistance necessary to enable a child to attend school should be deductible as well. In one such case, a family was allowed a medical deduction for the cost of hiring a guide to accompany their blind child at school. This deduction was allowed because the services of the guide mitigated the disability of blindness.[5.12]

If a parent needs to place a child in a private school for which the public school district will not pay, the deductibility of the tuition continues to hinge on the purpose of the placement and the nature of the curriculum. Problems need to be anticipated here because of the inevitable overlap between educational and therapeutic goals. For analytical purposes, we can minimize such confusion by framing the question this way: Would the placement have been appropriate or this service necessary for a student who did not have this disability? If the answer is yes, meaning that the placement or service would have been necessary or desirable even if the student were not disabled, then you are unlikely to get your deduction. If the answer is no, that is, this specialized service would not be required or appropriate except by a student with a disability, then you should get your deduction. If the answer is maybe, further thinking and analysis are demanded to justify the deduction.

Although the issue of student placement will continue to be important, cases involving special services within a mainstreamed educational environment are likely to predominate in the future. In evaluating such cases, the analytical framework used in the older tuition and discrete services cases will continue to be applicable, even as the specific services involved grow and change. One such new issue is assistive technology. With the introduction of computers into the classroom, several new categories of isolated special education costs can be foreseen. Schools often refuse to provide peripherals or software that permit students with disabilities to access or effectively use mainstream classroom or computer lab equipment. Families may thus incur the costs of providing the access technology their children need.

Items ranging from specialized software to alternative keyboards or screen-output devices designed for use by people with disabilities should be deductible. Again, the point is not that they are used for education or in an educational environment, but rather that they are designed and used to mitigate the effects of disabilities. When this is their defining feature, it should not make a material difference whether they are used in school or at home.

Assistive technology devices and services vitally illustrate the possibilities. Let us discuss an example. In educational settings, augmentative communication devices are probably the most widely sought type of technology.[5.13] Although their purchase may be motivated by educational considerations, the expense would be deductible as a health care cost. As a device designed to mitigate a communications disability, the alternative communication aid qualifies as therapeutic under any conceivable standard. Even without acknowledgment by school authorities of the need for the device, the necessary justification should not be hard to formulate. With an augmentative communication aid, the answer to our question is a resounding no. Without the disability, such a device would not be needed for educational or any other purposes. Put another way, a student who does not have a communications disability could have no imaginable use for such a device!

What if a standard computer is needed to drive the device? Many students without disabilities use computers. Perhaps this student would have used a computer even if there were no disability. Such a situation presents a case in which the answer to our question is maybe. Our analysis must therefore focus on identifying the factors that turn that maybe for students at large into a no for the particular student in question. The key facts relate to the use to which the computer is put. If used solely to drive the augmentative communication device, that is strong proof of its assistive nature. There is no need to limit the computer's use to classroom communication. If it is also used to facilitate noncurricular social communication with other students, this only serves to underscore the device's role as a tool for mitigating the communication disability.

Even when a school cannot provide needed technology devices and services, the IEP process represents a good opportunity to get the key facts on the record. Many parents and advocates understand that the yearly IEP meeting provides the record on which appeals from adverse school system decisions are based. Parents who lack the means for an appeal or who do not expect to win one can in any event use the IEP conference as a forum to create a documentary record for their tax claims.

How can a viable tax deduction exist for the technology if the school's denial of our request would be sustained on appeal? The school's refusal to provide technology is often correct from the standpoint of the education law, but this does not mean that parents who seek to supplement what the school provides are not entitled to a tax deduction for their expenditures. What the education laws require schools to do is considerably narrower than what the tax law will support families to do for themselves.

When a school's inability or unwillingness to provide special education or related services interferes with the learning process, instructional support of some kind may be necessary. With such traditional educational services, the line between an ordinary educational expense and a special educational cost becomes acutely difficult to draw with precision. For example, consider a student with an information processing disability who falls behind in reading or other academic subjects. Similarly, a student may fall behind in math or history if his or her vision is insufficient to see equations on the board, or if his or her hearing is inadequate to follow a teacher's explanation of a historical event. As a result, tutoring, remedial reading, or other supplementary educational efforts may become necessary. Although standard in nature, these extra services are directly attributable to the need to overcome the effects of the disability. If the math teacher had simply spoken the equations while writing them, or if the history teacher had written the critical dates on the board while lecturing, the student might have kept up perfectly well.

The costs of tutoring are hard to deduct because it is difficult to prove that poor educational performance is linked closely enough to the disability. After all, too many students who can see the board fail to understand math equations, and many students who can hear every word the teacher says think history doesn't matter because it happened in the past. How does one show that the need for academic tutoring resulted from the disability? Moreover, even if we can demonstrate that the disability gave rise to the need for the tutoring, how do we show that the services are therapeutic rather than merely academic? Indeed, the latter is a greater concern, since if the services are therapeutic, the role of the disability in their justification becomes largely self-evident.

In many instances when students with disabilities fall behind, we can safely assume that the school system's prior failure to provide accommodations is the major link between the disability and the need for remediation. The hypothesis that the lack of special education services is responsible for the deficiencies is confirmed if academic performance improves after the accommodations are provided. While the cost of such accommodations would frequently qualify for deduction, as they did in the case of a notetaker hired to assist a deaf student,[5.14] the academic remediation that compensates for the earlier failure is not necessarily deductible.

Justifying remedial services as therapeutic will prove easier in some cases than others. For example, if the child has a diagnosed condition that interferes with reading or other information processing functions, the remedial reading will frequently qualify as *treatment,* especially if the tutoring is offered by someone with specialized training in the area of learning disabilities, or if it involves specialized reading techniques.

If it seems like the distinctions the tax law compels are tortured ones, they are! The effort to tease out the medical, educational, and psychosocial strands of a child's experience belie the real complexities of growing up. Yet for the present, that is exactly what the tax law requires. Almost worse than this oversimplification is the way the law requires us to undermine the dignity of our children. Attributing the need for tutoring to the disability exonerates the school system and perpetuates negative stereotypes that adversely influence the expectations teachers have of their students and the expectations that students with disabilities develop of themselves. Why should a parent whose child's performance deficiencies are attributable to the failure of a school system to provide reasonable accommodations be forced to blame the disability in order to obtain tax subsidies for the attempt to provide compensatory services? Is the tax law not forcing us to blame the victim in order to gain its favor? Unfortunately, since we cannot claim a deduction for the failures of the school system, we are forced to play to the stereotypes by contending that the need for remediation is due to the disability.

Poor academic performance resulting from the inadequacy of special education services may be characterized as a secondary consequence of disability. However much these prior school system failures may account for the academic deficit, the connection between standard educational services and the underlying disability is typically too remote to satisfy the tax system's requirements of proof. This does not mean that there are no atypical cases, however. A family

faced with the need to mitigate these secondary consequences of a disability should not refrain from seeking deductibility, but should be aware that the road is
a rocky one.

As always, they should prepare careful documentation, which might include:

☞ a request to the school to modify the special education services or environment to solve the problem;
☞ an assessment from a qualified professional that
  the educational deficiency is attributable to the disability;
☞ a test or demonstration to show the child's heightened grasp or enhanced function after the environment has been modified; and
☞ an assessment, once the tutoring or other special
  help has been provided, of the student's ability to
  keep up if the environmental modifications continue in effect.

Such evidence does not ensure the deductibility
of standard tutoring, but it does create the best context for arguing that the objectives are therapeutic.
With these standard educational services, our challenge is analogous to what we face in attempting to
deduct devices or supplies that acquire their disabil-
ity-relatedness from how and by whom they are used.
The trouble lies in the difference between ordinary
goods and these standard educational services. Once
you have proved that the person with a disability can
read with the aid of a computer when she could not
do so before, you have at least shown that the computer affects a function of the mind or body. By contrast, even when you have shown that a student with
a disability benefits from ordinary, nonspecialized
tutoring, you have not necessarily demonstrated
either that the disability caused the academic deficiency or that impact on the disability is the reason
for the improvement.

Returning to the concept of secondary consequences, we know that students with disabilities face
many barriers to acceptance similar to those faced by
adults. The social, psychological, attitudinal, and
adjustment consequences of these barriers are not
easily predicted or catalogued. Children with disabili-

ties have all the usual problems connected with growing up, some of which have little relationship to their disabilities, while others are closely connected.

A wide range of professional practitioners now work with children in our society. In sorting out when their services are deductible, we apply basically the same standards discussed in Chapter 4. When the relationship between the problem to be mitigated and the service is ambiguous or uncertain, the credentials of the service provider may be particularly relevant. Likewise, when the service provider is not a member of a specialized discipline, the nature and purpose of the services themselves must be explained and documented with all the more clarity. And when the services qualify for deduction whether the child has a disability or not, then the disability doesn't matter at all. If a child needs the services of a psychologist to deal with adjustment or developmental issues, we don't need to get hung up over whether the child's disability is the cause or whether that disability is being mitigated by the treatment. The services are deductible as medical treatment whatever the need, and, indeed, whatever their outcome.

In the blurred area between education and therapy, parents need to be sure that the practitioner chosen is appropriate for the service being claimed. For example, as noted earlier in this section, the claim for deductibility of remedial reading services would be strengthened if the tutor chosen had expertise in learning disabilities.[5.15] Tutors may or may not be certified teachers, but licensing, while an important source of evidence, is not the issue here. The issue is your ability, utilizing whatever evidence is at your command, to articulate facts that make your claim credible. Here, as elsewhere, the facts often define the law.

(b)

Higher Education

For many families, paying for college education has become a major financial preoccupation. Higher education presents two specific issues for students with disabilities:

1. It may be even more vital to economic prospects than college education would be for other students; and

2. Higher education for a student with a disability may cost more than the same education for a student without one.

A number of tax law provisions bear on higher education costs for all students. For instance, the interest paid on Series Double E U.S. savings bonds is tax-exempt under the Education Savings Bonds Program if used for educational purposes.[5.16] The exemption applies only if a number of conditions are met: family AGI must be below designated, inflation-adjusted limits ($44,150 for a single taxpayer or head of household, and $66.200 for a married couple filing jointly for 1992, above which the exemption is subject to phaseout); the bonds must have been acquired after 1990 (but not in trade for older bonds); the proceeds must be used for eligible higher education expenses of the bond owner, a spouse or dependent; the owner must have been over the age of 24 when the bonds were purchased; and the educational expenses for which the bond proceeds are used must be paid in the same year the interest is received. Additionally, in case there were not enough restrictions already, no exclusion will be granted for redemption proceeds that exceed the amount of eligible expenses.

These conditions apply to all students, but the statute's definition of *educational expenses* poses potential hardships for students with disabilities. The exemption is limited to costs incurred for tuition and fees. Therefore, costs such as those for assistive technology and assistant or attendant services, often the major costs that students with disabilities at public colleges incur, appear not to qualify for the exemption. If bond proceeds are used to pay these costs, the bond interest may well be fully taxable.

This bond exemption provision is relatively new. Only time and perhaps litigation will yield a definitive interpretation of its scope. For example, perhaps the term *fees* will be interpreted more broadly than is customarily the case to include amounts paid for assistive devices or for assistants' services. Admittedly, such an interpretation would involve a considerable stretching of Congressional intent. The fees referred to in the statute are surely those that we pay to the school. While fees we pay to assistants are often necessary for our enrollment or attendance, this is not the kind of necessity the law contemplates.

Pending clarification, families who want the bond-interest exemption can do a couple of things. The most obvious is to use bond proceeds specifically for tuition and related school fees. Even this may not be so easy in all cases. If the student is receiving financial aid specifically to cover those costs, the family may have no discretion for diverting that aid to other purposes and using the bond interest to pay tuition. Worse yet, even if some means existed for swapping the funds around, doing so might not gain you anything. As we shall see, scholarships are not always fully tax-exempt either. Their exclusion from income also depends on how they are used.

Without burrowing too deeply into the legislative history of this well-intentioned bond program, it is safe to say that Congress never thought about the special concerns of students with disabilities when drafting this provision. Obviously, while Congress intended to limit the exemption to what it considered core costs of college and graduate-level education, no one ever actively decided against including the unique expenses of students with disabilities. It just happened that way. As it is, the provision helps all students, including those with disabilities, but if anyone had thought about this program from the disability standpoint, it could easily have accomplished more. Inertia being what it is, remedying the oversight may not be easy.

Another provision that all families should know about concerns home mortgage indebtedness. While the tax law limits the deductibility of interest paid on home equity loans in several ways, the amount of interest that can be deducted is greater when the purpose of the loan is to pay medical or educational costs.[5.17]

Scholarships are another area in which tax benefits play a role in meeting educational costs. The proceeds of scholarships, grants, and fellowships are excludable from income, provided they are used to meet specified costs. Shocking as it may be, since 1986 the law has not treated financial aid for room and board as tax-exempt.

In public colleges, as in public elementary and secondary schools, the value of free educational services and facilities provided to students is not income to them. However, when the student pays these costs with scholarship funds or other educational financial aid, we need to make sure that these funds remain tax-exempt. Whether the financial aid is excludable depends on how it is spent. Financial aid is excludable only if received and used for certain specified expenses. "Qualified higher education expenses" include tuition, fees, and other costs incurred in enrolling in or attending school, such as books, supplies, and equipment.[5.18] Financial aid used for other purposes, however legitimate, may be includable in gross income.

In connection with financial aid, some special issues once again arise for students with disabilities and their families. Students with disabilities may face extra costs for equipment and supplies or may need the services of assistants. The issue in these cases is to make sure that these extra expenses are within the law's definition of *qualified* expenses so they remain tax-exempt. To illustrate, when a college requires that entering students have personal computers, there can be no argument about whether such equipment is required for enrollment. The excludability of sums raised to pay for that equipment would not be a problem. Even if the computer system used by a student with a disability cost more than a classmate's, the financial aid to cover the add-on costs would still be tax-exempt.

With costs the school does not mandate, the exemption from tax for funds spent on equipment and supplies still applies. Provided they meet the statutory test, absence of an official school requirement for their acquisition is of no consequence. Nevertheless, students and financial aid donors should be alert to the possibility that these costs will seem remote, that is, that their necessity for and relationship to enrollment at the school or pursuit of a chosen course of study will not be immediately obvious. As long as the student is able to demonstrate that the equipment or supplies are necessary for enrollment or for completing her/his courses, exemption will not be jeopardized.

From this standpoint, disability is actually not a very significant factor. For example, a student who needs a powerful magnifier to read a biology textbook is no different from one who needs a microscope to conduct lab experiments. That one needs assistive technology makes no difference. Both need the equipment to complete the requirements for the course. This need is the test for the exemption.

Because the excludability of school financial aid depends on how the money is spent, students need to pay attention to documenting the use of their funds. In cases where financial aid applications or other documents connected with the aid specify the purposes for which it is given, this element of proof does not usually present any problem. However, most financial aid application forms lack categories or questions specifically addressing disability-related expenses. Normally, students can list their needs on financial aid applications, making the bookkeeping comparatively easy. If a student has not specifically requested funds for assistive technology or has received funds not expressly designated for this purpose, students should be particularly careful to keep records sufficient to prove that the funds they received were used for the purchase and upkeep of equipment.

The purchase of services presents a more complicated problem. Nothing in the law indicates that the purchase of reader, notetaker, personal assistance or other services comes within the statutory definition of qualifying higher education expenses. Of course, the services of a reader, sign language interpreter, or other assistant or attendant will frequently be tax deductible, but that is a different issue from preserving exemption for the financial aid used to pay for these services.

Let us hope that the word *fees* will be interpreted broadly enough to cover such costs, though they may not be paid directly to the college or university. Such an interpretation would be strained, so some statutory change is necessary to resolve the problem. In the meantime, if financial aid expended on services is includable in income, one's line of defense is the possible deductibility of these expenses. If the deduction offsets the includable income, the transaction comes close to being what accountants and investors call a "wash."

For students not considered degree candidates under the definitions used by their schools, the tax treatment of financial aid may be governed by more restrictive rules.[5.19] Even when received and spent for qualifying expenses, scholarships to non-degree track students are tax-exempt only if the source is either a nonprofit organization chartered under Section 501(c)(3) of the Internal Revenue Code, a unit of the federal or a state government, or a foreign government. Amounts that can be excluded from income under such scholarships are also limited to a fixed amount for each month of school enrollment, regardless of the actual tuition or other costs. This limitation can present problems for any student who has qualifying expenses exceeding the permissible exemption amount, especially students with disabilities whose qualifying expenses may well be high.

Education no longer ends at the classroom door. Continuing education, retraining and career change, upgrading of skills, and refresher courses are important parts of many people's working lives. Staff development and in-house training programs are components of an ever-growing number of work environments. Although the costs of such training, professional development, and continuing education raise tax questions for all workers, these issues are particularly important for workers with disabilities.

Two tax benefits deal with worker education and training. One of these is a fringe benefit of employment. Educational benefits provided to workers under employer-sponsored educational assistance plans are tax-exempt to their recipients. Before discussing this provision further, a word of caution: as of this writing (September, 1992), the Internal Revenue Code section embodying this provision has lapsed. It was authorized only through June 30, 1992, meaning that the exemption will not apply to educational assistance provided after that date, although if recent history is any guide, this fringe benefit will most likely be restored to the law, retroactive to that date.

Up to a maximum of $5,250 per year, education provided under an employer-sponsored *qualifying* Educational Assistance Plan is both deductible to the business and excludable from the income of the employee who receives it.[5.20] Consistent with requirements applicable to all fringe benefits of employment,

(c)

Vocational and Job Training

the plans must meet a number of legal conditions in order to qualify for this doubly advantageous tax treatment. Educational assistance plans can vary widely in the kinds of education or training they support, in the amount of reimbursement or direct purchases they provide for each employee, and in other respects.

The educational assistance plan does not place narrow limits on the kinds of education that can be supported. Unlike the employee business deduction, employer-sponsored plans need not be limited to training that contributes to worker job performance or skills.

Let us turn, then, to situations where employees expend their own funds for education and training. The costs of vocational training, professional education, and the development of new job skills are not generally tax deductible. Wisely or not, education that contributes to economic advancement is not encouraged by the tax system. Workers' educational expenses are usually deductible only when they contribute to the production of income in the present. Employees' educational expenses are deductible on the basis of their purpose. Broadly speaking, expenditures to maintain job skills or to preserve one's job are deductible. These would include training required by the employer for maintenance of one's job or rate of pay; training required by law as a condition for continuing in a particular job or profession, and training required to prepare for new duties within your current employment.[5.21] The maintenance and upgrading of skills for one's current work have to be distinguished from the seeking of training to prepare or qualify for new work. Expenses in the first category are deductible; those in the second are not. Similarly, expenses of qualifying for a job or preparing for a profession are not deductible, since they are incurred in order to enter a new field or line of work. Thus, the lawyer's costs for taking the bar exam are not deductible, but once admitted to practice, the costs for continuing education would be.

At a time when worker mobility and flexibility are increasingly prized features of the work force, clear boundaries do not always exist to distinguish a job-maintenance cost from a job-advancement educational expense. The answer depends on a mix of factors, including whether the training is a formal or legal prerequisite for entry into some new line of work, and the worker's intentions in seeking the training. If your primary intention is to preserve or enhance skills in your present job, you are not deprived of the deduction simply because the training might also contribute to later job prospects.[5.22] The very same course might be deductible at one time but not at another, as your motive for taking it changes.

Nor does the law demand that the training be formally required by the employer as a condition for keeping one's job. By the same token, an employer's agreement that the training is related to one's current job does not automatically resolve the matter in favor of deductibility.[5.23] Usually, if an employer assigns new tasks to a worker, the necessary training if paid for by the employee will qualify for deduction. Take the case of a data processing manager in a small manufacturing firm who is told that because of layoffs he will as of next Monday also be the director of personnel. Knowing little about human resources work, he rushes out to take an intensive course on the subject and buys a number of books and periodicals; his employer reimburses none of these expenses. Are these expenses deductible? The answer is yes, for at least two reasons. First, the increase of duties was decided by the employer and, realistically, was a condition for the employee's keeping his job. Second, the employee did not take this training with any intention to move into the personnel management field or get a personnel management degree, although, of course, he is free to put this work on his resumé.

In applying the same-line-of-work test, the law treats teachers more leniently than other workers. Classroom teachers who seek certification in different subject areas or who even leave the classroom for training in school administration are allowed to deduct the costs of such training.[5.24] Theoretically, becoming a school administrator represents career change. The law does not dispute this but simply makes an exception. Lest anyone become envious, remember how few breaks teachers get in our society.

When job-related educational costs qualify for deduction, they are treated as itemized deductions and claimed under the category *miscellaneous itemized deductions*.[5.25] Most typically, unreimbursed employee educational and training expenses are thought of under the heading of employee business expenses. We will learn more about this deduction category in Chapter 6. For now, it is enough to remember that a threshold applies to this deduction. For miscellaneous itemized deductions, including employee business expenses, the threshold is two percent of AGI, meaning we can only deduct these costs to the extent that they exceed two percent of our AGI. As usual, we also need to have enough deductions, under whatever category, to warrant itemization in the first place.

Workers with disabilities often incur job-related training costs that their nondisabled peers do not. For instance, if a firm installs a new computer system, basic training in the new system is typically provided to all employees, but this may not be sufficient for a worker with a disability. Consider a worker with a visual disability who uses speech synthesis peripherals to read the computer screen. With changes in the main office computer system, these adaptive components may require modification as well. Training on the new assistive devices, in addition to guidance in interfacing the new peripherals with the office system, may also be needed. When an employee with a disability pays for such extra training costs, they should readily qualify for deductibility.

In some instances, the worker who pays these expenses may have a choice as to which of two possible deduction categories to use. The expense may be deductible either as a miscellaneous itemized deduction or as an impairment-related work expense, which is discussed at length in Chapter 6. For the moment, a key element of strategy to remember is that impairment-related work expenses are not subject to the two percent of AGI threshold.[5.26]

The onset of a disability often leads to a change of career. As the law now stands, educational and retraining costs associated with career change are not deductible. Is this the wisest public policy in situations where the career change is a matter of necessity rather than choice, and when return to economic productivity is possible only in some new field? Clearly, the law should provide for the deductibility of retraining expenses incurred by people whose disabilities prevent them from continuing in their former line of work.

For most people in our society, education is a means to a better life for ourselves and for our children. After our formal education has been completed, most of us aspire to enter the working world. With that progression in mind, we turn next to the issues surrounding employment.

Employment And Business

(a)

Impairment-Related Work Expenses

Impairment-related work expenses[6.1] (IRWEs) were added to the Internal Revenue Code in 1986. The IRWE provision expands the range of work expenses for which people with disabilities can claim a deduction and establishes the principle that work expenses attributable solely to handicap qualify as deductible business expenses. On balance, IRWEs may be the most important provision in the tax law dealing specifically with disability.

   We all hope the day will come when employers recognize that the productive potential of workers with disabilities far outweighs the costs of providing assistive technology or other reasonable accommodations. Legal and attitudinal changes are moving us in that direction, but until employers accept responsibility for these costs, as they do for the equipment, facilities, and support services needed by other workers, effective utilization of the IRWE provision will remain one of the best interim strategies at the disposal of workers with disabilities for meeting job-related costs.

Although relatively new to the Internal Revenue Code, IRWEs are not new to the broader body of federal law. Their appearance in the tax code is predated by their use in the Social Security Act to define a category of expenditures used to shield income from "countability" under the SSI and SSDI programs.[6.2] In this context, the meaning of IRWEs differs somewhat from their meaning in the Internal Revenue Code.

The Code defines IRWEs as

> expenses of a handicapped individual as defined in Section 190 (b)(3) for attendant care services at the individual's place of employment and other expenses in connection with such place of employment which are necessary for such individual to be able to work, and with respect to which a deduction is allowable under Section 162 determined without regard to this section

What does this mean and how does it apply? We understand some of what this statute means, but because it is a new provision, for which the IRS has issued no regulations, and under which no significant rulings or cases yet exist to guide its interpretation, some of its meaning can only be determined over time. It is no exaggeration to say that readers of this book will help determine what this statute accomplishes by the costs they claim, the arguments they advance, and the education they provide. We will organize our discussion around six key questions about the IRWE provision.

Our first question is a general one concerning the mechanics and purposes of this provision. IRWEs are an itemized deduction available to employed people. Like other itemized deductions, IRWEs are claimed on Schedule A to the Form 1040 Individual Tax Return (the so-called long form). Workers who want to claim the deduction also have to file Form 2106 with their tax return. The IRWE amount is shown on Line 11 of that form and is carried over to Line 25 of Schedule A.

Specifically, IRWEs are a subgroup of the deduction category known as miscellaneous itemized deductions (MIDs), which are discussed in the next section. Unlike other employee business expenses, IRWEs are not subject to the 2 percent of AGI threshold for deductibility, but are completely deductible by those who itemize.[6.3] Accordingly, one purpose for the creation of IRWEs was to remove certain expenses from the 2 percent requirement. Another purpose of the IRWE deduction is to accord business expense status to some costs that previously either would not have qualified for deduction under any theory or would have qualified only as medical expenses.

Our second question is who is a handicapped individual? The IRWE provision (Section 67 (d) of the Internal Revenue Code) refers us to Section 190 (b)(3) for the applicable definition. As noted in Chapter 3, Section 190 (the section creating the architectural barrier removal deduction) contains the Code's most important reference to the term *handicapped,* defining it as a physical or mental disability which for the individual "constitutes or results in a functional limitation to employment" or which "substantially limits one or more major life activities."[6.4] Section 190 and its implementing regulations give examples of impairments that would meet these standards, including blindness and deafness (plus manual tasks, walking, breathing, learning, and working, as added by the regulations).[6.5] Handicapped persons are not limited to persons with these listed impairments, however. The definition of handicapped person is an open-ended one under which the conjunction of a physical or mental impairment and an activity or employment limitation appear sufficient to meet the test. The statutory definition is broad enough to include any physical or mental impairment that, for the individual, constitutes or results in such limitations.

The law does not require a diagnosis or medical assessment to justify the claim of impairment-relatedness for one's expenses. Of course, a factual question can always arise about whether an individual actually has an impairment. If the IRS disputes the existence of an impairment, medical evidence could be useful, but the important point is that no medical findings or certification are required to invoke the deduction.

Our third question is what types of expenses are deductible? The statute refers specifically to *attendant care services* and to *other expenses*. This reference to attendant care services is puzzling and disconcerting, especially since it is the only concrete illustration of what expenses the statute contemplates. Congress (which enacted the ADA only four years after the IRWE provision) surely understands that people with disabilities do not need *care* in order to work. Congress must have intended a broader definition than this term usually denotes.

In its application of this unfortunate terminology, the IRS supports such a broader reading. In its publication 907 the IRS includes readers, sign language interpreters, and services to help "the mentally retarded do their work" in its definition of attendant care services.[6.6] This list of service providers is meant to be illustrative only. Other services such as those provided by drivers, phone answerers, attaché case carriers, or other assistants are also covered. These services either fall within the definition of "attendant care services" or they qualify for the IRWE deduction as "other expenses." Eligibility for the IRWE depends not on the category of the service but rather on its impairment- and work-related nature.

Our fourth question is where must the services be performed? In order for expenses to be treated as IRWEs, they must be incurred "at" or "in connection with" the place of employment. Presumably this location requirement was intended to avoid disagreements or uncertainty over whether a particular cost was truly work-related. Congress apparently believed that including a location requirement would prevent people from claiming work-relatedness for costs that were personal in nature.

Based on this location requirement, some may be concerned that the statute limits deductible services to those provided on the employer's premises. However, by reading the statute that narrowly, we would deny deductibility in many cases where Congress obviously intended it. The scope of the location requirement hinges on the interpretation of the words, "in connection with," as in, "at or in con-

nection with the place of employment." The only sensible reading of the "at or in connection with" language is that Congress intended services to be
deductible wherever received, so long as they are
connected with one's employment.

An unduly narrow reading of the location
requirement would bear no relationship to the way
people actually conduct business and do their jobs.
Depending on the job duties, services may be needed
away from one's *place of employment.* Common sense
tells us that when a job requires the services of assistants or attendants in the field, these costs should be
deductible on the same basis as those incurred in the
office. One could also argue that, for someone whose
work involves time spent away from the office or
store, such outside locations are his or her place of
employment.

In today's increasingly demanding work environments, many employees find it necessary to supplement time at their place of work by doing work at
home. Accordingly, we must ask the questions: Does
the IRWE provision cover services we utilize at home
and, if so, is the range of such services as broad as
those that would be covered at our place of work?
Based on a reasonable construction of the words "in
connection with," the answer should be yes. This
interpretation is supported by Publication 907.[6,7]

But even if services received at home can qualify
as IRWEs, we still face the question of what services
meet this test. A reader, reading work-related material
to a person who is blind, is an obvious example of a
service that qualifies. Would an attendant at home,
whose services are needed in preparation for work
each morning, qualify as an IRWE? Such services are
clearly impairment-related; they are also work-related
in that we would be unable to prepare for or get to
our jobs without them. Can the statute be interpreted
to include such services? With considerable reluctance
and no small amount of disappointment, I am forced
to conclude that the answer is probably no.

Assuming services provided at home (such as
readers, typists, etc.) qualify as IRWEs, the law would
probably draw a line between services that directly
relate to the performance of our jobs and services that
relate to job performance only indirectly by facilitating our work. The limitation here stems from the

words "work expenses." Our tax law contains many instances of expenses which, though indispensable in order for someone to work, are denied deductibility because they are too *remote* or *indirect.* Commuting expenses, the costs of work clothes (except for uniforms, which are defined as articles of clothing that would not be suitable for use away from the work site), and many other costs fail to qualify for deductibility as business expenses on this basis. Put another way, they are considered personal expenses, even if incurred to facilitate work.

The IRWE statute clearly accords business deductibility to a number of expenses that would previously have been considered personal in nature, but the question remains how far Congress intended to go. Changing the law to make indirect expenses in the home eligible for the business deduction would be a far-reaching step. Without clear statutory language indicating the congressional intention to do so, the IRS and the courts are unlikely to conclude that Congress intended so significant an expansion of the traditional business deduction. The words "in connection with," do not amount to a sufficiently clear and unambiguous statement of such legislative intent. Indeed, the fact that "at or in connection with" relates to the "place of employment" suggests that Congress did not mean to significantly expand the deduction for work-related services in the home.

Prior to enactment of the IRWE statute, attendant care services provided at an individual's place of work might or might not have qualified as deductible employee business expenses. In light of that case-by-case uncertainty, it is perfectly plausible to conclude that Congress added the IRWE statute to clarify the deductible status of such expenses. In providing this clarification the IRWE statute performs an important service, though we wish it had gone further.

Unfortunately, the legislative history of the Tax Reform Act of 1986 (which created the IRWE) offers little guidance in ferreting out the drafters' intentions regarding possible deductibility of services in the home. Our conclusion, that the answer depends on the nature of the service, derives from a common sense reading of the statute and from the nature and context of prior law. None of the three congressional reports accompanying the Tax Reform Act gives any indication of an intention as far-reaching as we desire.[6.8]

Of course, the fact that an expense fails to qualify as an IRWE does not prevent its deductibility under some other category. Thus, if the attendant services qualify for the medical deduction, we could avoid the IRWE problem by simply handling them that way. Ironically, incorporation of the term "attendant care services" into the law via the IRWE statute probably strengthens the claim for medical deductibility of attendant services. See Chapter 4(d).

Taxpayers need to test the boundaries of the IRWE provision. Where support services can be shown as essential to the ability to work, the argument that the IRWE section ought to cover them needs to be made and developed in the judicial and legislative arenas. Because of how poorly the IRWE statute is drafted, this issue of indirectness will need to be squarely addressed in a number of forums.

Our fifth question about the IRWE statute is what is the meaning of the word *necessary,* as in "necessary for such individual to be able to work." One can interpret the word to mean that you would be unable to hold the job without the items or services in question, but once more such a reading is too narrow to make much sense. In fact, the term means that the goods or services help you do the job more effectively. Necessity here should be understood in terms of what purpose or need necessitated the purchase.

This interpretation is supported by the IRWE statute's cross- reference to Section 162 of the Internal Revenue Code, which deals with the deductions that are allowable "in the conduct of a trade or business." Trade or business expenses are deductible if they are "ordinary and necessary" expenses in conducting the business.[6.9] The thrust of the IRWE statute's reference to Section 162, therefore, is that the concept of necessity should be given the same meaning here as it has under Section 162.

In interpreting necessity, no one has ever claimed that expenses incurred in the conduct of a business would qualify as necessary expenses only if the firm risked going out of business without them. So, too, with the IRWE, necessity means that business considerations (in this case job considerations) motivated or necessitated the expenditure.

Because many IRWEs may be unfamiliar to tax preparers and officials, the necessity for these costs may be questioned both from the impairment-relatedness and work-relatedness standpoints. A certain amount of educational work may, therefore, be involved in supporting one's deduction claim. The elements of evidence required here are less rigorous than for a medical deduction claim involving the same services. If the services are "helpful and appropriate" (to use a phrase commonly applied under Section 162), they meet the IRWE section's test of necessity.

If your claim is challenged on necessity grounds, your response will depend on whether impairment-relatedness or connection to work is the thrust of the challenge. In practice, these strands (necessity, impairment-relatedness, and work expense) may not be easily separable. In some cases, a statement from the employer, a job description, or many other kinds of supporting evidence should be helpful in establishing one's claim. Useful as such sources of evidence may be, no one should ever read the word *necessary* to imply that an expense must either be mandated by the employer, contained in a job description, or motivated by the threat of job loss in order to qualify as an IRWE. Nor would it be appropriate to suppose that a job analysis is necessary to support one's claims. Consistent with Section 162, employees are entitled to reasonable discretion in how they define and meet their impairment-related work needs.

Nor does the government have any authority to second-guess our selection of services. Because businesses are accorded considerable discretion in deciding what to buy in order to meet their business needs, it follows that they are also permitted to make disastrous mistakes. They are not denied a deduction for their expenses simply because purchases were ill-considered or economically unsound. The lesson in this for IRWEs is that the law does not require an individual's choice of method for meeting impairment-related work needs to be the wisest one.

One situation can be anticipated where the IRS could conceivably question the necessity for some of our costs. The IRS can disallow business expense deductions on the ground that their amounts are *unreasonable,* but the application of this reasonableness standard has been largely confined to compensation (salaries, bonuses, stock options, etc.) that the business pays.[6.10] With IRWEs involving payment for skilled services, a danger exists that those unfamiliar with the range of services people with disabilities utilize will question whether the amounts are reasonable. Faced with such a challenge, it should suffice to prove that you got what you paid for. In the case of professional services, you can submit data on their cost or fair market value or other supply-and-demand information. The point here is to demonstrate that you are not using an IRWE claim to conceal or subsidize gifts to your friends.

Our sixth question is whether assistive technology is included within the scope of IRWEs. The statute makes no reference to technology. For that matter, it makes no express reference to *goods,* as distinguished from *services,* at all. Therefore, in order for assistive technology devices to be included, they must qualify under the "other expenses" language of the section.

The interpretation that technology is covered finds support in the statute's reference, not to attendant care and other *services,* but rather to attendant care and other *expenses.*[6.11] There is nothing in the law to suggest otherwise, and there has been no indication that the Internal Revenue Service views the IRWE statute as applying only to services. While services are clearly the focus of the IRWE statute, Congress would surely have used the term "other services" rather than the far more expansive "other expenses" if it had intended to exclude equipment or other goods from IRWE status. Since the law does not specify what other expenses it may have in mind, and since it does not exclude any category of expenses, the only reasonable conclusion is that equipment that meets the impairment-relatedness and work expense standards does qualify for IRWE designation.

Assuming that goods are covered, the IRWE statute becomes important for low- as well as for high-tech equipment. In this context, even simple standard items should qualify for the IRWE deduction if they meet the test of impairment-relatedness. Meeting this test should not present major obstacles. Essentially, an item's impairment-relatedness is a question of fact, based either on how or why it is used. Because the *why* will provide sufficient evidence in many cases, this standard for demonstrating impairment-relatedness is clearly easier to meet than the test for medical deductibility.

Why is the IRWE status of equipment so important? After all, wouldn't technology needed for work, whether impairment-related or not, be deductible as an employee business expense anyway? The answer is a qualified yes. While equipment qualifies for deduction outside the IRWE context, that deduction would be taken under the miscellaneous itemized deductions category, thereby subjecting equipment to the 2 percent of AGI deduction threshold. All in all, for reasons of economics and administrative simplicity, we need to establish that IRWEs include technology and whatever other "tangible property" we may need to do our work.

Even if technology is eligible for the IRWE deduction, computers or other capital equipment raise additional issues. Major questions occur around the time frames over which they can be deducted. Also with computers, a number of additional conditions must be met, whether the equipment is classified as an IRWE or not. These issues will be discussed further in sections (b) and (d).

The creation of the IRWE deduction has done a great deal to clarify the tax status of many expenditures incurred by workers with disabilities, but as important as IRWEs are, not every unreimbursed employee business expense is an IRWE. Because other unreimbursed employee business expenses are still important to working people with and without disabilities, we turn next to a discussion of these other costs.

(b)

Miscellaneous Itemized Deductions

As their name suggests, miscellaneous itemized deductions (MIDs) include a broad array of expenses. The category is an umbrella for many deductible expenses that are not covered under other specific provisions.[6.12] We have already encountered one important MID in our discussion of employee educational and training costs in Chapter 5(c). MIDs, like medical care expenses, are subject to a threshold or floor. In the case of MIDs it is not the 7.5 percent applicable to health care, but 2 percent of AGI. This means that once we have totaled our MIDs for the year, they are deductible only to the degree that they exceed 2 percent of AGI.

Unreimbursed employee business expenses are one of the most important MIDs. Many working people incur employee business expenses that their employers often pay. When our employer reimburses our expenses, we usually deduct the amount of that reimbursement above-the-line as an adjustment to income. But if our employee business expenses are unreimbursed, we deal with them as an itemized deduction under the MID category. Employee business expenses can extend to anything, from uniforms to professional memberships, from safety shoes to trade periodical subscriptions. Employee business expenses also include the non-IRWE costs that people with disabilities incur.

Even if something can not be clearly classified as an IRWE, it can often still qualify for deduction as a MID. Because MIDs dispense with the requirement of impairment-relatedness, they are in practice a broader category than IRWEs. Many of the job-related expenses workers with disabilities incur are not impairment-related. As an obvious example, if a professional with a disability purchases a journal to keep up with developments in his or her field, that expense is certainly work-related, but it is not impairment-related. A worker with a disability, therefore, may face situations in which work expenses need to be divided between IRWEs and MIDs.

For people with disabilities, MIDs may also represent an important fall-back position for work equipment that does not meet the test for impairment-relatedness. Nevertheless, there are problems surrounding the deductibility of home or personal computers as business expenses that have nothing to do with their status as IRWEs or MIDs.

Home computers are the flashpoint for a tumultuous struggle. The Internal Revenue Service takes the position that home computers (that is, computers used at home) are not normally deductible as an employee business expense.[6.13] In order for them to be deductible, home computers must be *required for the performance of one's job according to a strict convenience-of-the-employer standard, or their use may need to be a literal condition for the holding or keeping of one's job.* Recent tax court decisions have taken a more expansive view, however.[6.14] Pending resolution of the issue by the Supreme Court, people who wish to claim their home computers as employee business expenses should think about ways in which they can demonstrate the requisite high level of necessity.

Generally speaking, increased productivity is not enough, but if required work cannot be done in the office, its accomplishment at home is more than a matter of increased productivity. For workers with disabilities, the lack of suitable accommodations at the workplace may give rise to just such a necessity. Either because of lack of space, noise level, inadequate lighting, incompatibility of interfaces between standard office equipment and access peripherals, or other causes, work at home may be indispensable. Employer mandate or written job description do not appear to be decisive. That is, a statement or a letter from the employer that work at home is required, which many a boss would be more than happy to write, is not conclusive so far as IRS is concerned. Ironically, the poorer the job accommodations at the work site, the more likely the need for supplementary work at home. Even if an employee can successfully claim a deduction for a home computer on the basis of this necessity, additional complexities discussed in section (d) must still be confronted in connection with the period of time over which the deduction is spread. These are discussed in section (d).

A number of workers with disabilities are telecommuters. Some cannot travel back and forth daily to an outside work location, while others simply have skill levels, employment situations, or personal preferences that make this option possible. For those whose place of employment is genuinely their home, many of the problems surrounding the deductibility of technology or services at home should be easier to solve. Presumably, if a person can establish that the home is the place of employment, most or all of the deductions available for goods and services in a conventional office setting should likewise be appropriate.

In assessing the deductibility of various goods and services for people who work at home, the right to a deduction for a home office is not the central question. Because the law requires that to be deductible, a home office must be located in an area of the home used exclusively for business. Whether an individual who works from bed via a modem can successfully claim a home office deduction remains an open question. Precisely because of this uncertainty, we need to remember that the deductibility of one's attendant services or one's assistive technology does not depend on your success in claiming a home office deduction. One's "place of employment" is one's place of employment, whether one can deduct it as a home office or not. While success in claiming a home office eases the path to a number of other business deductions, failure of that claim does not preclude the deduction of these other expenses.

So far in this chapter we have been concerned with the deductions that can be taken by employed people. The costs incurred directly in the operation of a business are handled differently in some important ways. For self-employed people these differences in the treatment of business expenses can often result in a dramatically different bottom line. While there are some differences between what business expenses self-employed people and those who work for wages can deduct, the predominant explanation is procedural, namely, the difference between Schedule A (which people who work for wages or salaries use to itemize their business expenses) and Schedule C (which people who own their own businesses use to itemize theirs).

(c)

S elf-Employment

People whose business expenses derive from employment use Schedule A to the Form 1040 to deduct these expenses as itemized deductions. People in business for themselves may file Schedule A to claim itemized deductions on their personal returns, but their business expenses are listed on Schedule C, called Net Profit or Loss from Business. A self-employed person includes in her or his personal income only the profit from a business, trade, or profession (that is, what remains after the business's expenses are subtracted from its revenues). By filing Schedule C (or the equivalent form for partnerships or corporations), you deduct your business expenses even before determining your personal gross income, because business expenses are netted out prior to incorporating the business income (profit) into your personal gross income calculation. In effect, what results is the equivalent of an above-the-line adjustment to income for these self-employed business expenses, in the sense that their deductibility no longer hinges on whether you itemize. A self-employed person may or may not choose to file Schedule A, but that decision is based on the availability of personal deductions, such as health care costs, charitable contributions, home mortgage interest, and so on.

Schedule C is used by unincorporated businesses, technically known as sole proprietorships. Comparable forms are used if the business is structured as a partnership or a corporation. Owners include only the profit, or their pro rata share of the profit, in their personal incomes, although the question of how much that profit is can frequently be as elusive as any other tax question we may encounter.

Some people who work for wages are nevertheless allowed to deduct their business expenses above-the-line. The law confers this opportunity on performing artists with AGIs of under $16,000 and whose employee business expenses meet several other conditions.[6.15] This is a welcome exception to the general rule, given its applicability to persons with limited income who add great value to our society and who often endure considerable hardship. Ideally, such tax treatment could serve as a precedent for use in connection with others who also enrich our society, such as low-paid workers with disabilities or workers with disabilities who hold more than one job.

Like other costs incurred in the conduct of their trade or business, the impairment-related work expenses of entrepreneurs or self-employed professionals with disabilities become, in effect, above-the-line deductions by virtue of Schedule C (or the equivalent partnership or corporate returns). You still qualify for your personal deductions below-the-line, and you may either itemize or take the standard deduction as you see fit, but if you take the standard deduction, you do not forfeit any tax benefit from your IRWEs.

A possible source of confusion needs to be anticipated here. People who are in business for themselves may incur IRWEs, but they do not use the IRWE or MID terminology in deducting them on

Schedule C. IRWE terminology applies only to deductions claimed by employed persons on Schedule A. When a business deducts the costs of accommodating its disabled employees or operators, it assigns those costs to the applicable generic expense categories: personnel, equipment, and so on. At one time, there might have been a question as to whether a business's costs for goods and services to accommodate workers with disabilities qualified for deduction as "ordinary and necessary" business expenses under Section 162. No such uncertainty now exists. Indeed, the vital question today relates to when a business can convert its reasonable accommodation costs from capital to operational expenses, and when it can convert deductions for reasonable accommodation expenses to tax credits. These issues are addressed later in our discussion of the disabled access credit and the architectural barrier removal deduction in sections (g) and (h).

What is vital for all businesses to know is that the costs of goods and services to accommodate their employees (or, for that matter, their job applicants) with disabilities are deductible on the same basis as any other goods and services the business purchases.

As indicated in sections (a) and (b), the deductibility of technology and the timing of its deduction involve their own special issues, and this is true for businesses as well as for their employees. As a practical matter, the scope of our deductions and their timing must be addressed in a coordinated fashion if the optimal tax results are to be achieved. With this in mind, it is to the hideous complexities surrounding the timing of business equipment deductions that we must now turn.

To the numerous distinctions among expense categories already discussed in this book, one more must now be added. All expenditures made by individuals or businesses can be divided between capital expenses and what are called noncapital, operational, or ordinary expenses. Capital expenses (or expenses chargeable to capital account, as they are technically called) are those for durable goods, defined as tangible items expected to have a useful life of more than one year. Technology, whether assistive or not, is

(d)

Depreciation of Capital Equipment

treated as capital equipment if it is expected to remain in service for more than one year.[6.16]

The fact that something is capital equipment does not change its overall deductibility, and the same rules and tests apply as for other types of expenditures, but the status of capital equipment does change the time frame over which the deduction is taken. When businesses buy capital equipment, they do not deduct its entire cost in the year of purchase, even if they pay the entire cost in that year. Instead, the law requires them to spread the deduction over the life of the equipment; that is, the equipment or other capital asset is depreciated over its useful life.

The rules governing depreciation determine how rapidly businesses can write off (deduct) the cost of automobiles, plants, equipment, furniture, even rental tuxedos or other big ticket items. Without fear of exaggeration, there may be nothing in the tax code more complex than the rules governing depreciation.

The number of years over which an item of capital equipment can be depreciated depends on the category, or class life, to which it belongs, the depreciation method adopted (declining balance, straight line method, or other), the accounting convention employed (midyear, midquarter, etc.), and numerous other esoteric criteria. The IRS publishes schedules specifying the useful life of many categories of equipment. For computers, this time frame is typically either five or seven years, depending on the accounting decisions.

But there are exceptions to the requirement that capital assets have their deduction spread over a number of years. Businesses can choose (*elect* is the technical term) to deduct all or some of their capital equipment expenses in the year the items are placed in service. They do this with an election to expense, or a section 179 election, its official designation. If a business incurs Section 179 expenses of $200,000 or less in a year, it can elect to expense (that is deduct rather than capitalize) up to $10,000 of these costs.[6.17] In order for an item of equipment to be eligible for expensing, it must be used "in the active conduct" of a trade or business.[6.18] Individuals, too, can take advantage of the election to expense. For purposes of qualifying for the election, employed people are deemed to be actively engaged in the business of being employed, and hence are permitted to expense their business-related capital equipment costs.[6.19]

Few employed individuals would ever have occasion or means to spend more than $10,000 for assistive technology in a given year. But even at their typically far more modest expenditure levels, the choice between expensing or depreciating can be an extremely significant one.

Although the election is limited to a maximum of $10,000 per year, that ceiling can be further reduced by a number of factors. The most important of these limitations is that, irrespective of what the equipment actually costs, the amount that can be expensed is limited to the net income derived from trade or business.[6.20] In the case of an employed person, business income would include proceeds from their jobs plus any additional earnings from self-employment. It makes no difference that the equipment was not used in all the activities forming the earnings pool, so long as it was purchased and used for at least one of them.

People with low incomes who finance their work-related technology with savings or borrowed funds face a problem here. Most people would prefer to expense their equipment so as to recoup the tax deduction as quickly as possible, but the amount of the election will be limited, especially in the first year, by their low earnings. Put another way, their income will be too small to absorb the full value of the deduction. Even a high-paying job, if commenced late in the year, might not generate sufficient income to fully utilize the potential benefits of expensing.

At just this point, however, another wrinkle in the expensing provision comes into play. If we lose the right to expense some of the $10,000 because it exceeds our earned income, we are allowed to carry forward the remainder into subsequent years. Normally, whatever taxpayers do not or can not expense is depreciated, but this carry-forward option provides another method for recovering our costs more quickly than depreciation would permit. With any luck, combined income from Years One and Two will be large enough to allow us to complete the process of expensing. No limit is placed on the number of years over which this carry-forward is permitted, but you must deduct your carryover amount to the maximum extent available in each subsequent year. Thus, if your technology cost $3,000, but because of the earned income limitation, you were able to expense only $2,000 in Year One, you must expense the remaining $1,000 in Year Two if earned income permits.

Though most taxpayers who can do so would prefer to expense their equipment, even individuals with incomes sufficient to fully absorb the deduction in the year of the purchase may on occasion find it advantageous to opt for depreciation instead. For example, if you anticipate income growth in Year Two and beyond, particularly if such growth entails moving from a lower to a higher tax bracket, deferral of your deduction (which is in effect what depreciation does) ordinarily makes better economic sense. A deduction of any given amount is worth almost twice as much to a person in the 28 percent bracket as it is to a person paying at the 15 percent marginal rate (perhaps three times as much for a person who is self-employed, once self-employment tax is taken into account).

Before we get too deeply immersed in strategy, though, a few other technicalities, which heavily influence the decision whether to depreciate or expense, must be taken into account by purchasers of capital equipment, especially computers. Primary among these is the tax system's familiar suspicion about computers. Basically, the Internal Revenue Service believes that employed people who try to deduct computers for business use at home are using employment as a pretext. In section (b) we discussed how difficult it is to deduct a home computer, but even when deductible, the same suspicion has made expensing the device far riskier and more difficult.

Computers, cellular phones, and automobiles make up a category called *listed property*.[6.21] Without going into all the harsh ramifications of this status, the main point is that with listed property, the risk of what is called *recapture* is materially heightened.

What is recapture? When we expense a business asset, we are still required to continue using it for business during the period over which it would otherwise have been depreciated. If we do not use it in this fashion, we are subject to recapture, meaning that we must treat as taxable income, in the year the business use ceases, that amount by which our tax write-off from expensing exceeds the amount we would by then have deducted through depreciating the item.[6.22] Don't even try to understand this; no one else does either!

In essence, when we elect to expense equipment, we obtain a form of accelerated depreciation by getting our deduction faster than we would if we had used standard depreciation. If recapture is triggered, it means we have to pay back that difference and thereafter use a less advantageous depreciation method. So even after we have expensed our equipment, we need to continue using it for business or employment in order to avoid recapture.

For most capital equipment, recapture is not a serious practical problem. Realistically, most items bought for business use will continue in such use until they are abandoned. But with listed property, where the IRS believes that the intended use was personal all along, the question of what constitutes sufficient or "qualifying" business use to avoid recapture looms large.

In order for listed property to avoid recapture, its use must be more than 50 percent for business in each year of its depreciable life.[6.23] Even if the item of listed property was depreciated rather than expensed to start with, failure to comply with the more-than-50-percent-use requirement will result in the substitution of a slower or otherwise less advantageous depreciation formula. To ensure that it can find out whether listed property was used "predominantly"[6.24] for trade or business, the IRS requires specific record-keeping. Taxpayers are supposed to maintain logs documenting all use of the equipment.

Regrettably, because there are no cross-references between the IRWE and the listed property sections of the Internal Revenue Code, we do not know whether the status of an item as an IRWE in any way modifies its treatment as listed property. Nothing in the law gives us any reason to believe that a standard computer purchased as an IRWE by a person with a disability would be treated differently from any other computer for purposes of the listed property requirements. The definition of computers used by the listed property section includes certain peripherals within the meaning of this term.[6.25] Since the law makes clear that its definition of computer does not extend to other electronic devices or to all equipment with microchips in it, there may be considerable room for arguing that a variety of electronic assistive devices do not come within the definition of listed property.

Businesses do not face the restrictions on deductibility of computers that their employees do. Computers used at a regular place of business, and owned by the business, can be justified according to the simple "ordinary and necessary" test.[6.26] In addition, where computers are used at a regular place of business, whether by the owner or employees, they are not considered listed property.[6.27] If the business maintains an office in the taxpayer's home as its principal place of business, a number of the most onerous restrictions are relaxed. In light of the problems posed by attempts to deduct home computers, a number of accountants routinely recommend that their clients establish businesses.

For some people, starting a business will be a realistic option; for many others, it will not. For those who can start a business, remember that the intention to make a profit, not the actual existence of profit, is the test of its validity. Certainly, even from the tax standpoint alone, going into business for the sake of avoiding listed property rules would be a little like spending $1,000 in legal fees to contest a $25 parking ticket!

For people not in a position to start a business, some other strategy must be found. In the search for such a strategy, our old friend the medical expense deduction should not be overlooked. Especially with assistive technology add-ons, recourse to the medical expense category represents a much simpler way of getting our deduction in the year the equipment is bought. In the next section, we will discuss some of the overlaps between business and medical deductions. While there are cases in which the law specifies the deduction category we must use, the fact that we use a medically deductible device partly for business will not ordinarily interfere with our ability to deduct it under the health rubric.

Although people with disabilities can hardly expect their concerns to be a focal point in the debate over the taxation of home computers, sound policy arguments exist for changing the law to make exceptions to the listed property rules on behalf of assistive technology users. Consider, for example, the person who is forced to cease working prematurely because of a disability. As the law now stands, if such a person had expensed the equipment used in a business or employment, he or she might be subject to recapture through no fault of his/her own. Shouldn't it be sensible to make an exception where the equipment was used in good faith for the business purpose until business activities ceased? Certainly, precedents exist in the Internal Revenue Code for the waiver of other time requirements on account of disability. Such waivers exist in connection with moving expenses and with premature withdrawal of retirement funds. See Chapter 7(h) and (a).

Before leaving this discussion of the process of taking business deductions, a few words about the timing of deductions for services are in order. Services are not capital assets, and even if they were, they would ordinarily be received and hence deductible within the same year they were paid for. However, we sometimes prepay for services that we will receive in subsequent years. Extended warranties or service contracts on equipment are the most familiar examples of such prepayment. Ordinarily, we cannot deduct the entire fee in the year we paid it, but must pro rate it over the term of the agreement.

(e)

Work-Related Versus Personal Expenses

Sometimes we are reasonably sure that an item is deductible, but less certain about how it should be classified. This happens most often on that thin line between business (including employee business) and personal (including health care) expenses. In rare cases, the facts allow us a choice of which category to use, but far more commonly the law specifies which category applies. When the law does prescribe, we risk losing the deduction by trying to use a different category. Therefore, in many cases the question of whether something is deductible is almost too broad. The real question may often be how can the deduction be claimed?

A situation where we have no choice is typified by the costs for a guide dog, which are considered a medical expense, even if the dog is used solely when the taxpayer is conducting business. It is not a question of the IRS disbelieving that the animal is used only on business. Rather, the law defines this expense as inherently personal in nature.[6.28] The nature of such a cost is considered so personal that the motivation for incurring it is of no legal significance. In other cases, the expense will be assigned by law to the business category. For example, a person who takes a compulsory pre-employment medical examination treats its costs as a business expense.[6.29]

In distinguishing among the various expense categories, occasions for confusion abound. In Chapter 4 we encountered situations where expenses were distinguished as personal or medical in nature. Here, the word *personal* is used not in juxtaposition to *medical,* but in contrast to *business,* to distinguish between business and nonbusiness costs. These alternative usages of the word *personal* illustrate the point that you can never fully understand what a word or phrase means in the tax law until you know what facts or ideas its use is meant to compare or distinguish. As our example illustrates, the word *personal* can mean nonbusiness in some settings, nonmedical in others, and non-other things in still different contexts.

What makes the risk of confusion still more treacherous is that when the word is used in contrast to *medical* it means *nonmedical,* while when juxtaposed to *business, medical* is often precisely what it entails. Innumerable other words and phrases must be read with the same attention to context and with considerable sensitivity to ambiguity. We face a systemic problem in trying to follow this precept, since unless we know something about the other ways in which particular terminology is used, we do not necessarily know what ambiguities are possible.

(f)

The Targeted Jobs Credit

So far our discussion of employment has focused on the incentives provided by the tax law for people with disabilities who incur costs in order to work. However, the employment relationship consists of two parties, and it is vital for workers with disabilities, their vocational counselors, and their present and prospective employers to know that the tax law includes major incentives to employers for the hiring or the accommodation of workers with disabilities. Three especially pertinent provisions of the law are discussed in this and the following two sections.

The first of these is the targeted jobs credit (TJC).[6.30] Please note that as of this writing (September, 1992) the TJC has expired, so that it does not apply to hires occurring after June 30, 1992. As discussed later in this section, the provision is likely to be retroactively reenacted. Previously when Congress has extended the TJC, it has also taken the opportunity to make changes in the program.

The TJC is an incentive specifically tailored to hiring. Businesses routinely get a deduction for the wages they pay their employees. The TJC converts this deduction to a credit for what are termed *qualifying first year wages* paid to members of targeted groups. The credit is available for 40 percent of the first $6,000 of such wages. This means that for each member of a targeted group hired the business can transform up to $2,400 of the wages paid from a tax deduction to a tax credit. The reference to first year wages refers to the employee's first year of work, which can span parts of two of the employer's tax years. In that case, the business divides the TJC between the two years, but the total amount available remains the same.

The availability of this credit hinges on whether the worker hired belongs to one of the targeted groups whose employment the law is intended to stimulate. Although people with disabilities are likely to be represented in all of the targeted groups, two of these groups are composed almost entirely of persons with disabilities. These are Supplemental Security Income (SSI) recipients and persons referred for employment by state vocational rehabilitation (VR) agencies.[6.31]

In order to claim the credit, an employer must obtain certification that the person hired belongs to one of the targeted groups. This certification must be requested before the individual commences work, and the request for certification must specify which target group the employer believes the prospective hiree belongs to. Which agency is responsible for providing the certification varies with the target group involved. For most groups, the certifying agency (called the designated local agency) is the state employment service, but state VR agencies often perform this role for their clients.

State VR agencies are not free to certify someone simply because they have a severe disability and want and need a job. Would that it were this simple. Basically, they are authorized to certify only persons who are participating, in or who have participated in VR programs under the vocational rehabilitation system.[6.32] The individual must have been an active client under what is called an Individualized Written Rehabilitation Program (IWRP) in order to be eligible for membership in this target group. An individual may also qualify as a VR referral through the Veterans Administration (now the Department of Veterans Affairs).

If a job seeker with a disability believes that TJC represents an effective hiring inducement to a prospective employer, there is no harm in asking a VR agency to quickly open a case so that a referral can be made. It is not clear how willing such agencies are to cooperate in this way. Nothing in the tax law or in the Federal Rehabilitation Act appears to bar a state VR agency from taking such action. Inasmuch as an IRWP specifying the provision of an isolated service such as job placement alone would not be illegal, this kind of cooperation in the use of the TJC should be within the state VR agency's authority. More significant is the question of how well such agencies are prepared to advise employers with whom they do job development about the TJC provision, and how rapidly they can respond to a certification request from an employer on behalf of a job-ready client when time is of the essence. On the other hand, many critics have found fault with state VR agencies for overuse of TJC, particularly with developmentally disabled persons placed in low-wage, revolving-door jobs that end the day the credit has been used up.

Many technicalities surround TJC. In part, these reflect the intense ambivalence that has always surrounded the program. In fact, TJC is one of those provisions that has been adopted for specified periods of time, allowed to lapse, then reenacted. Its most recent authorization expired on June 30, 1992.[6.33] It will probably be reenacted at some point, but hires that took place before that expiration date will be covered whatever Congress later decides.

Among the key technicalities are limitations on the number of TJC claims a company can make. The

TJC is one of a half dozen credits comprising the General Business Credit (GBC).[6.34] A business's total GBC cannot exceed $25,000 plus 75 percent of its net regular tax liability for the year. You do not need to worry about what net regular tax liability is, but keep in mind that a business that says it cannot avail itself of TJC may be telling the truth.

One of the major limitations of the TJC is that it is not available for hiring anyone who has ever worked for the firm before. This limitation is understandable in light of the TJC's purpose of bringing people from underemployed groups, who would not otherwise be recruited or hired, into the work force. But for people seeking to return to work following a period of disability, some relaxation of this limitation might prove beneficial.

Firms electing to claim the TJC do so on Form 5884. Nothing in the law prevents TJC from being used in tandem with the provisions described in the next two sections. There are restrictions against using the credit in conjunction with other governmental programs that have subsidized the hire or helped to defray the new worker's wages.

(g)

The Disabled Access Credit

In this and the next section, we introduce two provisions of the law that, like the TJC, can be described as indirect tax subsidies. These provisions—the disabled access credit and the architectural and transportation barriers removal deduction—are not available to individuals with disabilities, but they are used by businesses to subsidize certain expenses that benefit people with disabilities. Even though people with disabilities do not use these provisions directly, everyone should know something about them.

Both provisions bear on the lives of people with disabilities in two settings: employment and public accommodations. Extensive consideration of these provisions is deferred to our discussion of public accommodations in Section (c) of Chapter 7. We discuss only their role in employment here.

The disabled access credit[6.35] (or small business public accommodations credit, as it is sometimes called) was enacted shortly after passage of the ADA.[6.36] It gives businesses a 50 percent tax credit for $10,000 in annual expenses (over a $250 base), incurred to meet the requirements of the ADA. Intended to encourage business compliance with this new civil rights law, the credit's applicability is limited to small businesses, which the statute defines as those with under $1 million of gross receipts in the previous tax year or those with fewer than thirty full-time employees.[6.37]

If an eligible small business incurs expenses for meeting the requirements of the ADA, the credit should be available for these expenses, up to the $10,000 maximum. Such expenses may be incurred on behalf of job seekers or employees with disabilities, and include the provision or modification of equipment, the removal of communication, physical, or other barriers, the provision of readers or interpreters, or a variety of other reasonable accommodations contemplated by the ADA.[6.38]

Employment and the obligations of employers are covered under Title I of the ADA. The credit is available for expenses arising under Title I in the same way that it is for public accommodations expenses made pursuant to Title III, the public accommodations title of the Act. No specific legal mandate other than that embodied in the statute itself is required for expenses to be eligible for the credit. Thus, to use the credit there is no necessity that a firm's ADA compliance efforts have been precipitated by a demand or a complaint, and there is no requirement that some oversight agency or judicial tribunal have issued a compliance order to the firm or have found it in violation of the law. Proactive measures are definitely within the credit's definition of "eligible access expenses."

The intention of the new credit to support and encourage prudent, proactive measures is underscored by two key provisions in the law. Under the ADA, firms with fewer than 15 employees are not subject to the employment provisions of the Act.[6.39] Yet nothing in the section creating the credit makes any distinctions between firms with fewer and firms with more than fifteen employees. If the credit were intended to apply only to firms facing mandatory requirements under the ADA, firms excluded from the jurisdiction of Title I would surely have been denied the benefit of the credit. In fact, compliance with the ADA by just such small businesses, whether legally mandated to do so or not, is exactly what the credit seeks to encourage.

Small businesses that are subject to the jurisdiction of title I have one practical reason to familiarize themselves with the disability access credit. Title I of the ADA requires businesses to provide "reasonable accommodations" to workers and job applicants with disabilities, but this obligation is waived when doing so would involve an "undue hardship."[6.40] Cost is a major element in determining whether a proposed accommodation would pose an undue hardship. In its regulations implementing Title I of the ADA, the U.S. Equal Employment Opportunities Commission (EEOC) has made clear that the question of undue hardship is to be determined on the facts of each case. A number of criteria are set forth that should be considered in making the determination.[6.41] What remains unclear is how cost is to be measured. Gross costs (the out-of-pocket expense of providing a particular acccommodation) are clearly greater than net costs (those that remain after all available tax benefits are taken into consideration). By using the credit, a $10,000 expenditure actually costs the company only $5,000 net.

Whatever definition of *cost* the EEOC and the courts eventually adopt, businesses owe it to themselves and their employees or job aspirants not to exaggerate the real costs of reasonable accommodations. Businesses do themselves a grave disservice by failing to fully familiarize themselves with tax provisions that can go a long way to solving the problem and avoiding the need for contention. Once available tax incentives are fully taken into account, a number of accommodations that bode financial hardship will prove far less costly than originally supposed.

Another important point to remember about the credit is that it can be used to meet the needs of established workers who encounter disabilities and want to continue working, or who reveal hidden disabilities after being employed for a period of time. It is almost always preferable for a business to keep an employee working rather than incurring the costs of disability retirement. For a small business facing this choice, the credit may prove particularly important, especially when "experience rated" insurance costs are taken into account. If the disabled access credit makes a job-retention accommodation affordable, the potential savings in health/disability insurance and worker compensation premiums may return in savings many times the cost of the accommodation. How frustrating it must be for a small business to know that means exist to restore a valued colleague to productivity but to lack the resources to make the outlays necessary for an accommodation? With effective utilization of the credit such frustration need be endured less often.

Until the Internal Revenue Service publishes its regulations interpreting the new credit, many questions remain unanswered. These are discussed in detail in Section (c) of the next chapter.

(b)

T he Architectural and Transportation Barriers Removal Deduction

The third employment incentive we discuss here is the Architectural and Transportation Barriers Removal Deduction (ATB for short).[6.42] This deduction is available up to a maximum of $15,000 per year for the removal of architectural and transportation barriers to the elderly and handicapped. Although the bulk of our discussion is again deferred to Chapter 7, some attention is warranted here, if only because the application of this provision to employment is underappreciated, even by many of those who recognize its value in facilitating access to public accommodations.

In this connection, nothing in the statute or in the regulations implementing it suggests that elderly or handicapped people are excluded from coverage because they are employees of the firm rather than its customers or clients. Indeed, the definition of handicapped persons used in the ATB section includes people with impairments that "constitute or result" in limitations to employment.[6.43]

The barrier removal deduction primarily pertains to structural changes made to buildings, vehicles, facilities, or equipment. It cannot be used to subsidize the costs of general renovation or new construction. Why is the ATB necessary at all? Wouldn't the removal of architectural and transportation barriers be deductible anyway, as a normal business expense? The answer is yes, but ordinarily such expenses are treated as capital costs, recoverable only when the property is sold or through depreciation over a number of years. With the ATB, businesses may elect to treat the expense as an ordinary deduction, up to the $15,000 annual limit, meaning that the deduction will be fully available in the year of the expense.

In defining architectural and transportation barriers, the law does not leave it up to each business to decide for itself what an architectural or transportation barrier is. Only qualifying barrier removal expenses are eligible for the deduction. For this reason, neither good faith efforts nor the removal of real barriers that do not qualify for the deduction guarantee the availability of this tax benefit. Since the issues are the same whether the barrier is removed to benefit employees or as a public accommodation, we will defer discussion of these restrictions to Chapter 7 (c). Another group of unresolved issues surrounds the interaction between the ATB and the ADA credit. This topic is also taken up in the next chapter.

(i)

The Child and Dependent Care Credit and the Earned Income Credit

The Child and Dependent Care Credit[6.44] introduces us to a new relationship between personal and business expenses. Sometimes, in order to work, we must incur expenses that are not deductible under the business, medical, or any other category. We may need to buy a suit in order to look respectable in the office each day, but work clothes (unless they constitute a required uniform) are not tax deductible under any theory. But when the personal expenses we incur in order to work are for the care of a child or a dependent with a disability, the tax law offers us some help.

From our discussion in Chapter 4 and in Section (e) of this chapter, the reader will recall that the law makes distinctions between medical care expenses (which are deductible) and such other services as personal care, companionship, household services, domestic services, etc. (which are not deductible). None of these categories has an established or technical meaning; they are ad hoc terms used to distinguish the expenditures at issue from costs that would meet the standard for medical care expenses. By contrast, the term "dependent care" does have a recognized meaning. That meaning is set forth in Section 21 of the Internal Revenue Code, which establishes the child and dependent care credit.

This tax credit allows a taxpayer to deduct—not

from taxable income but, as with all *credits,* directly from the tax owed for the year—as much as $720 for one qualifying dependent, up to $1,440 if there are two or more such individuals receiving care. The exact amount of the credit is computed under a formula that allows taxpayers to claim between 20 and 30 percent of their eligible dependent care costs, depending on their AGI. For taxpayers with AGIs of $10,000 or less for the year, the percentage of eligible care costs that can be claimed is 30 percent. For higher incomes, the proportion decreases by one percent for each additional $2,000 of AGI. Thus, a taxpayer with an AGI of between $10,001 and $12,000 would be entitled to a credit of 29 percent of dependent care costs, etc., until, at an AGI of $28,001 or above, the "applicable percentage" falls to 20 percent.

Once we have determined our applicable percentage, the next question is what figure do we apply that percentage to? Our credit is the applicable percentage of the eligible care expenses we incur in order to work.

Whatever our actual care costs may be, the amount of our eligible care expenses is restricted to $2,400 for the care of one qualifying dependent, $4,800 for the care of two or more dependents. One's actual care expenses may exceed these limits, but such additional sums will have to be dealt with in other ways, since they are not eligible for the credit. Of course, if our actual care expenses are less than $2,400 (or $4,800), then that lower actual figure becomes the one on which our applicable percentage is figured.

A number of other factors can limit our eligible care costs as well. For one thing, these costs cannot exceed our net income from employment for the year (which will be our wages if employed, or Schedule C profit if self-employed). In addition, people who receive tax-exempt dependent care services as a fringe benefit of employment may have to subtract the value of this fringe benefit from their actual care costs in determining the eligible amount.[6.45]

What expenses meet the definition of eligible care costs and when can we claim the credit? To utilize this credit several conditions must be met: 1) the person for whom the household services or other care is provided must be a "qualifying individual"; 2) the costs incurred by the taxpayer must be "qualifying costs"; and 3) certain technical and documentary requirements must be met.

Who is a qualifying individual? Any child under the age of thirteen qualifies automatically if the taxpayer can claim the child as a dependent. Older children, other dependents, and spouses qualify only if "physically or mentally incapable of caring for himself."[6.46] This standard of incapacity for self-care may not be so harsh in practice as it sounds. What the law has in mind are the well-being and protection of the care recipient. A person who is unable to complete tasks of grooming, eating, or going to the bathroom independently clearly qualifies. Presumably, so would a person who cannot readily escape from the home if a fire or other emergency were to occur, someone liable to medical emergencies who would not be in a position to summon help in time, or people in any number of comparable situations.

Whatever incapacity for self-care ultimately means, dependent care services don't have to meet the standard for medical deductibility in order to qualify for the credit. Here, the character of the need, more than the nature of the services, is decisive. If the household or dependent care services are legitimately incurred (that is, if the care was paid for and received), the IRS is not likely to contend that the recipient was not sufficiently disabled. The law contains no requirement for medical certification of incapacity or for a diagnosis. However, taxpayers would be well-advised to be prepared to specify the nature and severity of the disability or illness, if asked.

As to when we can claim our care expenses, the credit is only available for those care costs incurred so that the taxpayer can perform gainful work outside the home. If the parent, spouse, or guardian is out of the home for any reason other than to earn income, the care costs will not be eligible costs, no matter the justification for the absence. This requirement has been construed rather tightly. For instance, people taking educational courses cannot claim the credit, since they are not engaging in what the law calls gainful work.[6.47] Similarly, although there are no definitive rulings on the point, it appears that people who perform gainful work but who do so at home also cannot claim the credit. Although the expenses

are legitimately incurred so that they can be freed
from care responsibilities in order to do their work,
these costs are not eligible for the credit because the
taxpayer is not away from home.

Although working at home may be the only
viable work option for some people who have heavy
dependent care responsibilities, the law has not yet
caught up with these realities of contemporary life.
Absence from home of the income earner is central to
the statutory scheme. This is illustrated by the rule
that a taxpayer who is home from work because of
illness cannot claim the credit for care expenses
incurred while at home, even if prevented by illness
from personally furnishing the care, and even if still
earning income through sick pay or vacation leave
while at home.[6.48]

Several accountants have suggested a strategy
for dealing with this problem which may be worthy
of exploration. For a home office to be deductible, it
must be in an area that is "exclusively" used for business.[6.49] As such, the office technically ceases to be
part of the home. If the taxpayer maintains a home
office that has passed muster for deductibility,[6.50]
couldn't one therefore argue that the taxpayer is away
from home while working in that office? In advancing
such an argument, key facts to emphasize would
include the need to be in one's office at specified
times or for particular periods of time, the conduct of
the work in a room or portion of the house removed
from the location of the person receiving the dependent care, the role of the taxpayer in providing the
care at all times other than when working, and similar
factors.

The credit is available when the taxpayer's
absence from the home is occasioned by looking for
work, or if the taxpayer is receiving vocational training, including vocational rehabilitation training. But
this would do the taxpayer little good, unless some
sort of training stipend were being paid, since in the
absence of income from gainful work, there are no
net earnings for the credit to offset.

Married taxpayers must ordinarily file a joint
return in order to claim the credit. But when they do,
the earned income limit is the earned income of
whichever spouse makes less. If your spouse is the
nonworking care recipient with no earned income,

what happens then? The spouse with the lower income then has an earned income of zero. Does this mean there are no eligible care expenses? The answer is no. The law takes care of this by imputing (deeming) income to the dependent spouse. The spouse receiving the dependent care will be considered to have earned income of $200 for each month during which she or he is a qualifying individual. In this way, the earned income of the lesser-earning spouse could still be $2,400 a year. And if there are two or more qualifying individuals involved, the spouse's imputed earned income will be $400 a month, so that the family can get to $4,800 for the year.[6.51] That way, if the eligible care costs are that high, the earned income limit will not operate to reduce your available credit.

The same is true if the nonworking spouse is a full-time student. That spouse, too, will be deemed to have $200 a month of earned income. A full-time student is defined as someone who meets the educational institution's definition of "full-time" for at least five months out of the year.[6.52] Curiously, the law takes the position that, although full-time students can take night courses, no one who goes to night school, even if they carry a course load the school defines as full-time, can be considered a full-time student.

The law does not mandate that dependent care be provided in the home. People with disabilities may sometimes spend time in various day-treatment or day-care settings. If the family pays for this care, the credit can help to offset these costs. But except for children under thirteen, a person receiving dependent care outside the home will be a qualifying individual only if he or she regularly spends eight hours a day or more in the taxpayer's home. This essentially means the child over thirteen, the spouse with a disability, or the other dependent must come home each night. Temporary absences from home such as for vacations or medical care will not deprive you of the credit provided the regular pattern of living in your home is shown.

Wherever the dependent care is provided, the identity of the provider makes a difference. No professional requirements or qualifications limit your selection of a care provider. Even family members can be hired to provide the care, so long as they are not children of the taxpayer under the age of nineteen and so long as they cannot be claimed as a dependent by the taxpayer. The caregiver's tax identification number must always be provided to the IRS. For individuals this will typically be a Social Security Number; for agencies or organizations it will be a Federal Tax Identification or Employer Identification Number. A not-for-profit, religious, educational, or other tax-exempt organization may not have such an ID number, so there will be nothing to report. In that case, you indicate this fact on the tax form. When a taxpayer fails to obtain the tax number of a care provider, the credit will not be denied if the taxpayer can show "due diligence" in attempting to obtain it. An indication on the tax return that the provider refused to provide the information or that the taxpayer tried but failed to get it will usually suffice to show such due diligence. In that situation the taxpayer would provide whatever information is available—name, address, etc.

The dependent care credit and the medical care deduction need to be thought about together. Because the credit is available for household services and other nonmedical care expenses, it covers costs that would not normally be deductible under the health care rationale. If we had only the health care deduction at our disposal, we would typically be entitled to no tax advantages in connection with many of the dependent care expenses we incur in order to work. For instance, if we hire a babysitter to stay with a child or someone to cook for a disabled spouse while we work, we are typically entitled to no deduction since these expenses do not qualify as medical care expenses and are too remote to be classified as business expenses. But through use of the child and dependent care credit, such expenditures can still receive a measure of tax subsidization.

Your approach should be to use the two provisions together in a way that achieves the largest total benefit. The first step in doing this is making sure to assign each possible expense to the appropriate category. If we try to claim as medical expenses items that should be treated as dependent care, we will get neither a deduction nor a credit. The government is under no obligation to advise us that by opting for a different tax strategy from the one we used, we would have achieved a better result.

With those expenses that could arguably be classified as either medical or dependent care, we may have a choice. For that reason, the second step is assuring that we make the choice that will yield us the lowest total tax. Expenses that might qualify as either type would include a nurse or other skilled person to provide the dependent care, or, in the case of dependent care provided outside the home, extra costs resulting from the need for specialized resources or facilities. We can never "double dip," but sometimes it may be to our advantage to choose the deduction, other times to claim the credit.

One factor to keep in mind in making this choice is that with the credit there is no requirement to itemize. This means that we can claim the credit while still taking the standard deduction on our income tax return. To claim the credit you must file Form 2441 with your Form 1040 (Schedule 2 if you file your return on Form 1040A). The procedure for claiming the credit is no different for itemizers than for those who take the standard deduction. People who do not itemize can still gain all the benefit of the credit. In situations where the standard deduction is used, choosing the credit in fact represents the only means for getting the tax advantage. In other situations where both the credit and the medical deduction are available, use of the health care deduction might represent the better strategy. As always, it depends on the facts, in this case the numbers.

The connection between the health care deduction and dependent care credit may also be important in allocation cases. When services have to be apportioned between medical and nonmedical components, it should frequently be possible to use the dependent care credit for some part of the nonmedical care costs. Generally, it makes most sense to claim your medical expenses first, then use the credit to the extent that your remaining costs and your income allow.

For a low-income family, the child and dependent care credit can sometimes erase the year's entire federal income tax liability. As a practical matter, the credit is limited to the amount that would do this, since any amount beyond this would do you no good. What is the point of having a $500 credit if your tax liability before application of the credit is only

$450? The government is not going to refund the extra $50. Beyond what was withheld from you during the year, there is nothing more for you to get back.

Credits such as this are known as nonrefundable personal credits. But these are not the only kind. There actually are *refundable* personal credits, which allow taxpayers to get back more than was withheld, credits that in effect do reduce taxes below zero. The outstanding example of this is the earned income credit (EIC).[6.53] For low-income families with children (in 1992 families with AGI or earned income of $22,370 or less), this can result in a maximum refund of well over $1,000, even if the family had no tax liability for the year without regard to the impact of the credit.

We will not discuss the EIC at length in this book because the disability of a family member has little impact on its utilization. One important point should be noted, however. Normally, your child cannot be a qualifying child for purposes of the EIC if she or he is over 19 years of age (24 if a full-time student). An exception is made to this age requirement if the child is "permanently and totally disabled" at any time during the year.[6.54]

Permanent and total disability is defined in more or less the usual way, in terms of inability to engage in any substantial gainful activity by reason of a mental or physical condition that is expected to last for a continuous period of more than one year or expected to result in death. If such a disability exists, and if the child meets the other conditions for qualification, the child's age will make no difference. For workers who bear the responsibility for the care of their seriously disabled adult children, this can sometimes make a difference.

(j)

E mployee Fringe Benefits

We have already touched several times on the interplay between fringe benefits and tax planning. In today's economy, fringe benefits are nearly as important as salary in the evaluation of compensation packages, in the negotiation of union contracts, and increasingly in the international competitiveness of American business. From the standpoint of workers with disabilities, the role of fringe benefits can be magnified in several ways.

Benefits such as health insurance protect us against costs that might otherwise be staggering. And they either cost us nothing out-of-pocket or cost far less than we would pay for equivalent benefits purchased individually, assuming we could purchase comparable coverage at all. Day-to-day life offers many more mundane examples of valuable fringe benefits, ranging from the subsidized lunches offered by some employers to the childcare that many progressive employers now provide or subsidize.

There is another reason why fringe benefits are as valuable as or more valuable than wages. While some fringe benefits carry no particular tax advantage, other fringe benefits can be excludable from the recipient employee's income. The law provides this treatment for a number of fringe benefits, including health insurance,[6.55] educational benefits (up to $5,250 per year, assuming it is renewed on the same basis), dependent care assistance (again subject to maximum annual limits),[6.56] and a number of others. Plan limits on the amounts of various fringe benefits are a separate issue from limits on how much of the benefits will qualify for tax exemption. Assuming they are what the law terms "qualifying" fringe benefits (meaning that they are provided under an employer's Plan that conforms to myriad legal requirements), the fringe benefits we receive are excludable from our taxable income while still deductible as business expenses to the employer.

With those fringe benefits that are exempt from tax, we need not worry about such issues as what theory of deductibility to use, whether we have enough deductions for itemizing, or what forms and schedules to fill out. Fringe benefits make life simpler all around. Fringe benefits of the tax-exempt sort are referred to as "pre-tax" dollars. If we can make necessary purchases with pre-tax dollars, we need not trouble ourselves with any tax issues. Knowing this can help people with disabilities when employment fringe benefit plans offer options that are responsive to their concerns.

One place where fringe benefits may prove particularly instrumental is in the area of medical plans. If one needs to obtain assistive technology that would qualify for a medical deduction if purchased privately, why not try to acquire it as a fringe benefit?

Not all fringe benefit plans are amenable to this strategy. We look for either a "cafeteria plan,"[6.57] under which workers can select from among various benefit options, or a "self-insured" health plan, under which the employer has discretion over what benefits to pay. Health plans that operate through the payment of premiums to outside insurance companies, that is, health care plans of the sort we would traditionally describe as insurance policies, typically lack the flexibility to accommodate the approach suggested in this section. Self-insured plans may utilize outside insurance companies for administrative or case management purposes, but the key point of distinction here is that the employer actually pays the medical bills and retains the right to decide what expenses are covered.

Before attempting to use a health care plan to obtain assistive technology, one would want to be certain that the benefits available under the plan are sufficient to cover the technology. Also be reasonably confident that using the plan in this way would not jeopardize the finite benefits needed for other foreseeable health care costs. Assuming that one is covered by a suitable plan, one would basically make one's technology request in the same way that other plan benefits would be requested.

A high probability exists that plan administrators will reflexively deny that assistive technology is covered. Their initial negativity is likely to be based on one or both of the following: their fear that the expense is not one for which the employer would be permitted to claim a deduction, or their fear that whether deductible or not, the requested expenditure does not fall within the terms of the plan. But the employee need not rely on an administrator's word for this, since such plans must be maintained in writing and should therefore be available for review and discussion.

Should the plan prove not to allow for the purchase of assistive technology, consideration might be given to a suitable amendment. After all, no one was thinking about this type of expense when the plan was written, so the restriction may have been unintentional. If the plan poses no obstacle, whether in its original form or after amendment, the tax law won't either. Where something is properly deductible as a mcdical expense, there is no reason in the law why a fringe benefit plan should not cover it. Provided that procedural requirements governing plan amendment are observed, no danger exists that plan provisions authorizing payment for expenses qualifying for medical deduction would jeopardize the plan's tax status in any way.

Nevertheless, employer or plan administrator reticence are understandable. Whatever may be the merit of the request, it is likely to be novel to those administering the plan. Convincing them that the proposed expenditure does qualify as a medical expense may constitute a major hurdle. Moreover, if an outside plan administrator or a managed care company is involved, other strong institutional opposition is likely to be encountered.

Where good faith differences of opinion and real uncertainties persist, an advance ruling from the IRS could be the best strategy for breaking the logjam. The Letter Ruling (or Private Letter Ruling as it is frequently called) is one vehicle for accomplishing this. The employer or the employer and employee jointly may request a ruling. If the issue involves only an interpretation of law, and no factual determinations need to be made, a ruling could provide a way to get a definitive answer before making any final decisions.[6.58]

The role of Letter Rulings is beyond the scope of this book. Suffice it to say that, in cases where the facts are not in dispute, where their legal interpretation is required, where the legal points in question are not under active review by the IRS through the regulatory process, and where certain other conditions are met, it may be advisable to seek a ruling from the IRS that will give the plan administrators the guidance and, hopefully, the assurance they may need.

Persuading an employer should be easier now than it used to be, because under ADA, if the equipment is employment-related, the law may require the employer to provide the equipment anyway. Precisely because of this potential obligation, one caution should be offered to workers who utilize fringe benefit plans as a source of technology acquisition. We must be careful not to use our fringe benefits to subsidize our employer. If fringe benefits are used to pay for work-related technology, we are paying for equipment that arguably ought to be provided by the firm. To avoid this the fringe benefits strategy is best pursued where non-work-related technology is at issue, including assistive technology for our dependents whose health care is covered under the fringe benefit plan.

seven

Miscellaneous Provisions

This chapter introduces a number of provisions of the tax law that affect the lives and prospects of people with disabilities. They are too varied to be easily characterized. Some have broad implications for quality of life; others are of concern to only a small number of people, but each is important and can make a major financial difference to someone. We begin with a provision that may be of great interest to people who are forced to leave work due to the onset of a disability.

(a)

Early Withdrawal Penalties

The acronym *IRA* is familiar to many people, but what may surprise some is that this does

not stand for individual retirement *account,* but for individual retirement *arrangement.* The individual retirement account
is one of the many forms an individual retirement arrangement can take. IRAs are, in turn, only one of more than a half dozen programs to put aside retirement funds. All these approaches involve the deferral of income tax on the funds until they are withdrawn in later years. Many people participate in employer-sponsored retirement and pension programs. Such programs represent one of the major fringe benefits that people obtain through employment. The programs that employers offer take many forms. Depending on whether one works in private business, in education, in government, or for oneself, such designations as 401 (k) plan, tax-sheltered or tax-deferred annuity, defined benefit and defined contribution plans, Keogh plan, or simplified employee pension are familiar.[7.1]

Whatever the designation, all these pension plans have three things in common. They are all defined by law and must meet certain criteria in order to qualify for the special tax treatment they are accorded. They all allow taxpayers to put money aside for retirement on a tax-deferred basis. They do this on the theory that an individual's tax rate will be lower after retirement and that tax deferral during the earning years is a significant incentive for people to save for their old age.

Employee pension plans have something else in common, too. If funds are withdrawn early (prematurely), they are taxable when withdrawn. To discourage early withdrawal, they are taxed at an especially high rate. In addition to the regular tax that results from their inclusion in gross income, a penalty tax is imposed on the amount of the premature withdrawal.

This penalty tax, or additional tax as it is officially known, is called the Section 72 tax.[7.2] It is 10 percent of the amount prematurely withdrawn. Moreover, it can not be avoided if one's taxable income for the year is below the threshold for owing any taxes. To the extent incurred, the additional tax is due, regardless of your regular tax liability for the year.

For people with disabilities who withdraw their retirement funds early in order to meet urgent adjustment needs, the additional tax can be a heavy burden. Because the penalty can not be avoided by having little or no taxable income, it works its greatest hardship precisely on those who need the funds the most. In this light, it is good to know that the penalty can sometimes be avoided when disability and medical expenses are involved.

What makes a withdrawal premature? Generally speaking, people must not withdraw their retirement funds before they reach age 59 1/2. This timing rule applies to IRAs and most other retirement programs. With an employee pension or retirement plan, you have to look carefully into the provisions of the plan before concluding that withdrawal prior to age 59 1/2 is automatically considered premature. Depending on the plan's provisions for disability retirement and other variables, earlier retirement may be possible without penalty in some instances.

People who leave work because of a disability face many readjustments. Considerable income loss can occur, and the host of personal and family adjustment issues to be confronted all but defy imagination. Major expenses can be foreseen at the same time that income falls. Some expenses, such as medical or therapeutic care, may be covered by insurance. Others, including home modifications, assistive technology, and rehabilitative training, are rarely supported by health or disability insurance. Third-party support may be available for some of these costs, but typically savings, including retirement savings, represent the only source of necessary funds.

Faced with rising costs and falling incomes, many people are forced to dip into their savings, including the retirement funds that represent a major share of the savings of many working people. If this becomes necessary, it is good to know that the penalty can be avoided when disability is the reason for the withdrawal.

Section 72 of the Internal Revenue Code gives a strict medical definition of disability, defining it in the familiar terms of inability to engage in substantial gainful activity because of a medically determinable condition expected to result in death or to be of "long and indefinite duration." Medical certification sufficient to satisfy the Secretary of the Treasury is also required in the customary fashion. Once disability is established, the additional tax "shall not apply to any distribution . . . attributable to the taxpayer's becoming disabled. . . ."[7.3] The regular income tax on the distribution is not diminished or waived, but at least the 10 percent penalty can be avoided. To the degree the distribution is used for medical care or other deductible purposes, even the regular tax may be reduced or eliminated.[7.4] Depending on one's nonreimbursed medical expenses and other variables, taxable income may end up being rather small, even though gross income was increased by the amount of the distribution. After all, the funds would typically not have been withdrawn unless some urgent need for them existed.

Some people assume that if they are permitted early retirement on disability under the terms of their company's retirement plan, they are automatically exempt from the penalty tax. This is not true. The fact that a person is allowed to retire early under such a plan, while tremendously valuable as proof, does not mean that the legal definition of disability for this tax benefit has been met.

In establishing the nature of these legal requirements, two factors must be kept in mind. For the exemption to apply, the taxpayer must not only prove the existence of a disability but must also show that the withdrawal is attributable to the disability. What is the meaning of the word *attributable?* Beyond being disabled, are there any further requirements, for how the withdrawn funds are spent or why their withdrawal is necessary?

While we have little guidance concerning any requirements that may apply to our use of the distribution, the most sensible reading of the word *attributable* is that but for the disability, the withdrawal would not have been made. In other words, the withdrawal is attributable to the disability in the sense of being the result of or being caused by such disability. Nothing in the law or on Form 5329 (which is used to claim the penalty exemption) suggests any requirement for documentation or detailed information on how the withdrawal has been spent. Nor do the rulings issued on this subject predicate waiver of the penalty tax on a taxpayer's submitting information on how the funds will be expended.[7.5] Meeting the definition of disability is enough. Of course, if someone returned to work during the year, or otherwise demonstrated a capacity to engage in substantial gainful activity, the exemption might be jeopardized—not because of how the money was used or why it was withdrawn, but because the individual failed to meet the applicable definition of disability.

What about the individual who is ready to go back to work after several years? At the time of retiring, that individual may indeed have had a medically determinable illness that was of "long-continued or indefinite duration," yet might be able to return to work after a number of years. If this person claimed the exemption, would the subsequent return to work trigger an obligation either to reinvest the previously withdrawn retirement funds or to pay the 10 percent tax on the earlier withdrawal? Again, there is no definitive answer, but the overwhelming likelihood is that it would not. This view finds support from several sources. As to the retirement funds themselves, no requirement to restore them exists once a withdrawal tax has been paid. Since they were included in GI when withdrawn, we do not have to worry about them anymore. As far as the penalty tax is concerned, the same result should hold. As long as the definition of disability was met in the year the withdrawal took place, a subsequent return to work, or even subsequent medical improvement, should not nullify the right to the exemption.

Further ambiguity is added to the recovery scenario by the possibility that in some instances the purpose of the withdrawal may be to purchase expensive assistive technology to facilitate returning to work. We are again required to apply logic in suggesting an answer, but if the individual meets the definition of disability through the end of the year in which the withdrawal is made, there should be no legal problem. There may be a practical problem, however, if the circumstances indicate that a capacity for substantial gainful activity existed at the time of the withdrawal. Here, such terms as *long-continued duration* may become the focus of interpretation.

The real problem underscoring this discussion is the failure of the law to keep up with the reality of disabled people's lives. From the standpoint of the tax law, disability is a one-way street: those who leave work because of disability are never expected to return. Scenarios involving eventual return to work were simply never considered by those who wrote or administer the law. In Chapter 9, we discuss how this gap can be filled without depriving people of the penalty exemption, and without opening loopholes for manipulation or abuse.

People who retire on disability should also be alert to other means for protecting early withdrawals from the 10 percent penalty. For example, depending on the terms of the retirement plan, certain other distributions before age 59 1/2 may qualify as nonpremature.[7.6] In particular, people over the age of 55 who retire under employer-sponsored plans can avoid the premature withdrawal penalty by taking their pension payout in equal monthly installments over their life expectancy, as determined by actuarial tables. Provided retirement occurred after age 55, it makes no difference to the law (although it may under the employer's plan) whether disability was involved. Such early retirement options should be thoroughly investigated by employed people prior to retiring.

Altogether, there are about a half dozen ways in which the penalty tax can be avoided. In certain cases, some of these may represent alternative strategies for workers with disabilities to avoid the penalty tax. Perhaps the most important of these involves withdrawals made to pay medical expenses.[7.7] Unlike the penalty exception for disability itself, the penalty waiver for medical costs depends entirely on how the funds are spent, however.

For people who make premature withdrawals from qualified employee plans, amounts spent for deductible medical care expenses are not subject to the additional (penalty) tax. Deductible medical expenses are, of course, the health care expenses that exceed 7.5 percent of AGI. Since the amount of withdrawal is included in gross income, the odds are that we will end up with a larger AGI than we would have if no withdrawal was made. The threshold for deductibility may rise as a result of adding the amount withdrawn to our income, but if the medical expenses can not be met any other way, that is the price the law requires us to pay.

If the entire withdrawal is used to pay medical costs, then much or all of the increase in our income will be offset by the medical deduction. Remember, though, that if some portion of that withdrawal is used in getting to the 7.5 percent deduction threshold, that portion of the withdrawal will not be deductible. Remember, too, that the withdrawal increases AGI, so that the threshold will be higher after the withdrawal than before. A further point to remember is that the exemption from the additional tax is limited to withdrawal amounts actually spent on medical care. This means that if the withdrawal exceeds the amount spent on medical care, the difference is subject to the additional tax.

An interesting twist here is that we do not need to itemize in order to claim the exemption. The law refers to the amount that would be deductible, not to the amount we actually deducted, and it further states that the penalty exemption is available whether the taxpayer itemizes or not.[7.8] Why would someone with medical care expenses that exceed the 7.5 percent floor not itemize? And if one's medical expenses were large enough to require dipping into retirement savings, wouldn't the person be certain to have itemized deductions that exceed the standard deduction amount? In most cases, the answer is likely to be yes, but this will not always be the case. Even when itemization is mathematically possible, technical factors may preclude doing so, such as use of the standard deduction by a spouse who has already filed a separate return for the year.

There are two limitations on the health care exemption to the additional tax. One is that it does not apply to IRAs. For early withdrawals from IRAs, use of the funds to pay medical expenses will not suffice to invoke the penalty waiver. Only retirement plans that people participate in through employment are eligible. This restriction evidently derives from a mistrust of IRAs, perhaps because, though in the hands of a custodian such as a bank or brokerage company, they are self-managed. Because some employer-sponsored retirement plans bar early withdrawal unless proof of medical expenses or needs is forthcoming, these plan and oversight requirements were probably thought to offer adequate protection against abuse. Moreover, most people covered by retirement plans also have medical insurance and disability coverage, meaning that they would have less frequent occasion to withdraw their retirement savings to meet medical needs.

The other limitation on the availability of the

health care exception to the penalty tax has to do with timing. In order for the withdrawal to be exempt from the additional tax, the medical care costs must ordinarily be incurred in the year the withdrawal is made. For people whose withdrawals are made too late in the year to pay their medical expenses in the year of the withdrawal, this limitation could work a hardship. Warned of the risk, people can take precautions, including timing the withdrawal early enough in the year, or if circumstances permit, making the withdrawal only after the major bills have come in so as to avoid the risk of withdrawing more than must be spent.

The health care expense penalty exemption can help in the acquisition of assistive technology. As discussed in Chapter 4(c), since assistive devices are often deductible as medical expenses, the health care exemption applies to withdrawals made to purchase medically deductible assistive technology. In this case, one usually has the advantage of knowing in advance of making the withdrawal exactly how much money will be needed. All things being equal, one should also have control over timing, and thus be able to ensure that the expenses are incurred and paid in the year the funds are withdrawn.

Although the health care withdrawals exemption to the penalty tax is of greatest importance to people who have suffered significant income loss due to illness or disability, the law does not limit its applicability to people who are disabled. People who do not meet the test for disability can still avail themselves of the medical expenses exemption to the additional tax.

Anybody using this approach should be mindful that the withdrawal, by increasing gross income, will also make AGI larger. This means that the threshold for deductibility will be higher. Additionally, even if all the withdrawn funds prove deductible as medical expenses, only taxable income will be reduced; AGI will still be elevated. People who need to keep their AGIs low should take this residual impact of the withdrawal into account. For instance, as we learn in the next section, AGI is a key factor in determining the availability and the amount of the credit for the permanently and totally disabled.

Contained in Section 22 of the Internal Revenue Code, this provision grants a tax credit of 15 percent of something called (appropriately enough) "the Section 22 amount." This credit can be for up to $750, but for most people it will not yield anything close to this, and indeed frequently even for those who qualify, it will yield nothing at all. Two groups of people qualify for the credit: those age 65 and over and those younger than 65 who have retired early because of permanent and total disability.[7.9] For elderly people who claim the credit, disability is not an issue. Their age (65 or over), the amount of their income, and the source of that income determine their eligibility for the credit. Disability becomes an issue only for those under age 65. When they reach age 65, they can change to the elderly category, making disability as such no longer relevant.

For purposes of this credit, the definition of disability has three elements. First, it must be of a nature that prevents the individual from engaging in substantial gainful activity (i.e., performing work that is substantial and is normally done for pay or profit). Second, the disability must be expected to result in death or to last for one year or more. Third, it must be the result of a medically determinable physical or mental condition, the nature of which is proved by medical certification. In this connection, the form that the taxpayer submits to claim the credit (Schedule R for Form 1040 filers, Schedule Two for users of Form 1040A) includes a section to be filled out by the physician.

People who retire on disability prior to age 65 confront a potential dilemma in claiming the credit. To be eligible to claim the credit in the year of retirement, the individual must have "retired on disability before the close of the taxable year and when he retired was permanently and totally disabled."[7.10] Here the words "when he retired was . . . disabled" become problematical. For someone whose disability results from a progressive illness, this provision can yield harsh results. If the individual retired immediately after confirmation of a diagnosis but before the condition reached a point when meaningful work was impossible, would the worker be considered disabled within the meaning of the law? In other words,

(b)

T he Credit for the Elderly and the Permanently and Totally Disabled

would the credit be available in the retirement year if the individual had retired prior to becoming unable to work? There is no definitive answer to this question, but common sense tells us that if you became unable to perform substantial gainful activity in the same year you retired on disability, then you should qualify for the credit in that year.

Meeting the three-pronged definition of disability does not guarantee that one will benefit from the credit. Some complex calculations of income and its sources are also necessary before we know how much, if anything, can be claimed. Computation of the amount of the credit begins with determining the *initial amount*. For people over 65, this figure is $5,000 for a single taxpayer, $7,500 for a couple filing jointly if they are both qualifying individuals. However, $5,000 is not necessarily the initial amount for taxpayers under age 65 who claim the credit because they are disabled. The taxpayer with a disability may have an initial amount lower than $5,000. In such a case, the initial amount is either $5,000 or the disability income amount, whichever is less. If the disability income is lower than $5,000, it becomes the initial amount. If it is higher, the $5,000 applies. If both members of a married couple filing jointly qualify for the credit, but only one is under 65, the initial amount is either $7,500 or the disability income plus $5,000, again whichever is less.

Disability income is the amount received by an individual, leaving work because of disability, as wages, or as payments in lieu of wages, under disability or health insurance plans. Various kinds of payments fall under this definition. One needs to look at the terms of the employer's health or pension plan to know exactly how the payments received are categorized. As a general rule, if the payments are excludable from gross income, they do not fall within the definition of disability income (and hence do not need to be subtracted from $5,000 in determining the initial amount). If the payments are taxable, they probably do meet the definition of disability income (in which case they supersede $5,000 as the initial amount). Of course, if an individual under 65 has no disability income, the initial amount is $5,000.

No sooner have we computed the initial amount than we must begin hacking pieces off it. We reduce the initial amount to arrive at the Section 22 amount, which is the figure on which the 15 percent credit is based. We get from the initial amount to the Section 22 amount by subtracting a number of items including Social Security, Railroad Retirement, Department of Veterans Affairs, and other nontaxable government benefits from the initial amount. We do not need to subtract benefits paid through insurance or employer benefit plans if they come under Section 104 (a)(4) of the code. In the end, the distinction between revenue items that do and do not need to be subtracted gets a little murky, because includability in gross income is not as useful a test here.

After we have subtracted these nontaxable benefits, we need to implement one more reduction. This is a reduction based on overall income, from whatever source. If adjusted gross income (AGI) of the qualifying individual (the person claiming the credit) exceeds $7,500 for the taxable year (or $10,000 for a couple filing a joint return), we also have to subtract one-half of the excess. Once this is done, we have arrived at our Section 22 amount.

The amount of the credit is 15 percent of the Section 22 amount. If our initial amount was $5,000, there was nothing to subtract, and if our AGI was under $7,500, then the Section 22 amount would also be $5,000. At 15 percent of that, the maximum credit would be $750. It also follows that an individual with an AGI of over $17,500 can not claim the credit. This is because we reduced our initial amount by half the excess of AGI over $7,500. At $17,500, the excess is $10,000. Half of that is $5,000, which if subtracted from the highest available initial amount leaves a Section 22 amount of zero.

As these restrictions on the amount and availability of the tax benefit make clear, this credit is targeted to lower-income people. For some people, the availability of the credit can make a significant difference, but many who could benefit from it will already have taxable incomes near zero before the credit comes into play. This credit would be dramatically more effective if it were a refundable credit such as the earned income credit discussed in Chapter 6(i).

Although eligibility for the credit is predicated on inability to engage in substantial gainful activity, this does not mean that you will lose the credit if your

AGI includes any money from earnings. In the retirement year itself, there may be wages or self-employment income from before the onset of the disability. Even after the disability retirement, remember that whether an individual engages in or is capable of engaging in substantial gainful activity are questions of fact. Performance of some light work will not jeopardize entitlement to the credit as long as the work does not demonstrate a capacity to do anything substantial, and as long as it is not work of a kind that anyone would ordinarily be paid to do. The converse is also true. If you do not receive pay, such as for performing volunteer work or for occasionally helping in a family business, the applicable test for entitlement to the credit is whether the work you are capable of doing is of a nature anyone would pay to have done. What you do, not whether you receive some nominal pay, is the deciding factor.[7.11]

Like many other tax provisions, this credit was designed on the assumption that people who are permanently and totally disabled at one time will always be so. The notion that medically disabled people could return to function through the use of technology has little place within the framework of the law. Accordingly, we can foresee a variety of situations that the law gives us little guidance for evaluating.

We will not go into these issues in depth. Essentially, they are the same issues surrounding return to work that we discussed in the previous section. One question, however, should be addressed. Can an individual who retires on disability, then returns to work, and then retires on disability yet again following a relapse or progression of the condition, claim the credit for a second time in connection with the same medical diagnosis? Nothing in the statute indicates that such a repeat claim would be barred. Each claim for the credit is judged on its own merit.

Even within the framework of an ongoing disability, a qualifying individual may be able to claim some or all of the credit in one year but not in another. As we indicated earlier, this can happen when taxable income is already too low for the credit to have any significance. But it can also happen at the other end of the spectrum when income is too high. Because availability of the credit is predicated in part on AGI ($17,500 AGI is the upper limit), a taxpayer's itemized deductions are not taken into account in determining the credit's applicability. This credit could be far more useful if taxable income, at some appropriate level, were substituted for AGI because AGI does not reflect medical or living expenses in any way. It certainly does not reflect most of the expenses of living with a disability. Substitution of taxable income for adjusted gross income would at least take medically deductible expenses into account. Short of eliminating the use of AGI in computing this credit, we recommend that Congress adopt a modified AGI under which costs for assistive technology, attendant services, rehabilitation services, and possibly one or two other items would be subtracted from AGI for purposes of determining whether the $17,500 ceiling has been reached.

(c)

P ublic Accommodations

In Chapter 6 (g) and (h) we discussed two important provisions: the disabled access credit and the architectural and transportation barriers removal deduction. We discussed their value in promoting employment, but their greatest significance lies in facilitating access to public accommodations.

Title III of the ADA requires that "covered entities," including "public accommodations" and "commercial facilities," make their facilities and services "accessible to and usable by" individuals with disabilities.[7.12] Exactly what businesses are required to do is a complex matter, well beyond the scope of this book. Many excellent resources exist to explain the requirements of the law.[7.13] What should be emphasized here is that when businesses take measures to comply with the ADA, and indeed in many instances when they make accommodation efforts not predicated on the ADA, the tax law offers substantial incentives for their actions.

Why any business fails to make its facilities, services, and products as accessible as possible is puzzling. The exigencies of competition dictate nothing less. With the population aging, and with some estimates indicating that by the turn of the century as many as one in five Americans may have a disability, the economic benefits of accessibility are increasingly apparent to all who have investigated the subject. Still, we know of many reasons why accessibility has not proceeded as rapidly or as fully as some expected. Today's out-of-pocket costs count for more than tomorrow's hypothetical revenues. Increases in the marginal costs of production or doing business pose competitive risks, particularly in highly competitive market sectors. Ignorance of the definitions of accessibility and reasonable accommodations leads to exaggerated fear of the costs or difficulties involved. Misunderstanding of disability generates fear. Apprehension of discomfort engenders avoidance. Yet all over the country, the implementation of new laws and the evolution of new awarenesses are combining to yield profound change. It is heartening to know that in this process the tax law offers encouragement and support.

The Disabled Access Credit

The disabled access credit, sometimes called the small business public accommodations credit, was enacted in 1990 just three months after passage of the ADA as Section 44 of the Internal Revenue Code.[7.14] Its full name is Expenditures to Provide Access to Disabled Individuals. It was enacted for the twofold purpose of allaying the fears of small businesses about the potential costs of ADA compliance and to encourage such compliance through tax subsidization. While the disabled access credit does clarify and reinforce the deductibility of certain expenses, most of the costs it covers would be deductible as "ordinary and necessary" business expenses even if the credit did not exist. Other costs it covers, because they involve capital expenses, would not be deductible but would be added to the basis of the property and recovered through depreciation over a number of years. What makes the credit important, therefore, is not so much its creation of new deductions, but rather its acceleration and enrichment of those that already exist.

Section 44 of the Internal Revenue Code provides a tax credit for the "eligible access expenditures" incurred by "qualifying small businesses." The amount of the credit is 50 percent of the eligible costs that exceed $250, up to a maximum of $10,250 per year. This means that the maximum value of the credit is $5,000 per year (50 percent of $10,000).

A *qualifying* small business is defined as one that in the preceding taxable year had gross receipts of $1 million or less *or* one that employed no more than thirty full-time employees. For purposes of this credit, gross receipts for any year do not include returns and allowances, while full-time means working thirty or more hours per week in twenty or more weeks. Note that these are alternative definitions. Meeting either one will do. Thus, if a small business generated $10 million a year in gross receipts but had fewer than thirty full-time workers, it would qualify for the credit. Likewise, it would qualify if it had fifty employees but gross receipts under $1 million.

What expenses constitute *eligible* access expenditures? Broadly speaking, eligible expenses are those amounts expended to comply with applicable requirements under the ADA. The word *comply* should not be misinterpreted here. The law does not mean that the firm must be the target of a complaint or demand, the object of a compliance or enforcement effort, or the subject of a judicial or administrative order. In the provision of public accommodations, just as with employment, businesses are free to act on their own initiative to meet the standards of the ADA. It is not even necessary that an individual who will benefit from the public accommodation efforts be identifiable at the time the compliance activities are undertaken. The reverse is also true. The fact that a business takes measures to implement ADA requirements only under threat or compulsion of legal action against it will not result in the credit being denied.

Despite the broad sweep of Title III, many businesses and many kinds of accommodations remain outside its jurisdiction. But the fact that an entity or a particular service is not covered by the ADA does not necessarily mean that the credit is unavailable to subsidize measures aimed at going beyond the law's requirements. In this connection, it should be noted that although Title III of the ADA did not become effective until January 26, 1992, the disabled access credit has been available for eligible access expenditures incurred since its November 5, 1990 enactment date. If Congress had intended to tie eligibility for the credit to coverage under Title III, the likelihood is strong that it would not have granted the credit for expenditures occurring more than a year before any Title III mandate was operative. Nothing in Section 44 suggests that availability of the credit is limited to public accommodations that come under the jurisdiction of Title III.

Thus it appears that the size of the firm and the nature of the actions it takes are the principal determinants for applicability of the credit. But one other variable must surely be present. We noted earlier that the right to use the credit does not hinge on the identification of particular individuals who will benefit from the access expenditure. But since the credit is intended to facilitate access for persons who are protected by the ADA, the projected beneficiaries of a firm's public accommodation efforts must at least be persons who meet the definition of disability under the Act. As noted in Chapter 3, the ADA defines a disability as: "a physical or mental impairment that substantially limits one or more of the major life activities of such individual."[7.15]

For the broad range of commercial facilities and places of public accommodations covered by Title III, familiarity with the disabled access credit may prove important when complaints or compliance proceedings occur. Like Title I of the ADA, Title III requires the facilities it covers to make "reasonable accommodations." Whether a proposed or requested accommodation is *reasonable* depends on a number of factors, including its cost. When the particular accommodation would constitute an "undue hardship," the covered entity is not required to provide it. The regulations promulgated by the U.S. Department of Justice to implement Title III do not make clear whether the gross cost of a particular accommodation or only its net cost after all tax benefits and other available subsidies have been taken into account is the proper figure for use in determining burdensomeness. Logically, since the net cost is the real cost, the after-tax figure is the one that should be used. Whatever answer the courts ultimately give, public accommodations owe it to themselves and their customers or clients to understand the tax law provisions that will minimize the costs of some accommodations to the point of making them feasible, or that will enhance the credibility of claims of undue burden in those instances where the costs are truly prohibitive.

Specifically, the credit defines four major categories of eligible expenditures. These include:

☞ removal of architectural, physical, communication, and transportation barriers that prevent access to or use of the business by persons with disabilities;

☞ provision of services such as qualified interpreters and qualified readers, taped texts and other "appropriate methods" for making materials available to people with hearing or visual impairments;

☞ acquisition or modification of equipment or devices for individuals with disabilities; and

☞ provision of "other similar services, modifications, materials, or equipment."[7.16]

With the exception of barrier removals, the other categories of access expenditures mentioned in this list most nearly correspond to what the ADA calls "auxiliary aids and services."[7.17] Because auxiliary aids and services frequently represent the means for providing reasonable accommodations, we will use the term *reasonable accommodations* throughout this section. Depending on the context, barrier removal, auxiliary aids and services, or other measures can all represent reasonable accommodation strategies.

One expense category explicitly denied eligibility for the credit is construction expenses in connection with facilities placed in service after the effective date of the credit (November 5, 1990).[7.18] Retrofitting of buildings placed in service before that date would be eligible for the credit, provided the measures taken meet the standards for barrier removal.

In order to qualify for the credit, expenses must be *reasonable* and *necessary* for accomplishing the access goal. Since regulations to implement Section 44 have not yet been issued, we do not know precisely how these words will be interpreted, but it seems unlikely that the IRS will attempt to substitute its judgment for that of the taxpayer concerning how a particular access need should be met. One cannot imagine the IRS rejecting the provision of materials in braille because it believes the costliness of braille compared to cassette tapes to be an unreasonable expense. Reasonableness here should be read to mean what is reasonably necessary in order to accomplish the access goal. Since providing materials in braille would be an effective method for achieving a legitimate access goal in certain cases, the only question that should come up around reasonableness is whether the amount spent exceeded what braille production could reasonably be expected to cost.

One way to think about the reasonableness requirement is as an attempt to prevent businesses from using ADA compliance as a pretext for subsidizing other business expenses. What happens if an accommodation made for customers with disabilities also benefits the firm in other ways? Although we must again await the IRS regulations to learn what standards of proof will be employed or what evidence of motives will be required, it is little short of unthinkable that an otherwise eligible expenditure would be denied the credit simply because, like most good accommodations, it happened to benefit other nondisabled people as well. Nevertheless, while most expenditures for which the credit is claimed will be sufficiently clear-cut in their purpose and sufficiently targeted in their impact to avoid serious uncertainty, situations of a more ambiguous nature are also likely to come up.

For example, many retail stores have recognized the widespread customer preference for dual output cash registers. These are registers that simultaneously output price information via visual display and synthetic speech. If a grocery store adds spoken output at its checkout stands, its motives may naturally be suspect. How could it prove that its action was motivated by the desire to accommodate customers with visual impairments, and if it could prove this, would such an accommodation be an eligible access expenditure?

In such a case, the existence of a specific request from a customer or would-be customer might be useful. Also, advertising the existence of the speech output to people with sight impairments would enhance the validity of its claim. Another strong piece of evidence might be found in how many of the store's registers are equipped with the new technology. If the store modifies all its registers, that might suggest a general business purpose. On the other hand, if it modifies only one register and makes periodic public address announcements regarding the availability of this amenity, these practices too would tend to support its claim.

All these factors go to proving the store's motivation and good faith, but none of them helps it to know whether such an installation falls within the definition of an eligible access expenditure. In this connection, Congress directed the IRS to develop regulations implementing this new credit. These are expected to be issued by early 1993. The law provides that in order to be *eligible* for the credit, access expenses must meet standards promulgated by the Secretary of the Treasury and the Architectural and Transportation Barriers Compliance Board.[7.19] This approach gives rise to a major concern. Though well-intentioned, the IRS can hardly be regarded as an appropriate entity for deciding what constitutes a satisfactory public accommodation. Grounds exist for fearing the promulgation of definitions and standards that unduly narrow the scope of the credit. In specifying this regulatory process, Congress followed the precedent set with the architectural and transportation barriers removal deduction, which we discuss later in this section. Because the parallel regulatory schemes raise similar problems, we shall return to the forthcoming disabled access credit regulations after we explore the legacy of the IRS's architectural and transportation barrier removal regulations.

It is hoped that the way taxpayers have used the credit since its passage will assist the Internal Revenue Service in drafting standards that reflect the broad diversity of effective solutions in various employment and public accommodations contexts. Whatever the regulations ultimately contain, they are likely to be organized around lists of access expenditures deemed eligible for the credit. Even if such a list is restrictive and serves inadvertently to narrow the scope for creative and innovative accommodations, enormous opportunity will still exist for a wide array of measures designed to bring people with disabilities more fully into the mainstream of commerce and economic life on the part of the commercial facilities, professional offices, and other entities covered by Title III of the ADA.

Pending the regulations, a host of situations can readily be foreseen in which simple measures or modest acquisition costs can yield significant enhancement in accessibility and usability. A desk slightly raised to accommodate a wheelchair, a high-intensity lamp or other magnifier for a person with partial vision, a telephone amplifier for a person with impaired hearing: these and infinite other accommodations cost little and come within the spirit of the access credit.

Services, too, represent a considerable portion of likely access expenditures. Like the purchase or modification of equipment and devices, the needed services should often become clear in the dialogue between public accommodation operators and individuals with disabilities. Regrettably, Section 44 makes no provision for consumer input into the selection of accommodations strategies. Nevertheless, to the extent that the ADA does contemplate a consultative and cooperative decision-making process, we hope that the regulations implementing the credit will do likewise. That is, the regulations will best serve the spirit of the law if they give the benefit of the doubt to those access expenditures which resulted from consumer input into the public accommodation operator's decision-making process.

Ironically, one factor that may inhibit use of the disabled access credit is its applicability only to small businesses. Some small firms may incur access expenses they cannot absorb. This would happen if their tax liability for the year, before computation of the credit, were not large enough to absorb the entire amount available. Since this is a nonrefundable credit, the business would ordinarily lose the benefit of any access expenditures that would reduce its tax below zero. Or would it? In this case, maybe not.

The disabled access credit is one of a number of tax credits, including the targeted jobs credit discussed in Chapter 6(f), which comprise the general business credit (GBC).[7.20] As noted in Chapter 6(f), limits apply to the overall amounts businesses can claim under the GBC. Thus, occasions can arise when a firm may not be able to claim all its eligible access expenditures, even though they are within the $10,250 limit, because the combination of all its GBC credits exceeds the maximum the law allows. But if the GBC creates a problem, it also provides a solution. In situations where either the insufficiency of taxable income or the overall limits on GBC credits prevent a small business from claiming the disabled access credit for all of its eligible access expenditures, a procedure known as *carryover* is available. This means that businesses can carry their unused disabled access credits, up to the $10,000 annual maximum, back to prior years or forward to future years.[7.21] We will not go into the accounting intricacies of the GBC here beyond urging small businesses to remember that carryover can preserve benefits of the Section 44 credit that otherwise might be forfeited.

Even with carryover, small businesses may incur expenses that cannot be absorbed until several years into the future, or that will not meet the IRS's forthcoming standards for the credit, though incurred in good faith and to good effect. Should this happen, it is important to know that other tax strategies may be available to fill the void. We discuss the most important of these alternatives next.

The Architectural and Transportation Barriers Removal Deduction

Section 190 of the Internal Revenue Code provides for a tax deduction of up to $15,000 per year to businesses that take measures to remove architectural and transportation barriers to the handicapped or elderly. Originally enacted in the mid-1970s as a time-limited provision, the barrier removal deduction was made permanent in 1986. When Congress enacted the disabled access credit, it simultaneously reduced the barrier removal deduction ceiling from $35,000 to $15,000. What the Internal Revenue Code giveth, the Internal Revenue Code taketh away.

Although the barrier removal deduction is useful in facilitating access for workers with disabilities, its foremost significance lies in the realm of public accommodations in affording access to customers, clients, and other users of the facilities or services the business offers. Like the disabled access credit, the barrier removal deduction operates not by creating new deductions, but by transforming certain barrier removal expenses from capital to ordinary expenses, which results in their becoming deductible in the year incurred rather than being depreciated. To the degree that barrier removal costs exceed the $15,000 annual limit for the deduction, or to the degree that such costs fail to meet the highly technical requirements surrounding qualification for the deduction, discussed below, barrier removal expenses simply revert to the status of capital expenses. When that happens, they are treated no differently from any other expenses for the modification of facilities or vehicles that a business might incur.

The deduction is broader than the credit in being applicable to businesses of any size. This means that larger firms are able to use it while smaller firms may look to it as an alternative or fall-back strategy. The deduction is also broader in being available on behalf of "the elderly" as well as the handicapped. Here elderly has the usual meaning, over 65 years of age.

On the other hand, the deduction is narrower in scope than the credit because it is available only for the removal of architectural and transportation barriers. As such, it does not include other barriers such as communication barriers, and it does not extend to reasonable accommodations such as provision of equipment or services.

As discussed in Chapter 6(h), the barrier removal deduction is available for the removal of architectural and transportation barriers (that is, for modifications to facilities or vehicles) designed to make them more accessible to or usable by the handicapped or elderly. For purposes of this deduction, a handicapped individual is defined as a person who has,

"a physical or mental disability (including but not limited to blindness or deafness) which for such individual constitutes or results in a functional limitation to employment or . . . which substantially limits one or more major life activities of such individual."[7.22]

By way of illustrating some major life activities that would meet this definition, the IRS regulations implementing Section 190 list: performing manual tasks, walking, speaking, breathing, learning or working.[7.23] This list is not intended to be exhaustive. Limitation in any function would qualify.

Not all barrier removals will meet the standards for the deduction. Only *qualifying* barrier removal expenses do. Qualifying barrier removal expenses are those that meet strict definitions promulgated by the Secretary of the Treasury (with input from the Architectural and Transportation Barriers Compliance Board). These regulations do two things. First, they list specific barriers, removal of which will justify a claim for the deduction. Second, they provide detailed guidelines for the design specifications with which such barrier removals must conform in order to qualify for the deduction.

Standards exist for such barrier architectural features as grading, walks, parking lots, ramps, entrances, doors and doorways, stairs, floors, toilet rooms, water fountains, public telephones, elevators, controls, identification signs, warning signals, platform edge strips, and others.[7.24] Thus, if a business seeks to claim the barrier removal deduction for making a public walkway more accessible or usable, the resulting walkway must by at least 48 inches wide and must have a slope of no greater than 5 degrees. Similarly, elevators must have controls that are tactilely identifiable, and public telephones must be reachable by people in wheelchairs. In most cases, specifications for height, width, length, and other parameters are very precise. The regulations make no provision for good faith or "substantial compliance." In those cases where such precisely delineated guidelines are not met, the deduction will generally not be granted.

Because of the exacting nature of these guidelines, barrier removal planning and implementation are best done with the assistance of architects, contractors, or others familiar with the regulations and experienced in their application. Taxpayers planning to claim the deduction should also maintain thorough records, including architectural blueprints, building permits, and documentation of cost.[7.25] Documenting the cost of a barrier removal is especially important because the deduction is not allowed for general construction, renovation, alteration, or routine maintenance of facilities, even when these activities result in heightened accessibility.[7.26]

Use of strict design guidelines may sometimes have unfortunate results, including raising the costs for barrier removal, or causing firms who have made prudent modifications to their facilities to lose the deduction. Nonetheless, the reasons for such precise requirements are readily understandable. The regulations adopted by the IRS derive from standards developed by the American National Standards Institute (the ANSI standards).[7.27] ANSI standards were developed with considerable input from the design and disability communities. Their specificity in large measure reflects the best assessment available of what represents a satisfactory result and what will work. The good faith of a business firm is of little value to the wheelchair user who still cannot use the bathrooms or readily get the chair into or out of the building. Property owners and the building industry simply do not know enough about disability to be wisely entrusted with the decision of what constitutes an adequate barrier removal measure. The government can not be faulted for wanting to avoid the use of taxpayer funds to subsidize accommodations that may be ineffective or even unsafe, however well-intentioned.

No regulations could hope to anticipate all the barriers with which a business or its patrons might be confronted. For this reason, it is important to note that situations do exist where firms can get the deduction for the removal of barriers not contained on the IRS list. The regulations contain what may be called an "other barriers" category. Other barrier removals qualify for the deduction if they meet three conditions.

☞ The barrier must be a substantial barrier to access or use by handicapped or elderly people;
☞ It must actually have been a major barrier for one or more classes of such persons; and
☞ Its removal must be accomplished without creating any new barrier to access or use.[7.28]

To illustrate the application of this category, suppose that a retail chain receives complaints from elderly or mobility-impaired people that the beautiful plaza fronting its flagship store is treacherously icy in the winter. The firm decides to install a roof or awning over the plaza to shield it from the elements. Installation of a roof is not on the IRS list of barrier removal measures. If the firm had decided to solve the problem by regrading or resurfacing the walkways, it could have consulted the design guidelines in the regulations to know exactly what it had to do in order to qualify for the deduction. Here, because it selected a method for which there are no guidelines, it may have to hold its breath, hoping that the residual category will apply.

Would the awning qualify for the deduction?

That depends on whether it satisfies the three conditions for other barrier removals: Were the patches of ice a "substantial" barrier? Is there an identifiable group within the target population whose access or use was actually impaired by the barrier and who benefited from its removal? Do the stanchions that were erected to support the new roof constitute a barrier to this group or anyone else? If the answers to these questions are in the affirmative, the awning should certainly qualify for the barrier removal deduction. If the answer to any one of them is distinctly no, then the deduction is far less certain. Such cases will tend to be decided very much on their particular facts.

The architectural and transportation barrier removal regulations were issued in 1979.[7.29] Since then, the ANSI standard on which they were largely based has been revised,[7.30] but the IRS regulations have not. Consequently, one of the major problems we face in applying the barrier removal deduction is the law's failure to take account of barriers and removal strategies that modern technology bring within our reach.

The problem is particularly acute in the area of transportation barriers because technology has dramatically changed our understanding of this concept. The Internal Revenue Service's regulations do not give much guidance on the criteria that transportation barrier removals must meet. The concept applies to modifications made to vehicles used by the business to provide transportation to its customers and clients. As such, transportation barriers are understood to be narrowly limited to features of motor vehicles that limit their accessibility to or usability by handicapped and elderly persons.

Today we understand that the lack of access to directional or location information in public places ranging from airports to hotels, shopping malls to amusement parks, represents a major barrier to the mobility and independence of people with sensory impairments. People who cannot see miss information that is only flashed on electronic displays; those who cannot hear miss information presented by public address announcements. Advances in technology and design have made it increasingly feasible to overcome these barriers at relatively little cost through use of FM or other infrared loops, "talking signs," dual-output digital information systems, and a number of other promising but still experimental technologies.

Is the law flexible enough to recognize these barriers and accord deductibility to these measures for removing them? Initially, the answer depends on whether they qualify as "architectural" or "transportation" barriers in nature. The law says they are not transportation barriers because that term refers to vehicle modifications. Are they then architectural barriers? One's first inclination might be to say no, because they do not involve any structural features of the facility. On the other hand, if we recall the list of barriers for which the IRS has promulgated definitions, several of them do relate quite clearly to access to information. Most notable among these is the specification for warning systems, which to qualify for the barrier removal deduction must provide both aural and visual information.

Arguing by analogy, and using the three-pronged test for other barrier removals discussed earlier, the deduction claim for installing high-tech systems for making information available to persons with visual or hearing impairments in public accommodations settings might well be sustainable. But whether or not a particular barrier removal effort succeeds, the larger issue is that our tax law should fully encourage creative responses to access challenges, not leave taxpayers in doubt as to the tax consequences of their efforts.

Although it is important to use the regulatory process in ways that will ensure the sincerity and the efficacy of claimed barrier removal or reasonable accommodation efforts in the public accommodations arena, grave danger also exists that regulations that seek to list in advance what are qualifying barrier removal expenses or eligible ADA access expenditures will stultify what should be a dynamic unfolding process. In its implementing regulations for the disabled access credit, the IRS should strive to avoid the kinds of pallid lists that can never keep pace with rapid technological and social change, and that can only result in arbitrary distinctions between equally valid accommodations strategies. At the very least, the IRS should include a residual or "other access expenditures" clause that reflects the enormous range of issues and the enumerable effective responses for defining and meeting the challenges of access. If the IRS defines what it considers eligible ADA compliance measures in the same way it defined qualifying barrier removal expenses, every likelihood exists that great harm will be done, albeit unintentionally, to the goals of the ADA, which brought the access credit into being.

The architectural barrier removal deduction was amended (by lowering the maximum deduction) in the same legislative bill that created the disabled access credit. Yet neither section contains any reference to the other, and neither affords guidance on their interaction. What does emerge clearly is that effective tax planning in the public accommodations area will require the coordinated and complementary use of both provisions.

Coordinating the Credit and the Deduction

The simplest cases will be those in which only one of the provisions is applicable. A business too large to utilize the credit would not be in a position to use the disabled access credit. Small businesses, however, will be confronted with the need to decide whether one or both provisions apply: if only one, which one; and if both, which or in what order they should be used.

In those cases where both apply, nothing in the law suggests that a firm is not free to choose whichever will yield the best bottom-line results. Moreover, where the total expenditures involved exceed the applicable limits of each provision, nothing in the law suggests a firm is barred from using both. For example, suppose a firm implements barrier removal measures at a cost of $25,000 that qualify both as eligible access expenditures under the credit and as qualifying barrier removals under the deduction. Pending issuance of the IRS's access credit regulations, nothing has been found in the law to suggest that the small business in question could not apply the first $10,000 (above the $250 threshold) to the credit, and the remaining $15,000 to the deduction.

At the other end of the spectrum, cases can still be foreseen in which good faith and successful efforts to accommodate people with disabilities will fall between the cracks and be favored by neither tax benefit. Nonetheless, for the bulk of businesses who enter into the ADA process with good faith and open minds, these important tax provisions go a long way toward ensuring their efforts will prove economically viable as well as legally and morally just.

(d)

T he Additional Standard Deduction

Taxpayers who are aged (over 65) or blind get a slightly larger standard deduction than other taxpayers.[7.31] In addition to the *basic* standard deduction, these two groups are also entitled to an *additional* standard deduction. Indexed to inflation like the basic standard deduction, the additional standard deduction for 1992 is $900 for a single or head-of-household status taxpayer, $700 for a married person. A taxpayer who is both over 65 and blind gets two such additional standard deductions. For a married couple filing jointly, each of whom is both blind and over 65, the additional standard deduction will add $2,800 to the basic standard deduction of $6,000 in 1992. Because their standard deductions are larger, the amount of the itemized deductions these taxpayers need in order to itemize becomes correspondingly larger.

The determination whether an individual is 65 years old or blind is made as of the last day of the year. In this sense, the additional standard deduction is like the exemption for a newborn baby. Even a baby born at one minute before midnight on New Year's Eve qualifies as a dependent for that year. Except for people who do not know or cannot prove their date of birth, establishing eligibility for the additional standard deduction on the basis of age presents no problems. Eligibility based on blindness is established by medical certification, either on a yearly or a permanent basis. Blindness is defined by a strict medical standard. The individual must have visual acuity of no better than 20 over 200 in the better eye with a corrective lens or must have a field of vision no greater than twenty degrees. This is the traditional definition of legal blindness, widely used since enactment of the Social Security Act in 1935.

Unfortunately, from the standpoint of describing the kinds of vision loss that people experience, and from the standpoint of identifying those people who face major functional limitations due to loss of vision, this definition is increasingly unsatisfactory. Whereas the definition reflects loss of acuity or the occurrence of tunnel vision, it takes no account of some of the most prevalent forms of vision loss among the older population today. For example, macular degeneration may initially result in a decline of central vision, not in a loss of peripheral vision. Such people may have vision that covers a wide enough angle, but is lacking at the center of the visual field. The functional consequences for daily living may be the same, but the law chooses to deny these people the status of blindness.

The advent of contact lenses and other new vision correction techniques have raised questions about the definition as well. Contact lenses qualify as corrective lenses if they can be routinely worn for prolonged or indefinite periods of time, the way routine eyeglasses can be.[7.32] If they can be worn only briefly or for specific tasks, their corrective impact is not taken into account. Magnifiers that do not function as lenses (i.e., are not inserted into the eye or worn as glasses) are not taken into account, nor are electronic visual aids, such as closed-circuit TV magnifiers or other assistive technology devices. Since such devices only restore function, it is entirely appropriate that they not be confused with approaches that have a medical effect.

Another problem with the definition of blindness is its assumption that visual function is static. In fact, with many syndromes and for many individuals, fluctuating or episodic vision loss is the norm. In view of the many forms vision loss can take, and in light of the nonstatic nature of many people's vision, consideration should be given to amending the law in one of two ways. Either a more flexible functional definition of blindness should be substituted for the present test, or people with conditions involving recurrent instances of significant visual impairment should be classifiable as blind. Of course, the advisability of modifying the definition of blindness for tax purposes depends in large measure on whether the additional standard deduction represents sound public policy.

The special tax status accorded by the law to blind people is a subject of considerable importance. It has occasioned debate and discord in the disability rights movement. Some background helps put this debate into context.

Many readers will recall that for approximately

forty years the Internal Revenue Code authorized two personal exemptions for blind people, compared to the one exemption that everybody else could claim. This second exemption, which actually began as a deduction, dates back to World War II, when blind people were widely recognized (and to a certain degree held up as role models to "able-bodied" war workers) for making valuable contributions to defense production. Of course, people with every conceivable disability participated in the defense of the country at that time, but they were not necessarily identified or recognized as being disabled. The extra exemption was devised partly in gratitude, but in major part from a recognition that blind people incurred expenses to work and to live that other tax-payers did not. Whatever its original merits, this exemption nevertheless provoked considerable resentment among members of other disability groups, who felt that people with any disability should be entitled to the same benefit.

The Tax Reform Act of 1986 dealt with this issue by striking a compromise. Unwilling either to abolish the benefit entirely or to extend it to other groups, Congress changed the law, replacing the extra exemption with the additional standard deduction. For blind and elderly people, the change from an extra exemption to an additional standard deduction typically meant a reduced tax benefit, including total forfeiture of any advantage if the individual chooses to itemize. If the compromise left some blind taxpay-ers dissatisfied over the curtailment of their tax advan-tage, it also failed to mollify many critics who contin-ued to feel that blind people were still receiving benefits to which others should also be entitled.

To put these views in context, let us remember that the additional standard deduction yields only a small tax advantage. For a single taxpayer in the high-est tax bracket (many of whom itemize anyway), the additional standard deduction yields a maximum tax savings of less than $300, while for most taxpayers the benefit is far less, often zero. A sum this small hardly seems worth worrying about, but that argu-ment cuts both ways and is applicable to the defend-ers and the critics alike. Anyone who allows defen-siveness of or resentment about this provision to interfere with effective coalition-building or coopera-tion is making a dreadfully short-sighted mistake.

While the add-on costs of being disabled vary from individual to individual, the undisputed fact is that disability carries with it certain economic costs. All too often these are "opportunity costs," but in almost every case they include out-of-pocket costs of some nature. A provision such as the additional stan-dard deduction represents an effort, admittedly crude and limited, to recognize these costs through the tax system. Logically, if this effort and recognition are warranted for people who are blind, they are equally applicable to those with other disabilities. Federal rev-enue concerns are likely to prevent broadening the availability of the additional standard deduction in the foreseeable future. Perhaps a smaller additional stan-dard deduction, applicable to all people with major life-activity disabilities, would ultimately strike the best balance among competing objectives. Economic survey and data analysis techniques have progressed to the point where such costs, including opportunity costs, can be assessed on an aggregate or average basis. The issues surrounding broadened application of such a principle in the tax law are further discussed in Chapter 9.

(e)

Y our Home

Home ownership is central to the American dream, but the economic importance of the home goes far beyond the emotional or symbolic meaning. For many people, the home, in addition to being the largest investment they ever make, is the centerpiece of their tax planning strategy. Perhaps no individual deduction is more sacrosanct than home mortgage interest. Even the most vigorous advocates of the "flat tax" (an income tax system that allows few or no deductions and taxes everyone at the same rate) stop short of calling for abolition of this tax benefit.

For people with disabilities, home ownership presents three special issues. One of these, reduction of or exemption from local real property taxes, is dis-cussed in Chapter 8. The others relate to the medical deductibility of home modification expenses and the availability of capital gains tax exclusion when the home is sold.

*Making Your
Home Accessible*

For people with various disabilities, home modification can become a necessity. Advances in technology and design have allowed many more people to make their homes accessible and to retain the full use and enjoyment of their property. Implementation of necessary home modifications can be enhanced by a clear understanding of the subsidization available for such measures.

As mentioned in Chapter 4(c), the costs of home modifications necessary to mitigate the impact of a disability can usually be deducted as medical care expenses.[7.33] Even when people rent their homes, the costs of modifications for accessibility are deductible.[7.34] The deductibility of home modification expenses is predicated on the same theory that underlies other disability-related health care deductions. The modifications make the home accessible and usable, thereby mitigating the functional impairments associated with the disability in question. Thus, a ramp or elevator facilitates movement into and out of the house or between floors for people who would otherwise find this difficult or impossible.[7.35] A visual alert system allows people with hearing impairments to know of the arrival of visitors.[7.36] Grab bars in the bathroom, appropriately designed cabinets in the kitchen, electromagnetic or widened doors, and a host of other features do the same for people with various impairments.

While the deductibility of home modifications is subject to the usual tests and thresholds, some unique factors come into play in determining the amount of our deduction. Even though our home modification expenses may exceed 7.5 percent of our AGI, the allowable deduction may be reduced. Several restrictions that do not apply to other medical expenses affect the deductibility of our home modification costs. By far the most significant of these is the rule that home modification expenses are deductible only to the extent that they do not increase the value of the property.[7.37] This means if you spent $1,000 on home modifications that qualify for the medical deduction, but increase the value of your home by $900 in doing so, your allowable deduction would be only $100, the amount by which your costs exceeded this increase in value. If the increase in value were equal to or greater than the cost, you would have no allowable deduction at all. For a renter with no financial interest in the property, the impact of modifications on its value has no tax consequences.

Accordingly, one key question is will a proposed modification increase the value of your property? Usually it is fairly simple to answer this question. The Internal Revenue Service publishes a list of modifications that it regards as not increasing the value of property.[7.38] Most of the common home modifications are on this list. If your modification is on the list, you can deduct all your costs if all the usual requirements for deductibility are met. Remember that this determination of whether a modification does or does not increase value is a legal one. The IRS is not placing any limit on the amount you can ask for or get when you actually sell. If the modification contributes down the line to a higher sale price than you expected, you do not have to pay back the deduction.

If you cannot determine whether your proposed modifications will increase value, or if you know that they will, you must document the amount of the change. One possible source of the necessary information is an appraiser who can give an estimate of the property's value before and after the work is done. Depending on a number of factors, including availability of blueprints, drawings, and pictures, such an appraisal may or may not require a personal inspection. Certified appraisers can be expensive, however. You could easily end up spending as much on appraisal fees as you save in taxes.

Another less costly option is to obtain an estimate from a knowledgeable local realtor who is often in a position to write you a letter or make a report based on knowledge of property values in your area. If the IRS subsequently disputes this assessment, the services of an appraiser may yet be necessary to resolve the dispute, but from the taxpayer's point of view, the realtor's good faith estimate is sufficient for openers.

Another restriction on the deductibility of home modification expenses also serves to distinguish these from other health care costs. The IRS does not ordinarily question one's medical care choices. Thus, if your costs for goods or services are legitimate, the IRS does not contend that you should have chosen less costly alternatives. If you require surgery, you may choose to have it in the cheapest or the most expensive hospital. If you need to consult a physician, you are free to choose the specialist who charges the highest fees. There may be problems if you choose to go away from home and claim a medical deduction for your travel, as discussed in Chapter 4(f), but aside from such situations the choice is yours. This principle remains true with home modifications, but is subject to one major complication. With improvements to real property, the tax law limits their deductibility to an amount that is "reasonable."[7.39] Much, therefore, hinges on the interpretation of this word.

This issue tends to come up in cases involving swimming pools. Even if its installation is motivated by a medical need, the government understands that there are some people who take this need as an opportunity for making aesthetic or other nonmedically-necessary improvements to their property. Courts have used various methods to sort out the elements of reasonableness and necessity in these cases.[7.40] The IRS and ultimately the courts have the authority to limit the deduction to the amount *reasonably* necessary to fulfill the health care objective.

As a practical matter, reasonableness and overall justification can never be totally separated. The danger is that excessive modification costs will call into question the justification for the underlying claim. With most home modifications, this is no danger. The person who installs handrails or grab bars in the bathroom is not at risk, unless the bars are solid gold. It is hard to use such an installation as an excuse for beautification or luxury. But with other modifications and improvements (perhaps most notably swimming pools), sufficient variety exists in choice of design and materials to raise a real question about intent. Yet again, we face the inescapable fact that most people would like to have a swimming pool if they could afford one.

We mentioned earlier in this section that rental tenants can also claim a medical expense deduction for their home modifications. The entire cost is deductible in these cases because the rental tenant has no financial ownership interest in the property. Increases in the property's value that result from the modifications do not benefit the renter when the house is sold. This assumes that the relationship between the tenant and the landlord is what the law calls *arms-length*. If not, things get more complicated.

Landlord-tenant relationships raise another issue. On occasion, landlords try to condition their approval for home modifications by tenants on the agreement of the tenant to restore the property to its original state when the tenant moves out. Whether or not this is legal is a complicated question, but even when it is illegal, it sometimes happens. As a practical matter, tenants who do not have the resources to go to court, or who do not wish to alienate their landlords may find themselves with no alternative but to agree.

When tenants accede to such a demand, the result may be a doubling of their accommodation costs, as they pay for both doing and undoing of the work. What is the tax status of these restoration costs? The tax status of such payments is not entirely clear. While illegal payments are generally not tax deductible, the key point to remember is that the illegality of the landlord's demand has no bearing on the deductibility of the tenant's expenses. It may be illegal for a landlord to demand the payment, but if the tenant made the payment in good faith, including under duress, its tax status is not affected by the separate question of whether the owner had a right to demand it. Since no direct answer has been found in the law, advice on the tax status of these expenses must be given cautiously. When demanded by the landlord as a condition of being permitted to make the home modifications, the costs of the restoration are accurately described as part of the costs of making the modifications. There is no plausible basis for saying that the money was expended for any other purpose. The money would not have been expended except for the need to make the premises accessible. For this reason, one should be able to argue that the costs of the restoration are deductible, just as those of the modification itself are. These extra expenses are not unreasonable since they were necessary in order to achieve the modifications.

Property owners may on occasion simply demand extra rent as a condition for allowing a tenant to make necessary modifications. In most cases such charges would be discriminatory, but even the most energetic enforcement of the Federal Fair Housing Act[7.41] and of state and local anti-discrimination or rent regulation laws will not solve the fundamental problem. Given the limited supply of accessible housing, the market price of unsubsidized accessible housing is likely to remain higher than for other housing. That being so, is there any way that the differential rent people pay for access for themselves and their families could qualify for the medical deduction?

In Chapter 4(d) we learned that the increase in rent attributable to the need for a larger apartment to accommodate a live-in caregiver qualifies for the medical deduction[7.42] Shouldn't the same logic apply where the issue is accessibility rather than space, and where the person accommodated is the one with the disability? No decisions or rulings on this point have been discovered, but under limited circumstances, the argument is worth considering. Take the case of a taxpayer or member of her family who becomes a wheelchair user. The family's rented apartment or house is inaccessible, and the necessary modifications, such as a ramp and widening of the front door, are technically unfeasible or extremely costly. As a result, the individual who uses the wheelchair cannot readily leave or enter the home, and among other consequences is prevented from getting necessary medical treatment. Accordingly, the family moves to another rented home, substantially like the first in size, amenities, and neighborhood, and differing from the first home only in being accessible and costing more. In such a case, the taxpayer can prove: what rent he would have paid in the absence of the accessibility need; what the motivation for the move was; and why it was medically necessary. If the claim for deductibility of rent differentials is to prevail, a case with airtight facts such as these is probably necessary.

The home modification issue also has important ramifications for people who operate small businesses out of their homes. When a home-based business or professional practice makes its portion of the home accessible for customers, clients, or other business visitors, either the disabled access credit or the barrier removal deduction discussed in section (c) could apply. It should make no difference that the business or professional office is located in the home of its operator as long as the home is the location where the customers or clients transact the business or where meetings are held.

With home-based businesses, determining the amount of eligible access or qualifying barrier removal expenses may be tricky. You may have to allocate the costs between those relating specifically to the business premises and those relating to the rest of the house.

If customers are routinely allowed to use a particular bathroom, the costs of its modification would qualify. If the house has only one bathroom, modifying it for business purposes necessarily redounds to the benefit of household members and private guests as well.

Thus the house with a single bathroom or with only one entrance illustrates the impossibility of making the business premises more accessible without also benefiting the residential uses of the house. This additional benefit does not deprive the business operator or professional practitioner of the potential tax advantage.

Two alternative theories can be suggested for resolving the question of whether and how costs should be allocated. One theory is that since the purpose of the modification is to facilitate access to customers or clients with disabilities, the entire cost should qualify for the deduction or credit. The alternative theory is that an allocation must be made, based on the proportion of the bathroom's or ramp's use by clients versus occupants, the proportion of the house's square footage that the business occupies, or on a similar allocation formula. Although we would encourage taxpayers to use the first approach, it seems likely that in these mixed-use cases some allocation will be required.

Taxpayers who try to claim their entire cost should develop appropriate documentation, including evidence to prove their intention in making the modifications was to enhance accessibility of the business and evidence that no other feasible way exists for doing so (or that other ways are inordinately more expensive). If an allocation has to be made between the portion of the cost applicable to the business and the portion applicable to residential use of the house, most home-based businesses are familiar with methods for doing this, since home businesses routinely make such allocations of utilities, taxes, mortgage or rent payments, sewer and water charges, and so on.

The health care deduction cannot be used for home modifications other than those intended to mitigate the functional limitations of its occupants. It is regrettable that no tax law provision subsidizes the costs of making our homes accessible to family members, friends, or other visitors who do not reside in them and who do not visit on business. On the other hand, just as a business motive will not be invalidated by incidental benefit to nonbusiness users of the property, so also the medical deduction will not be denied simply because the modifications have to be made in a way that benefits business users of the common areas.

Gain on Sale of Your Home

When we sell a home, we normally pay income tax on the amount of our gain or profit on the sale. This profit is called a capital gain. Some confusion surrounds the subject of capital gains these days. In the wake of recent political debate over whether our nation should enact a *capital gains tax,* some people have gotten the misimpression that no such thing as capital gains exists in our law. The current debate concerns whether capital gains should be taxed at a lower rate than ordinary income. Since 1986, both capital gains and ordinary income are taxed at the same rate, but the distinction between these two types of income has never ceased to exist.

For individuals over the age of 55 who sell their principal residence, Section 121 of the Internal Revenue Code provides that the first $125,000 of gain on the sale is excludable from income. In other words, that much of your profit is untaxed. A number of conditions must be met for this exclusion to apply. Among other things, it is a one-time benefit, meaning that a taxpayer can elect to claim this exclusion only once in a lifetime. Another condition relates to certain time periods in ownership and occupancy of the property. In order to exclude the gain from income, the seller must have owned the home for at least the five years preceding its sale and must have occupied the house as a principal residence for at least three of those five years. This five-year requirement is called the *holding* requirement. The three-year occupancy is the *use* requirement.[7.43]

The use requirement can pose a hardship for

people with disabilities who need to be away from home for extended medical treatment. Fortunately, the law provides some relief in such cases. Provided an individual actually uses the property for at least one year during the five-year holding period, time spent away from home receiving institutional care is not counted for purposes of meeting the use requirement. The use requirement is partially waived in such cases. This waiver provision applies to people who become "physically or mentally incapable of self-care."[7.44]

As to the kind of care that triggers reduction of the use period, the law does not list the range of facilities or institutions that qualify. It does indicate that nursing homes licensed "to care for an individual in the taxpayer's condition" are included.[7.45] The kinds of facilities that meet the definition clearly include hospitals (including rehabilitation hospitals), nursing homes, and other traditional medical care settings. Inclusion of rehabilitation hospitals is particularly important. Rehabilitation can involve lengthy stays at such facilities for individuals with spinal cord or head injuries, as well as other injuries.

For some people who are away from home to receive "qualifying care" even for short periods, this provision can make the difference between getting and not getting the $125,000 exclusion. Let's say that you used your home for two years and eleven months during the five-year ownership period. Normally that's tough luck; no exclusion. But what if two months of the time away are attributable to care that meets the law's definition? In that case, the waiver still applies because you occupied your home for a year or more, though less than three years.

Accordingly, it may be useful to speculate about whether the provision could be extended to other facilities. Ideally, we would like to argue that the waiver should extend to periods of time away from home for rehabilitation treatment and services, for assistive technology assessment and training, or for other services valuable to people with disabilities, particularly to those newly disabled in later life, after age 55. Unfortunately, it appears that the law was intended to apply narrowly. One barrier to the inclusion of a wide range of rehabilitation centers and facilities is the law's requirement that *qualifying care* be provided in licensed facilities, such as nursing homes. This licensure requirement limits the range of facilities to which this provision could be extended. Beyond limitations on the type of facility, the statute clearly contemplates in-patient care. Finally, the statute contemplates absence from home for extended or indefinite periods of time since brief absences do not constitute failure to use the home as a principal residence.

This is one of those rare cases in which if Congress had thought about the issues confronting people with disabilities, the provision would probably have still ended up in much the same form. Nevertheless, if someone wants to litigate for broadening the range of situations under which absence from home will trigger the waiver, the argument would go something like this: If a person obtains rehabilitative treatment or services that are intended to restore the individual's capacity for self-care, why should periods of absence from home to receive such care be treated differently under the tax law than periods of absence that occur when the incapacity cannot be mitigated? This question can be posed even more forcefully if the individual would have been institutionalized for custodial care if he or she had not obtained the rehabilitation services. Then the question becomes: Why would the tax code want to give a break to people who accept nursing home life while denying it to people who try to take measures that would restore them to their homes and to a higher level of function in the community?

(f)

Charitable Contributions of Equipment

For many years, tax incentives have played a central role in the support of charitable, cultural, religious, educational, and other nonprofit activities in this country. The law does this by allowing a deduction (itemized in the case of individuals, a business expense for commercial firms) for the amounts, up to certain limits, that individuals or businesses contribute to organizations that qualify as tax-exempt status under Section 501(c) of the Code.[7.46] Hardly a week goes by in which the average household or business does not receive solicitations from organizations seeking contributions for providing services to people with disabilities, to those with specific medical diagnoses, or to those who are impoverished as a result of "handicap" or illness.

Many programs and organizations that provide services to people with disabilities, including a number of nonprofit organizations in the assistive technology field, have relied on the tax deductibility of contributions as a major element of their fund-raising strategy. Within the disability community, considerable ambivalence surrounds this extensive reliance on charity. On the one hand, many worthwhile services would not be available without appeals to the public. On the other hand, as fundraisers well know, successful invocation of pity and sympathy are often more effective fund-raising tools than are depictions of dignity and personal fulfillment. Yet, however much some might prefer that government or our own evolving resources be the primary source of support for disability-related services, charitable contributions are likely to continue to play a major role in all facets of the human services system for some time.

For this reason, it is important for individuals with disabilities and for consumer or service-provider organizations to know of a key provision in the tax law bearing on assistive technology. Section 170(e)(3) allows businesses that donate inventory equipment to certain nonprofit, tax-exempt organizations to get larger deductions than normally expected.

Inventory refers to items that a business would ordinarily sell. As a general matter, when a business contributes inventory equipment as an in-kind (that is, non-cash) contribution to a tax-exempt organization, it is entitled to a deduction equal to the production cost of the equipment. The donor is not entitled to a tax deduction equal to the normal selling price, since, among other things, there is no guarantee that the equipment would ever have been sold. Thus, the potential profit that a firm foregoes by donating rather than selling its inventory becomes part of its contribution, but not a part that the tax law is prepared to subsidize.

An exception exists to the rule limiting the deduction for contributions of inventory equipment to the amount of its production costs. When a corporation (specifically, what is called a C corporation, not the subchapter S variety) donates inventory equipment to tax-exempt organizations that help "the ill, needy or infants,"[7.47] these donors can take a larger deduction than usual, up to half the market value (what the equipment would have been sold for) or twice the production cost, whichever is less. To illustrate, let's say a C corporation makes a computer that has a production cost of $100 per unit and normally sells for $500. If it gives one of its products to a museum, it gets a tax deduction of $100 equal to its production cost. If it donates the computer to a *qualifying organization* that serves any of the three populations just mentioned, it gets double that, a deduction of $200. Why $200? Well, half the market price is $250, which is more than double the production cost, so $200 is the upper limit. If the market price of the computer were $150, that would be the limit, since in that case the market price would be less than double the production cost.

Again, much as we may deplore the terminology, organizations that serve people with disabilities often qualify under the applicable definitions of serving the "ill." If their work focuses on low-income people, they might qualify under the "needy" criterion as well. And if they serve young children with disabilities, then the "infants" category could also apply.

All else being equal, corporations that want to make contributions of inventory equipment would probably prefer to give it to a recipient that qualifies them for the largest possible deduction. A number of technicalities limit the availability of this opportunity. These mainly have to do with certain criteria the recipient organization must meet, beyond the identity of its target population. The recipient organization must not resell the equipment; it must use it for the benefit of the covered groups (as opposed, let's say, to using the equipment for its general administrative purposes); and it must give the donor certain assurances in writing. In fact, this is one of those provisions that seems so hedged round with qualifications and restrictions that one could be forgiven for thinking that what Congress and the IRS gave with one hand, they tried to take away with the other. Nevertheless, many firms and many nonprofit organizations use this provision to mutual advantage.

A number of clearinghouses and similar organizations have sprung up to systematize, coordinate, and simplify the use of this deduction. They accept corporate contributions of equipment and give non-profit organizations the chance to choose what they most need from among the donated items. Accountants who grieve over unsold inventory need to be fully familiar with all the applicable provisions. And nonprofit groups, including in many cases consumer organizations composed of people with disabilities, also need to be cognizant of these provisions when they seek corporate support.

In assistive technology no less than in other spheres, recycling is a concept whose time has come. People with disabilities often have items of equipment they no longer need but which could still benefit others. Regrettably, the tax law does not encourage the recycling of such equipment. While individuals can, of course, claim a charitable deduction for the value of property they contribute to nonprofit organizations, the rules for determining the value of donated equipment often result in its being worth little or nothing. This is particularly so where a tax deduction has previously been taken for the equipment (either as medical care or as a business expense) when it was purchased. Accordingly, until the law is changed, people with disabilities who understand the importance of stretching assistive technology resources will also need to recognize that tax benefits will not be a major part of the rewards they receive.

(g)

Sheltered Workshops, Supported Employment, and Training Programs

A provision in the tax law dealing with the income of sheltered workshop employees might be of interest to a few readers. This provision deals with the right of a taxpayer to claim as a dependent a child who works in a sheltered workshop, making it easier to claim an exemption for such a child than would be the case if the child were working in some other setting.

Normally, as discussed in Chapter 2(b) and (c), a taxpayer can claim a personal exemption for a dependent such as a child only if that dependent's income is lower than the "exemption amount" for the year in question. This is called the income test for dependent status, and it is one of five tests that must be met to claim someone as a dependent. However, we noted in Chapter 2 several exceptions to the income test, which, if applicable, allow a person whose income exceeds the exemption amount to still be claimed as a dependent. One of these exceptions is when the dependent's income derives from employment in a sheltered workshop.[7.48]

Specifically, gross income derived from sheltered workshop employment is not taken into account in determining whether the dependent's income exceeds the exemption amount ($2,300 for 1992). Several conditions must be met, however. The sheltered workshop employee must meet the definition of permanent and total disability that applies to the credit for the elderly and permanently and totally disabled;[7.49] the purpose for the individual's presence at the workshop must be to obtain medical treatment or services; the facility must be operated by a tax-exempt nonprofit organization or by a unit of state or local government; and the wages paid to the worker must be primarily intended as a part of treatment and be no more than incidentally intended as compensation for employment.

This provision does not mean that the other tests for dependency (e.g.,the support test, the relationship test, etc.) are waived. Nor does this provision mean that the sheltered workshop income is tax-exempt, only that it need not be counted for purposes of the income test for dependency.

Since sheltered workshop wages are low—often below minimum wage pursuant to exemptions granted by the U.S. Department of Labor—it can generally be assumed that people work in them because of their inability to obtain higher wages in a competitive setting. Work in a sheltered shop (or even in a related but usually lower-paying facility such as a work activity center) may still be motivated by the desire for some income, particularly if benefits under certain government programs can be supplemented without risk of ineligibility. On the other hand, sheltered workshops do provide a variety of therapeutic interventions, which certainly explain many placements of people by rehabilitation or other agencies in workshop settings. How this variety of factors relates to the Internal Revenue Service's definition of "medical care" is open to some question. In practice, there is probably little to worry about. If someone claims an exemption for an adult child whose modest income derives largely or totally from sheltered shop wages, it seems unlikely that the Internal Revenue Service will question the motives for the placement.

In recent years, a placement option called "supported employment" has largely replaced sheltered workshops as a placement option for vocational rehabilitation clients deemed unsuitable for competitive sector work.[7.50] In some cases, the wages, training stipends, or other payments made to supported workers may be excludable from income. If these payments are made pursuant to programs funded or administered under Part A of Title VI of the Federal Rehabilitation Act, they qualify for such exemption.[7.51] In this connection, IRS Publication 907 refers to payments made under the Employment Opportunities for Handicapped Individuals Act." Few people know what this 1965 law is, but its most recent embodiment was as Title VI A of the Rehabilitation Act.

At the risk of adding to the complexity, remember that this book is being written in September, 1992, a few weeks before the scheduled reauthorization of the Federal Rehabilitation Act due to take effect October 1. Therefore, by the time you read this, be alert to the possibility that many provisions of the Rehabilitation Act will be renumbered, not to mention changed.

Apart from programs under Title VI A, the Rehabilitation Act contains a number of other programs under which people can receive training stipends, transportation allowances, or other funds. Outside of rehabilitation, a number of other government manpower and training programs also provide for various stipends. With respect to all of these, their tax status depends on the purpose for which they are given. If they are provided as part of a legislatively enacted program to promote the general welfare, they are excludable from income; if provided as payment for work, they are subject to tax.[7.52]

Determining which category a given payment falls into may not always be easy. Where there is doubt, several features of the program will ordinarily provide guidance for resolving the uncertainty. For example, a program in which the level of payment is based on need rather than strictly on the number of hours of participation would typically be regarded as intended to promote the general welfare. By contrast, a program designed to give short-term employment to people who had exhausted their eligibility for unemployment compensation would probably be categorized as providing employment, and hence the payments received for participation would be includable in GI. Another group of relevant factors involves what the trainee actually does. A program consisting mainly of classroom training is not a jobs program, even when the training is designed to facilitate subsequent employability. A program consisting mainly of on-the-job training may or may not be an employment program, depending on such circumstances as the eligibility criteria for participation, the linkages between productivity and pay, and the underlying rationale for the existence of the program.

Beyond vocationally oriented programs, government payments are tax-exempt if they are considered to be welfare payments or payments based on need.[7.53] Payments from nonprofit organizations are subject to this same set of distinctions. Even payments from private individuals are exempt from taxation if they are gifts and not payments for services.[7.54] Although they may result in the donor's having to pay gift tax, they do not result in any includable income to the recipient. Essentially, what defines a gift is what is termed a disinterested motive, the lack of any obligation to pay or of any expectation of future action from the recipient. Among families and friends, many a gift comes with emotional strings of all sorts, but these are not the kinds of obligations the tax law has in mind.

(b)

M oving Expenses

People who move their residence in order to take a job or to engage in self-employment can claim their moving expenses as an itemized deduction.[7.55] As usual, a number of conditions must be met. We will not go into all the details of what is required in order for a moving expense to qualify for deductibility. For people who become disabled within two years after moving, one of the key conditions can be waived.

For moving expenses to be deductible, you must be employed full-time or engaged in full-time self-employment at your new location for a specified period of time, either for 39 weeks within the first year after moving, or 78 weeks out of the first two years. There are a few exceptions to this work requirement. One exception is for people who are prevented from meeting the work requirement because of disability. In that event, the moving expense deduction will not be denied, even though the taxpayer has failed to meet the work requirement.[7.56]

A person who already has a disability at the time of moving would not necessarily be barred from claiming the exception if the disability became sufficiently more severe to prevent fulfilling the work requirement. Motivation or intention might become an issue in such a case, however. If the taxpayer moved with the knowledge or expectation of being unlikely to work for 39 (or 78) weeks, then the IRS might understandably contend that retirement was the real purpose of the move. But if the expectation and intention were to continue work for at least the required period of time, then the failure to do so because of the disability should not result in disallowance of the moving expense deduction.

Where the onset of a disability results in the interruption of work, use of the exception should not be imperiled by the fact that the individual is eventually able to return to work after rehabilitation, training, or a period of adjustment. The statute does not require that the disability be "permanent and total."

Sometimes a disability can result in job loss because of the unwillingness or inability of the employer to provide necessary accommodations. In a case such as this, one of the other exceptions to the work requirement may come into play. This is the exception for a person who loses their job through no fault of their own or willful action on their part.[7.57] The inability or unwillingness of an employer to make reasonable accommodations, if it led to job loss, would represent a case of job loss coming within this exception.

The moving expense deduction is not subject to the 2 percent of AGI threshold that applies to miscellaneous itemized deductions. Moving expenses should not be confused with job-seeking expenses, even though both may involve transportation, lodging, and other similar components. Moving expenses are not subject to the 2 percent of AGI deductibility threshold that applies to MIDs, but job-seeking expenses are. Furthermore, job-seeking expenses are deductible only when one is looking for a position in the same field or line of work as previously pursued, whereas the expenses of moving to a new job or business location are deductible whether or not they involve a change of career. Finally, you cannot consider moving expenses deductible until you have obtained a new job or made definite or concrete plans for self-employment; anything prior to that point is job-seeking.

Because we may not know until two years after moving whether our moving expenses qualify for deductibility, questions may arise about when to claim the deduction. Most people claim the deduction in the year of the move, but if they subsequently fail to meet the work requirement, they will either have to file an amended return for the year of the move or add the previously deducted amount back into their income in the later year's return. Moving expenses are claimed on Form 3903.

eight

State and Local Taxes

This brief chapter is designed to make readers aware that state tax provisions frequently include features of importance to people with disabilities. Any attempt to comprehensively review these provisions for all states would require a chapter twice as long as this entire book. In your tax planning, keep in mind that state or even local law provisions may influence your decisions or hold out the possibility of lowering your costs.

So far, we have been concerned with federal income taxes. The federal government levies other taxes, including excise and inheritance taxes, but every state and local government also levies taxes as well. In many cases, these include provisions to which people with disabilities need to be alert.

Major state and local taxes can be divided into four groups: income taxes, sales and use taxes, real and personal property taxes, and business taxes. When federal income tax provisions offer no particular advantage, the provisions of state and local law may still provide the possibility for savings.

(a)

S tate Income Taxes

Most states impose income taxes on their citizens. In high tax states, these can bring the combined federal and state income tax rate for people in the highest brackets to over 40 percent. In other states, even when rates are low, the introduction or manipulation of such taxes can ignite massive political conflict.

In order to understand how state income taxes work, we have to remember they are usually keyed to the federal tax code. That is, they use figures from our federal return's AGI, or taxable income, and they use federal forms such as Schedule C, as reference points. But they typically use our federal tax information as points of departure, incorporating their own deductions, exclusions, credits, surcharges, and so on. Thus in virtually every state income tax system, your adjusted gross income or taxable income, as determined on your federal return, is carried over to the state return as the starting point for certain additional calculations. In some instances you simply take your federal taxable income and apply the state rate to determine how much state income tax you owe, but in most cases it is a little more complicated than that.

For example, states may use their own standard deduction amounts, differing from the federal, in which case your taxable income for state tax purposes will not be the same as for federal. Some states exempt some items from income that the federal law does not, again resulting in a lower income than you had on your federal return. Or states may use a different threshold for state income tax liability, meaning that someone who owes federal taxes may not owe any to the state, or conversely that someone whose income falls below the minimum for federal income tax liability may still be obliged to fork over something to the state. Some states have tax credits that have no counterparts in the federal formula, such as renter's credits. Among all these variations, some states have exemptions or exclusions for people with certain disabilities.

For people with disabilities, investigating these nuances is vital. The way the state law is structured often influences federal filing strategy. Let's say the state gives a $500 extra standard deduction for people who are blind and deaf. Since you typically have to use the same method (itemization or standard deduction) on both federal and state returns, this state standard deduction might induce someone to choose the standard deduction over itemization, whereas if only the federal choice is in question, itemization might be the better choice.

It would be impossible to report such provisions on a state-by-state basis. A survey of provisions bearing on people with disabilities in the tax laws of ten major states demonstrates their great diversity of amount and approach.[8.1] What we can do here is remind taxpayers with disabilities that they should take two steps in their tax planning. The first is to ascertain what, if any, disability-related provisions exist in your state. The second is to determine what impact on your federal and state tax strategy such provisions may have.

(b)

ales Taxes

As with income taxes, most Americans live in states that impose sales taxes. Some forty-five states impose such taxes, directly and through a variety of local or regional taxing authorities. These combined rates can currently range to over 8 percent. States vary enormously in what they exempt from sales taxes and in the procedures for obtaining these exemptions. But every state does have some exemptions of special interest to people with disabilities. In particular, a number of states define "prosthetic devices" in ways that extend to a variety of assistive technology devices. At least three states include major exemptions for devices of various sorts used by people who are blind or deaf, and a number of states have vaguely worded exemptions that could apply to many devices used to mitigate various disabilities. Once again, the range of definitions, provisions, and procedures is far too broad to enumerate here. A major state-by-state study of sales tax provisions in relation to assistive technology was published in 1990.[8.2]

Anyone purchasing assistive devices or supplies for them should investigate their state sales tax law with a view to doing three things. First, you need to find out if any exemption exists or if the state tax agency or state courts have interpreted any exemption in a way that would cover your purchase. Second, if an exemption applies, you need to find out the procedure for claiming it. In some cases, this will be done by presenting evidence of disability or of intended use to the seller, who will then refrain from collecting the tax. In other cases, it will be done by obtaining an exemption certificte from the state tax agency, or by filing for a refund after the tax is paid. Third, in any case where the statutory language suggests the possibility of an exemption, you should consider applying for an appropriate ruling. Almost all state tax agencies make provision for issuing such rulings, and they are often remarkably easy to obtain. Of course, when the state sales tax does not apply, neither do the county or special district sales taxes that are tacked on to the basic state rate.

Interstate mail order represents one sales tax avoidance strategy with which many people are familiar. Remember, though, in many cases, state use taxes come into play when the sales tax is not paid. When a purchase would have been exempt from the sales tax, then use taxes will ordinarily not apply either.

For a number of reasons, sales tax is likely to be collected on a growing number of interstate mail order sales in the years to come. This trend makes knowledge of your state sales tax more important than ever.

(c)

R eal Property Taxes

Real property taxes (i.e., on land and buildings) are the bedrock of municipal revenue raising in this country. We all pay them, directly if we own the property, indirectly if we rent our house or apartment. Two issues surrounding these taxes are of importance to people with disabilities.

The first is the possibility that the tax rate is reduced for people with certain disabilities. This may be a matter of either state or local law. An exemption from some or all of the tax may exist for people with certain disabilities (particularly veterans), for people over a certain age, for people with specific disabilities, or for people with disabilities and low incomes. The exemption may be structured in a number of ways, including by manipulation of tax rates, of assessments, or by exemption from tax of a certain portion of the property's assessed value. Procedures for claiming the benefit vary widely. Taxpayers should be especially alert to procedural technicalities, such as the need to periodically renew one's claim, the obligation to file one's claim during only one or two brief periods of the year, or the requirement to formally request a reassessment or reclassification of one's property.

The tax break may be available based on who owns the house or who lives in it. In some cases, an owner with a relevant disability also needs to be the occupant; in other cases, perhaps not. There is no substitute for checking if any pertinent provision exists in your state or locality.

The second issue with real property taxes relates to what happens when home modifications are made to mitigate the consequences of a disability. In Chapter 7(e) we discussed the medical deductibility of home modification expenses and the extent to which these costs must sometimes be added to the "basis" of the house. If the modifications increase the property's value, there is a danger that the house could be reassessed. If it is reassessed for a higher value, the real property tax might go up. A property owner who makes such modifications must, therefore, anticipate the possibility, fortunately not common, that this could occur.

Effective anticipation of this problem involves looking into both law and practice in your community. How often and according to what precepts does your community reassess property? What is the state and local law, and what are the local practices of assessors concerning home modifications that enhance the value of the property? Is there a procedure for getting an advisory opinion from local tax officials before undertaking the modifications? If there are periodic assessments, when will the next one occur? Are special district taxes, such as those levied for schools, keyed to assessments? In the event upward reassessment is possible, are there any legal provisions that limit or prevent this where the increase in value is attributable to the home modifications?

In those instances where the modification is on the IRS's list of those that do not increase value, a solid basis for contesting any upward reassessment exists. In other cases, if local tax authorities are obdurate, the involvement of independent appraisers may be necessary, but much depends on local rules for appealing unwarranted tax increases. Whether a tax increase that resulted from an increase in the value of real or personal property would violate the ADA or a state human rights statute is an interesting question. In some cases it seems likely that such an increase would violate Title II of the ADA regarding governmental entities and public services..

(d)

B usiness Taxes

Many people with disabilities pursue small business ventures. Like other entrepreneurs, they face an array of state business taxes, ranging from gross receipts taxes to licensing and registration fees. Often in fact, the line between a tax and a user fee or administrative charge is difficult to determine. Many states provide exemptions to one or more of their business taxes for persons with various disabilities. Exemptions from gross receipts tax, waiver of business license fees, exemptions for people with specific disabilities, for people over a certain age, or even for people living in specific counties have all been encountered.

nine

A Program for Reform

Throughout this book, we have discussed provisions and interpretations of the law that both create tax savings opportunities for and pose barriers for people with disabilities. This chapter focuses on the latter. Throughout this book, we have identified and explained provisions that fall short of their potential to benefit people with disabilities. Sometimes their deficiency is attributable to outmoded notions of who "the disabled" are and of what they need; other times these shortcomings result from what we might call inartful drafting. In still other instances, they derive from a failing common to all statutes: inability to foresee situations and circumstances that occur after the statute is written. In none of these cases have we criticized a provision that seems to have a valid or substantial revenue-raising or public policy purpose simply because it operates to the disadvantage of people with disabilities. We will not recapitulate these technicalities here, but instead will highlight those key areas where changes in the law could result in significant benefits for taxpayers with disabilities, their families, and society as a whole.

Before discussing these key reforms, it will be helpful to place our proposals in the context of the never-ending debate over tax policy in this country. Many tax provisions work to the disadvantage of specific people. The fact that a provision works to the disadvantage of an identifiable group of taxpayers does not automatically make it unfair. Nor are efforts to modify a provision or discrepancy guaranteed to succeed, even when manifest unfairness is recognized. More than simple unfairness is usually required to bring about change. In other words, the fact that a specific proposal for change would benefit people with disabilities, even to the point of rectifying unfairness, is not enough to guarantee its adoption. The tax law has many objectives and many constituencies. Change does not come easily.

Any tax system has two basic objectives: to raise revenue for the government, and to do so in a "fair" way. Particularly in a voluntary system like ours—one in which the citizens calculate their own taxes and forward the amounts due to the government—fairness, or at least the public perception of fairness, is essential to compliance. If too many people consider the system unfair, voluntary compliance breaks down and the costs and difficulties of enforcement rise. Unfortunately, there is little consensus on the definition of fairness today.

Our tax system also has a number of subsidiary objectives. Through its provisions, the Internal Revenue Code encourages certain activities on the part of individuals and businesses and discourages others. For example, the tax law encourages private individuals and businesses to make charitable contributions by making them tax deductible. By making medical expenses deductible when they reach a certain level, the law cushions people against the adverse economic consequences of high medical costs. By denying a business expense deduction to illegal bribes, the law seeks to discourage corruption.

The law makes its choices and distinctions about what expenses are favored and which are not, on the basis of an almost infinite number of considerations. Underlying almost every tax provision of any general consequence, though, is the argument or belief that the provision is in the interests of society. Much of this belief is rationalization, but much is not. Thus, current tax law provisions targeted to people with disabilities can be traced in large part to some concept of benefit to society. To advocate for change is to argue that the measures that will most benefit society are different now than they were when these provisions were enacted.

Our federal income tax system has been criticized over the years for taking too aggressive a role in trying to encourage or discourage various sorts of economic activity and personal behavior. Critics argue that it should confine itself to raising revenue. This criticism reaches its zenith in advocacy of a "flat tax." Whatever the merits of this criticism, we are likely to experience increasing reliance on tax law as an instrument of public policy for some time to come. It is not hard to see why. Funds for new and existing programs are scarce because of the huge federal deficit. Faced with an inability to fund their favorite programs, politicians of all stripes argue for the use of tax policy to subsidize and stimulate what they regard as worthwhile activities. Even when they profoundly disagree about what should be done, today's political leaders increasingly share the view that tax policy is an appropriate vehicle for accomplishing their goals. People disagree on what activities should be supported by tax subsidies and how these subsidies should be structured to yield the desired effects. However, few participants in the public policy debate appear to seriously question the premise that tax law is a powerful tool for channeling the economy and for influencing social conditions and personal behavior.

Because any given policy-based tax provision has fiscal implications, questions of tax policy and revenue are not easy to separate. The creation of a new tax benefit may either cost the government money or actually result in increasing federal revenues. The raising or lowering of tax rates has revenue implications that bear heavily on the policy goals that motivate the rate revision. Tax policy decisions frequently have unexpected consequences in terms of both their effect on economic decisions and behavior and their impact on revenue. Historically, tax increases have sometimes raised governmental revenues, and at other times decreased them. The same is true with tax cuts. Often little agreement exists on the appropriate criteria for measuring society's gains and losses, or even on how to measure the indirect impact on governmental revenues and expenses. All in all, tax legislation is an inexact science.

As it relates to advocacy for change, this inexactness cuts two ways. On the one hand, it underscores the importance of being as thorough and precise as possible in researching and justifying proposed reforms, since extravagant claims erode credibility and lead to disillusionment. The difficulty of prediction does not exempt proponents of change from the obligation to estimate as carefully as possible its revenue implications and its social and economic consequences. On the other hand, this inexactness also limits the specificity or the certainty with which any predictions can be made. No one can legitimately demand more proof or greater certainty than can reasonably be obtained. Anyone who imposes an unrealistic burden of proof on advocates for change is probably using the need for data as an excuse and would probably find some other ground for opposition to the proposal if hard and fast numbers were magically forthcoming.

Advocates, therefore, should avoid the temptation to make extravagant and unrealistic promises concerning their proposals. Neither should they be intimidated by the need for proof that their ideas will work. When stripped of its rhetoric and traced to its philosophical roots, much of our tax law turns out to be based on faith. Many of our most cherished assumptions cannot be proved.

One area where equity or fairness is a primary value is that of tax rates. What equity or fairness means is a matter of endless controversy. It is a concept whose prevailing definition has changed over the years. At one time, a "progressive" tax system, under which people paid at higher rates as their incomes rose, was considered the hallmark of tax equity. As recently as the late 1970s we had more than a dozen tax rates or brackets, reflecting increments of income. In the 1980s we veered away from this approach on the theory that lower tax rates and fewer tax brackets would stimulate economic growth and reduce tax-based distortions of economic decision-making. Now there are three brackets for individuals, four if you count the alternative minimum tax rate. One can only speculate what tomorrow's prevailing beliefs about tax equity will be.

Other equity issues surround the deductions, credits, and exclusions the tax law offers. Mainstream thinking holds that complexity is unavoidable in balancing the numerous and intricate policy goals of the tax law. Another widely held view is that this complexity serves mainly to provide opportunities for legal tax avoidance by those taxpayers who have the financial resources to afford sophisticated tax planning advice.

The impetus for changes in our tax law sometimes comes from surprising sources. The role of tax law in disability policy came into sharp public focus for the first time with the passage of the ADA. In order to ensure the efficacy of the new law and minimize any hardship that might result from its mandates, Congress quickly added the disabled access credit to the Internal Revenue Code. Although this provision is of profound importance to Americans with disabilities, it was not disability advocates who brought it into being. Rather, the concerns of small business primarily account for its adoption.

When people with disabilities take the lead in advocating tax reforms, what fundamental considerations of equity do we invoke? Ideally, what we want is best described as a "level playing field," to borrow the current jargon of international trade. This means that the costs of living, working, and going to school should be no higher for someone who has a disability than for anyone else. At least, if these costs are higher, that difference should not be attributable to disability.

Compelling as this premise is, the level playing field metaphor raises as many questions as it answers. Why should society subsidize these costs when they happen to be higher as the result of disability? If the disparate costs of disability should be subsidized, why is the tax law the means to do it? Finally, if the premise is accepted that tax law should be used to level the playing field for people with disabilities, what technical changes and implementation strategies would best accomplish these goals?

Like any recommendations targeted to an identifiable group of citizens, tax law proposals aimed at benefiting people with disabilities inevitably strike some as special pleading or as narrowly self-interested. Apart from the fact that such charges can justly be leveled at almost anyone who has ever advocated on his or her own behalf, many of the proposals in this chapter have implications for many people beyond the population with disabilities, large and growing though this population is. Changes in the tax law create new equity issues. If you extend a benefit to or make an accommodation for one group, you create demands for similar treatment from others in the name of equity. When such a chain of events is set in motion, it disrupts a host of delicate balances and relationships, both political and economic. The potential reverberations are great.

Beyond equity, another major impediment has to do with how government does its accounting. Even if you can prove that a particular reform will have positive revenue implications three to five years down the road, you have not necessarily justified it. In the current environment, short-term revenue losses (tax expenditures, as such losses are called) represent the more pressing concern.

Tax administration must also be considered in the evaluation of any proposed change. No change in the tax law can achieve its goals without adequate mechanisms for implementing and administering it. A number of the changes that would contribute most to the goals of independence and full participation will require modifications in some of the precepts and practices that mark the administration of our law.

Before proceeding to our major recommendations, let us evaluate two existing provisions of the law in light of the fiscal and philosophical issues that dominate the debate over taxes. Impairment-related work expenses and the disabled access credit are readily justified because they promote the employment of people with disabilities. Because they come into play only after an individual obtains a job, their revenue cost to the government is largely offset by the taxes paid by the newly employed worker. There is no IRWE except when a person with a disability is working, and there is no TJC claim unless the targeted group member is hired. How then could anyone possibly question the IRWE or TJC provisions in application to people with disabilities?

But are these provisions truly revenue-positive or at least revenue-neutral for the Treasury, and do they really increase the number or quality of jobs held by people with disabilities? To answer these questions definitively, we need to know several things. First, would workers who utilize the IRWE provision find some other way to meet their work-related needs if the IRWE deduction were unavailable? After all, many workers with disabilities managed to get the goods and services they needed prior to enactment of the IRWE provision. Second, even if people who would not otherwise be working are enabled to do so because of the IRWE, what kind of tenure or upward mobility do they have? Since the IRWE is also justified as a long-term measure for people who are already working, it would also have to be evaluated in terms of how much income gain it generates in relation to its costs. A third question the conscientious observer must ask is what impact does the IRWE have on the distribution of job accommodation costs? Put bluntly, did employers who might otherwise have paid for reasonable accommodations decide not to do so once their employees could claim a deduction for these costs, or have some workers with disabilities chosen not to risk angering their employers with accommodation requests once they learned that the tax law would subsidize the costs of meeting their own needs?

While demographic, statistical, and anecdotal information can be marshalled to allay most of these concerns, in the end the decision as to whether there should be an IRWE provision comes down to faith. Our values uphold the notion that society as a whole benefits if one of the barriers faced by people with disabilities in their efforts to enter the economic mainstream is eliminated. Even if there are revenue costs to the federal treasury, they are modest and well worth incurring for the sake of the opportunities the law creates.

With a provision like the disabled access credit, the justification is different. No real question of revenue-neutrality operates here, since the credit clearly results in revenue loss to the Treasury, subject of course to the possibility of indirect savings through reduced demand under various unrelated government transfer payment programs. Given that the ADA expresses a public policy in favor of employment and access, the real question is how the costs of compliance should be distributed. But the credit represents a decision that the costs of ADA compliance by private entities should be subsidized by taxpayers. Fairness dictates a provision of this sort to avoid hardship to the small business sector. The credit also makes good practical and political sense in that it plays an important role in defusing any anti-ADA backlash.

R ecognition of Disability

In this book we have discovered a significant number of tax law provisions that deal explicitly with disability. Many other provisions touch on the subject by implication. Yet we have met with frustration on many occasions, largely because of the lack of coordination and the inconsistency among many of these provisions. Some provisions are well-intentioned but outmoded; others are unintentionally harmful. To the degree that our nation has a public policy on disability as expressed in a number of federal laws, including most prominently the ADA, we must insist that our tax laws be supportive of those values. In fact, lacking even internal consistency, our tax laws do not meet this goal. Instead, they present a confusing, poorly articulated, often unnecessarily obscure or ambiguous conglomerate of provisions, exceptions, rules, and definitions.

Accordingly, the first step is a comprehensive review and evaluation of all Internal Revenue Code provisions bearing specifically or significantly on the interests of Americans with disabilities. We believe that a high-level commission should be created by Congress to systematically conduct this review. It should be composed of Treasury Department specialists, leaders in the field of tax policy, congressional tax experts, leaders from the business, legal, and medical fields, and, most important, persons with disabilities themselves. The commission should be empowered to make detailed and authoritative recommendations to Congress and the Treasury Department on such matters as:

☞ the extent to which current laws accurately reflect the policy goals that gave rise to their enactment, and the degree to which IRS administrative practices, interpretations, information dissemination efforts, audits, and other procedures advance or retard these goals;

☞ the degree to which current laws include terminology that unwittingly perpetuates negative images of people with disabilities;

☞ the extent to which existing provisions achieve consistency and afford adequate guidance to taxpayers and to practitioners in tax planning, tax compliance, and related activities;

☞ the extent to which existing disability-related waivers, exemptions, deductions, credits, and other benefits actually reach the subgroups for whom they are intended;

☞ the actual cost benefit experience accrued under current provisions dealing with disability;

☞ the degree to which clarification of existing provisions could enhance their understandability and accessibility without substantively changing the law; and

☞ the cost benefit and other implications of major proposals for tax law reform in connection with citizens with disabilities.

As this list of topics makes clear, there are two overlapping sets of issues. One deals with changes in the law that may be appropriate and necessary. The other deals with clarifying, simplifying, and publicizing the current law in ways that will make it more usable and accessible, but that do not require any changes in its substance. Before turning to our recommended changes, it may be useful to consider some of the important clarifications that can be easily adopted, with little risk of disruption or of engendering controversy.

Changing Terminology for Changing Times

The Internal Revenue Code provisions bearing on disability were added in different eras and reflect various underlying assumptions. Precisely because they evolved in this piecemeal way, the case is strong and urgent for systematically reviewing the terminology used in the law. The issue here is not one of "political correctness." Rather, there are important values and interpretations at stake.

To the degree that the law defines disability negatively, it reflects assumptions that our law has disavowed in other formulations. A complete review of the terminology used in the Internal Revenue Code would be valuable, not only from the standpoint of consistency, but also because current terminology introduces unnecessary confusion, obscurity, and distortion into the interpretation and application of the law.

Many of the ambiguities noted in earlier chapters of this book could be resolved by this step alone. For example, the terms *handicap, disability,* and now *impairment* are used in ways that do not lend themselves to clear analysis or interpretation. Much of the uncertainty and guesswork would be removed from the tax planning process if the use of these terms were brought into line with their use in the ADA, the Federal Rehabilitation Act, the Individuals with Disabilities Education Act, the Technology-Related Assistance for Individuals with Disabilities Act, and other major statutory formulations. Adoption of any of these statutory definitions would have substantive effects, since each of them would broaden the definition of disability which is now so frequently used to identify inability to work. But Congress can prevent any such broadening, if it wishes to, simply by making *disability* and *inability to work* into separate eligibility conditions, rather than blurring and confusing them as the law now does. The law is still free to treat people unable to work because of a physical or mental illness in whatever way it chooses. Instead of defining disability as inability to work, all the law needs to do is say that a person who is disabled and who in addition is unable to work will be entitled to this or that benefit.

The disabled access credit is a model here. It applies to anyone who meets the ADA's definition of disability. Why not use the same definition of who qualifies in connection with the architectural and transportation barrier removal deduction? When one analyzes the barrier removal statute and its implementing regulations, the conclusion that it is meant to cover pretty much the same people becomes clear. So why not just say so and remove the element of doubt

that clouds consideration by businesses of when barrier removal efforts are deductible. Clarifying this
would involve no change in the law. It would simply
make the law clearer, especially to people who lack
access to experts who can assure them of its full
meaning.

A more disturbing illustration of inadequate
wording is presented in the IRWE provision. What
possible purpose could be served by mentioning
attendant care services as the one specific illustration
of the broad range of expenses the section is
designed to cover? The Internal Revenue Service has
interpreted the term *attendant care services* to include
readers and sign language interpreters who work with
vision- or hearing-impaired persons. What possible
reason could there be for characterizing these and
other assistant services as attendant care? Conversely,
what harm would be done by incorporating a more
expansive definition or more realistic examples of
covered services into the law? Since readers, sign language interpreters, and similar service providers are
covered by the IRWE provision, making that coverage
explicit would require no change whatsoever in the
law's content. The clarification would simply make
the law more accessible to workers with disabilities
and prevent employers, accountants, or others who
read the law from deriving a narrow and largely negative impression of what the United States government believes workers with disabilities can do or
what they need.

An even more disturbing illustration is the frequent use of the word *disability* in association with
the word *death,* as in references to conditions that are
expected "to result in death" or last for "twelve
months or more." This association may be necessary
in order to make clear who is eligible for the benefits
or waivers in question, but it hardly serves to convey
a positive image of disability, let alone an accurate
one. Yet it is probably fair to say that in the majority
of instances where the tax code uses the word *disability,* it does so in the same sentence as the word
death.

A similar point can be made about many other
provisions. To the extent that IRS rulings or court
decisions have clarified ambiguous provisions,
shouldn't the statutory and regulatory language be

updated to reflect the full potential of the law as it exists?

Of course, the line between clarifying and changing the law is often blurred. Apart from the distinction between procedural and substantive change, some would go so far as to argue that clarifications that make the law more accessible to ordinary people do constitute changes, since such access leads to greater utilization of the various tax benefits with resulting increases of tax expenditure by the Treasury. Needless to say, the issues raised by such a debate go well beyond disability.

R ethinking the Meaning of Disability

We turn now to changes in the law that we believe can be justified on revenue, economic, and social grounds. Yes, these changes would assist the individuals with disabilities who are their primary constituencies, but they would also benefit society as a whole. The first of these relates to the meaning assigned by the tax law to the word and the concept of *disability*.

Why is disability important in the tax law? As we have learned, the term *disability* is most often used in the tax code to denote an inability to work. People who are incapable of working because of a permanent and total disability can invoke such provisions as the credit for the elderly and the disabled; can be exempted from penalty taxes on early withdrawal of their retirement funds; can deduct the costs of moving without meeting the otherwise applicable duration-of-work requirements; and can qualify for a number of tax breaks that are unavailable to other taxpayers.

The tax law uses an all-or-nothing test in determining "disability" in these contexts. It recognizes disability only when permanent and total, and only when it renders a person completely unable to work. People who retain reduced capacity for work or people who manage to continue working at some level, even if adjudged medically incapable of doing so, are not considered disabled for tax purposes. They may qualify for other advantageous provisions, such as impairment-related work expenses, or they may benefit from expenses to facilitate their access under the disabled access credit, but they are not disabled according to the tax law's predominant definition of the term.

This all-or-nothing approach does not correspond to current realities. In many cases, the onset of a disability reduces the amount of work a person can do, changes its nature so that income is reduced, or imposes costs that take large chunks of income. Could the tax law do a better job of addressing these increasingly common situations?

Current provisions subsidizing income loss due to disability largely come into play only when that income loss is total. Such provisions could easily be revised to provide some recourse to people who are unwilling to accept total inability to work or whose ability to earn income is greatly diminished but not extinguished. Judging by the consistency of these tax law provisions with the philosophy underlying many means-tested federal financial assistance programs, we can fairly guess that this is not a road Congress currently cares to take. But until somebody asks, there is no way to know for sure. Looked at another way, yes, you can say that Congress did not intend to extend these benefits to anyone who was not "permanently and totally" disabled, but how can the drafters of a law be deemed to have had any intention with respect to a question they never considered, regarding an issue to which their attention was never directed? Rather than focusing on what Congress did or did not intend in years past, it is far more useful to consider that it simply never occurred to anyone that disability should be anything other than an all-or-nothing proposition when our current body of laws was developing. When most of the laws were written, disability was a one-way street. Now the traffic rules have changed. Congress may not want to change the road signs, but somebody should at least ask.

Circumstances surrounding the adoption of these provisions vary, but Congress generally believed that persons who became disabled would have no income. Therefore, giving them a number of tax breaks was the compassionate thing to do. In light of the definition of disability used by Congress, it is clear that there was another assumption at work: people who lost their earning power because of disability would either die or never work again.

As suggested previously, this all-or-nothing approach is not inconsistent with the structure of many of our income replacement and financial assistance programs. People who eke out small incomes are often punished disproportionately under these programs, losing far more in cash, medical coverage, and other in-kind benefits than they accrue from income. That may be appropriate for programs involving direct expenditure of public funds, but even with these programs, the counterproductivity of the all-or-nothing approach is becoming increasingly well understood. How much more does this approach tend to make a mockery of the values of hard work and self-reliance when applied to the tax law? Our approach needs fundamental reassessment given the large number of people able and eager to work, and given the advent of technology that makes the continuation of a full and productive life increasingly possible. The tax law cannot serve as the primary vehicle for removing the pervasive work disincentives in many of our means-tested social and transfer payment programs, but would it not make sense to modify some tax provisions to avoid penalizing those who want to return to work? For example, why not revise the credit for the elderly and the disabled to allow a credit based on the amount of income lost because of disability?

In general, the technical issues confronted in dissociating disability from total inability to earn income are no different from those encountered in trying to avoid its use as a synonym for death. If society chooses to subsidize the income loss of people who are disabled, once again it can do so without confusing the two issues. All we need to do is structure the law so that the equation consists of three elements: disability, income level or income loss, and tax benefit.

Uncoupling Disability from the Medical System

In recent years much attention has been paid to the limitations in our traditional medical model of disability. Many of the expenses that people incur to overcome or mitigate the functional consequences of their disabilities are deductible. We learned in Chapters 4 and 5 how a full understanding of the medical expense deduction facilitates its use in situations as far-flung as assistive technology and special education. Although it is appropriate for society's definition of medical care to continue expanding as new modalities and new professional helping disciplines emerge, continued reliance on this deduction category for disability-related expenses may do more harm than good in the long run. Even though the health care concept offers the flexibility to give us these deductions, it is time to recognize them for what they are: disability-related expenses, not medical costs. With gratitude for all that the medical expense deduction has afforded us, it is time to move on.

Continued reliance on the health care rationale for the deductibility of disability-related expenses, such as assistive technology devices designed or modified for use by an individual with a disability, has several major drawbacks. Use of the medical expense deduction often raises costs by requiring the involvement of physicians and medical institutions in situations where they increasingly have neither an indispensable role nor substantial expertise. The argument in favor of retaining mandatory medical involvement is that the physician is necessary to preserve the integrity of the system, because without such involvement no means would exist to protect the tax system from being used to subsidize self-treatment. Such fears have little basis in relation to assistive technology. People who do not need such technology are simply not going to buy it. The separation of such disability-related expenses as are deductible anyway from the medical expense deduction would make everyone's life much simpler. Take the issue of travel expenses, discussed in Chapter 4. Tax advisers and IRS auditors cannot be expected to appreciate the full distinction between convalescence and rehabilitation expenses. If disability-related expenses were broken out as a deduction category in their own right, the resulting focus and clarity could lead both to avoidance of needless controversy between taxpayers and the government and to fewer instances of failure to claim permissible deductions because of taxpayer or tax adviser misunderstanding of the fine distinctions. A deduction for disability-related costs, which need not be expanded unless Congress decides it should be, would make it possible to focus on the nature of those costs. Their nature and potential deductibility would no longer be submerged beneath the assumptions and rules surrounding medical care. The criteria for the deductibility of disability-related expenses could be addressed and decided independently. Even if the actual content of the law were not changed in the slightest degree, tremendous benefit would ensue for the processes of tax planning and administration.

A further compelling example of how the medical expense deduction obscures issues is found in the area of personal assistance or attendant services. Although a medical expense deduction can sometimes be secured for such services, as discussed in Chapter 4(d), the distinctions between attendant and household services are likely never to emerge clearly within the medical expense framework. Resistance to allowing a medical deduction for household expenses is understandable, but a number of worthy attendant services claims have probably been casualties to the larger issue surrounding household help. As long as claims for personal attendants must be argued against the backdrop of fear over erosion of the rules governing household services, the outcome of such cases will be far more problematical than they should be.

Another problem with continued reliance on the medical care deduction is its 7.5 percent of AGI threshold. This deduction threshold, however justifiable elsewhere, is not appropriate when applied to disability-related expenses. Congress created that threshold to give relief to individuals and families who faced major, if not catastrophic, medical costs. The costs that people with disabilities incur, although they may be large and concentrated in a short time span, are often recurrent and ongoing. They may not add up to 7.5 percent of adjusted gross income in any particular year, but in the course of a lifetime their aggregate cost and their cumulative economic effect are typically far greater than those of traditional medical costs. Moreover, for a population with high levels of unemployment and underemployment, and with generally lower personal and family incomes than the national average, ongoing disability-related costs can constitute a significant and chronic drain on economic self-sufficiency.

Congress may conclude that these disability-related costs should be deductible at a lower threshold than 7.5 percent, or it may decide that there should be no threshold at all for people whose AGI is low. On the other hand, Congress may conclude that the same 7.5 percent threshold that applies to medical care should be maintained. In any event, the question should be addressed. As long as these costs remain obscured by the medical expense deduction, they never will be.

An additional problem with the medical expense deduction as applied to the expenses of people with disabilities is one of timing. Medical care expenses are ordinarily deducted in the year they are incurred. While this can work to the advantage of people with a fairly large income who incur major expenses, it imposes a real hardship for people who incur such expenses in years when, because of the disability, their income is low. It also works a hardship on people who had a larger income in prior years or who incurred expenses in order to have the prospect of higher earnings in future years. If disability-related expenses were designated as a separate deduction category, attention could be given to the incorporation of carryover provisions that would allow the deduction to be applied to the years in which it would do the purchaser/taxpayer the most good. At the very least, certain assistive technology costs, if treated as income adjustments, would be deductible without regard either to decision to itemize or to the 7.5 percent threshold.

Implementing this proposal would be simple. Taxpayers who suffered a reduction in gross income, say of 25 percent or more over one or two years, and who could demonstrate a relationship between this reduction and a disability would be allowed to carry back the deduction for their assistive technology or other costs for up to three years. They would likewise be permitted to carry forward such expenses for up to three years for use when their income increased or, if there was no increase, for the accumulation over those three years of enough income to fully absorb the deduction. The concept of carryover is well-established and easily implemented. Although used primarily in business settings, its application to individuals is not unknown. The scope of the deduction would not need to be changed, only the time frame over which it is taken.

Again, as long as disability-related expenses remain buried in the medical expense deduction, this proposal can not be adequately addressed. Congress may decide that no carryover is warranted, that if people are entitled to a deduction that their incomes do not absorb, it is just too bad. Here, too, Congress should at least have the opportunity to focus on that question. Within the framework of the medical expense deduction, it never will.

The Itemized Deduction Approach

Under current law, most of the tax benefits for people with disabilities are structured as itemized deductions. This approach often results in inability of the intended beneficiary to derive any advantage. If an individual's deductions are not larger than the standard deduction amount, those itemized deductions might as well not exist.

Defenders of current practice argue that the standard deduction provides equity for people who do not itemize. With the standard deduction, they are allowed to claim a sizable tax benefit even if they incurred no deductible expenses at all. Now that the standard deduction is indexed to inflation, how can there be any injustice to people who are obliged to use it?

Injustice or no, there is a problem. If the purpose of a given deduction is to subsidize specific costs, what is the sense of conditioning its availability on extraneous factors in the individual's tax profile? Impairment-related work expenses provide a striking illustration of this point. Compare two workers with identical IRWEs of $2,000. One gets the deduction because when combined with unrelated deductible expenses, say for home mortgage interest, total deductions from all sources are large enough to itemize. The other worker has no itemized deductions beyond the IRWEs so claims the standard deduction, thereby geting no subsidy for the IRWE costs. For reasons unrelated to either the economic impact of the IRWE expense or to its indispensability in facilitating employment, one worker gets a $2,000 deduction while the other is in the same position as if the IRWE provision did not exist.

What is the public interest in restricting a deduction such as the IRWE to workers who have relatively large deductions? To be sure, this same question could be raised in connection with any itemized deduction, but it has a particular urgency for people with disabilities who are entering, reentering, or struggling to remain in the work force, when the sub-sidy represented by the IRWE can be the margin of success. In such cases, use of the itemized deduction may not represent the best strategy for ensuring that the tax benefit is targeted where it was intended, to those for whom it can make the greatest difference. Converting the IRWE from an itemized deduction to an income adjustment or giving taxpayers the option to treat it that way, would ensure that its availability is not made to depend on unrelated, essentially irrele-vant factors. Our law does not include a large number of such above-the-line deductions. Various policy rea-sons explain those that do exist. Here, the argument for moving IRWEs above-the-line is to ensure its avail-ability to the largest possible proportion of those who could benefit from it, especially low-income workers.

There would be a small revenue cost to the gov-ernment if the IRWE deduction were available to peo-ple who do not itemize, since some people would claim it in addition to their standard deduction. This loss, however, would be offset by the tax revenues generated by their employment. People who could itemize would continue to do so, since that strategy would remain to their advantage. Lower-income peo-ple who want to work would be helped to do so.

The issue is to make sure that low-income tax-payers who may desperately need the tax break do in fact receive what the law allows them. By changing the manner in which IRWEs and other provisions tar-geted to people with disabilities are handled, the goals of existing tax law can be far better accom-plished. What specifically should be done?

Several solutions are possible. One frequently discussed proposal is to make IRWEs and several other provisions into a tax credit, refundable or non-refundable as the case may be. Converted to a credit, the IRWE and possibly some other deductions would be available to taxpayers whether they itemize or not. Such a credit could reflect IRWE costs dollar for dol-lar, or could be structured to apply to 50 percent of those costs, as the disabled access credit does in the case of expenses incurred by businesses. If nonre-fundable, such a credit could reduce tax liability to zero. If refundable, the taxpayer whose tax liability for the year is already zero might still look forward to a refund, up to some specified maximum, as is the case with the earned income credit. Upper-income limits might be placed on who could claim this new credit, or the credit could decline as income rises, as does the child and dependent care credit. By these or other means, a high degree of assurance could be warranted that the new credit would reach the intended people and situations.

There are problems with this approach. Refundable credits such as the earned income credit make sense only if narrowly targeted to people in the lowest income strata. To make the IRWE a refundable credit would probably result in its availability being restricted to a target population of low-income wage earners; it would probably be unavailable or only partially available to people trying to enter or stay in what we call the middle class. People would be left out if their incomes were too large to qualify for a refundable credit, yet too small to meet their needs without benefit of a tax subsidy.

Other problems arise with the use of credits. No existing credits are open-ended. All are limited, either to a maximum dollar amount such as the credit for the disabled, to a certain proportion of the eligible expenditure such as the disabled access credit, by the income of the taxpayer claiming the credit, or in other ways. Personal credits, whether refundable or nonrefundable, are generally designed to benefit lower-income taxpayers. To be fully effective for IRWEs, a tax credit would have to be unlimited in amount, available to all taxpayers regardless of income, and available for a large proportion of IRWE expenses. A credit meeting all these conditions would represent an enormous departure from the structural pattern established throughout the rest of the Internal Revenue Code.

Another suggestion that occasionally comes up involves what can best be described as extension of the additional standard deduction so that it would apply to all people with disabilities, not only to those who are blind and elderly. Although this would contribute to greater tax equity among people with visual and nonvisual disabilities, it does not really solve any of the major problems we have identified. Economists can make a fair estimate of the economic costs of disability, and such an estimate can be used to determine the size of a new additional standard deduction.

See Chapter 7(d). However, a provision in a fixed amount would be only an average and would have no relationship to the actual costs incurred by any individual. Such a deduction would not be targeted to the particular kinds of expenses that we want to subsidize. It would be too imprecise and too impersonal an instrument to be effective.

When all the political, economic, administrative, and equity factors are taken into account, expanded use of income adjustments holds the greatest promise of meeting the need and balancing the conflicting interests at issue. What would happen if IRWEs and other currently deductible disability-related costs were treated not as itemized deductions, but as income adjustments that are deducted from gross income in the process of calculating adjusted gross income? Since adjustments can be taken whether a taxpayer itemizes or not, all taxpayers would be able to benefit from their IRWEs or other deductible disability-related expenses, and in many instances people with very low incomes might have their AGIs pushed below the threshold for tax liability. Only one substantive change in the law would be needed. Since some of the deductions in question would be taken out of the present medical expense category, a new adjustment to income would have to be created to include them, as well as IRWEs and a number of other currently itemizable deductions. Apart from this regrouping, neither definitions nor tax rates would need to be changed.

The transfer of these tax benefits from the itemized deduction category to the income adjustment category would not be unprecedented. Models for treating IRWEs as above-the-line deductions (i.e., as income adjustments) exist with certain employee business expenses. In particular, certain employee business expenses of performing artists are handled as adjustments to income rather than as itemized deductions. We believe that the impairment-related work expenses of individuals with disabilities can and should be handled this way as well.

As attractive and simple as this approach is, it fails to grapple with the problem of timing. It is important to assure that everyone who is entitled to a deduction gets it, but unless this issue of timing is also dealt with, tax equity for people with disabilities is a long way off. Worse, the public policy goals that gave rise to the creation of these deductions will continue to be frustrated in all too many cases. Therefore, unless we are to end up with the same timing problem, the new adjustments must be eligible for carryover.

Timing

No one knows how many people with disabilities lose their IRWEs or disability-related medical deductions because they can not itemize. Although transforming those itemized deductions into adjustments to income would prevent many people from losing the deduction, they would benefit little if their incomes were insufficient to absorb the tax savings. The tax law cannot increase people's income, but by spreading a deduction over enough years, the law can effectively increase the pool of income that the deduction offsets. This approach represents the best solution for many of the tax inequities resulting from dramatic income fluctuations associated with the onset of disability during the working years or from high disability-related costs that are concentrated in a short period of time. The move above-the-line also represents the best mechanism for making the tax code relevant to low-income individuals who incur IRWEs or other disability-related costs.

As discussed in Chapter 6(d), depreciation of capital equipment may amount to a form of carryover in some cases, but depreciation is no solution to the problem. Depreciation is available only for business expenses, so would not cover expenses under the medical care category. Moreover, depreciation would never be available to cover assistive technology or other services when they are paid for with savings or borrowed funds. Finally, even for capital equipment, depreciation permits only carry-forward, not carry-back, since property is depreciated beginning in the year it is "placed in service." Thus, a straightforward carryover provision is needed.

So far, none of the changes we have recommended requires change in the definition or scope of any deduction. Congress might elect to make substantive modifications in the course of implementing these procedural and technical changes, but lawmakers would not need to make such changes in order to embrace these precepts. We now turn to provisions that do require substantive changes in the law. Each of the recommendations that follows does involve changes in the content of the law, changes that affect the definition of several key concepts.

In Chapter 6(j) we discussed the role that employee fringe benefits can play in technology planning and other decisions made by workers with disabilities. The law needs to be clarified in several important ways in order for fringe benefits to be maximally useful. To understand what these are, it is necessary to offer some brief background on regulations governing fringe benefits under the tax law.

F ringe Benefits

To qualify for the dual tax advantage of deductibility to the employer who pays them and income exemption to the employee who receives them, fringe benefits are of value to both employers and employees, especially when they qualify both for deductibility to the employer who pays them and for exclusion from the income of the employee who receives them. In order to qualify for this double tax benefit, benefits must generally be provided under approved fringe benefit plans. To be approved, fringe benefit plans must meet various legal requirements concerning their form and content.

The two major laws dealing with self-insurance, retirement, and other fringe benefits are the Employee Retirement and Income Security Act (ERISA) and the Internal Revenue Code. Fringe benefits of employment are also covered by the ADA, although the scope of that coverage remains to be determined. To the extent that a particular fringe benefit plan might be found in violation of the ADA, linkage of ADA compliance with preservation of the plan's tax-favored status could prove a powerful tool for enhancing implementation of the ADA.

Likewise, health plans should be required to make clear that any cost that would be deductible if incurred by the worker can be covered by the plan without jeopardizing its tax status. We must emphasize that this proposal would not require firms to offer any specific type or level of coverage. However free they are under current law to make such coverage decisions, that is how free they would remain. All that this recommendation would do is incorporate into the law the clear statement that a health plan's status cannot be jeopardized by providing any goods or services that would be medically deductible if paid for out-of-pocket by the worker. Plan governance documents and materials submitted to plan participants should also make this point clear.

Personal Assistant Services

Although a substantial proportion of the services of personal assistants are deductible under the health care rationale, the path to successful deduction of these costs presents many obstacles. There are several ways through which the tax law could productively subsidize these critical components of a full life without risk that people will simply find ways to deduct the costs of household servants or chauffeurs.

First, since we already have a child and dependent care credit, why not consider creating a self-care credit? To be consistent with the parallel to the dependent care credit, this new self-care credit could be limited to those personal assistant services needed by the recipient in order to earn income. However, a broader definition would be far more helpful. Consideration should be given to a self-care credit that extends to all assistance services, not just to those that facilitate earning an income. Assistance services eligible for the credit should include those incurred to achieve a better quality of life, to facilitate education, and, most of all, to forestall institutionalization.

Since a new credit of this scope would cause anxiety among law- and policymakers, the credit could be established on an experimental time-limited basis. If necessary, the new self-care credit could be limited in one or another of the ways that all existing credits are limited. The full credit could be made available only to people with adjusted gross incomes (or with taxable incomes) below a certain figure. Or it could be granted only for those personal assistance costs that exceed a threshold figure such as 10 percent of AGI. The credit could be restricted to a proportion (perhaps 50 percent) of eligible assistance costs. The nature of qualifying costs could be limited. In this event, priority should be given to those attendant services costs that enable the recipient to avoid hospitalization or long-term institutional care.

Standards of proof could readily be developed and applied, such as methods for determining who is at risk of institutionalization. Such methods already exist in a number of human services programs as a way of targeting the resources of those programs to "at risk" populations. A number of states already operate state-funded programs that enable people with severe physical disabilities to obtain the services of in-home attendants. The standards used by these states in their determination of the nonfinancial components of program eligibility could be used as the basis for developing eligibility criteria for the self-care credit.

A key point when discussing personal assistance (or "attendant care" services) is that governmental programs and policies favoring the institutionalization of elderly or disabled people over life in the community must change. They are beginning to change and will continue to do so. As a more balanced public policy emerges, the tax law must be revised so that it is supportive of these important new priorities, not antagonistic to them. A self-care credit for those assistant services costs that demonstrably help avoid institutionalization is as rational a place as any to start.

Rethinking the Public-Private Partnership

More than at any time since the 1930s, social and human services programs are experiencing dramatic budget cuts. As a result, the disparity between the eligibility criteria set forth in the authorizing legislation and the eligibility criteria determined by appropriations levels is widening at a rapid rate. Might we not give some consideration to a dramatic measure that would strengthen the partnership between the governmental and private sectors? If an individual meets all the conditions for receiving a given service from the government except the financial eligibility requirements, why not give that individual a tax credit or deduction if he or she pays for the service? If something is important enough to be provided with public funds to those who cannot afford it, it is almost always worth subsidizing through the tax system for the person who pays for it personally.

A number of the measures we have proposed raise new challenges for documentation and proof. One dimension of the public-private partnership is the ability of the two spheres to respect one another's definitions. In cases where taxpayers would qualify for a particular governmentally-subsidized service except for failure to meet the income eligibility standards associated with the program, methods should be developed for using the nonfinancial components of such eligibility determinations as evidence in appropriate tax contexts. Since taxpayers would be collecting and bringing forward this documentation themselves, no issues of privacy need arise, and no material revisions of laws controlling the intergovernmental transfer of information would be needed. All that would be necessary is for various state, local, and nonprofit services programs to be willing and able to certify nonfinancial eligibility in those cases where it exists.

Business Incentives

In Chapters 6 (f)-(h) and 7(c), we discussed three provisions aimed at business that are of great potential importance to people with disabilities: the targeted jobs credit (TJC), the disabled access credit (DAC), and the architectural and transportation barrier removal deduction (ATB). We characterize these provisions as having great "potential" importance, because each has a number of internal problems that substantially limit its impact. Each could become immensely more useful with some simple, noncontroversial amendments.

Assuming its reenactment in much the same as its previous form, people with disabilities will continue to represent two important target populations of the TJC. This is due to the inclusion of state vocational rehabilitation (VR) agency referrals and supplemental security income (SSI) recipients among the targeted groups. If the objective of the law is to encourage businesses to hire persons with disabilities, these target groups represent a far too restricted segment of the population with disabilities who want and deserve to work.

TJC has had a checkered history, including allegations of its misuse by business and doubts about the tenure of employment it facilitates. It is not our purpose here to evaluate the credit, but merely to suggest that if it does remain on the books, it could be more responsive to job-seekers with disabilities and their prospective employers. The credit should be available for the hire of any job-seeker with a disability. Limitation to persons referred by state vocational rehabilitation agencies serves little purpose because such agencies are no longer the central funnel through which people with disabilities enter the work force. In the ADA era, people with disabilities will enter the work force in many ways, some under the umbrella of a formalized rehabilitation program, many not. It is anachronistic to believe that a state VR agency is uniquely equipped to certify the fitness of a person with a disability for employment, or that only such an agency can certify the fact of disability.

The target group composed of SSI recipients should be expanded to include Social Security Disability Insurance (SSDI) beneficiaries who meet the same tests of disability as SSI recipients. The problems they face in finding (in their case, usually in returning to) employment are similar to those confronted by SSI recipients. The same individual sometimes receives benefits simultaneously under both programs. Common sense argues for the inclusion of this group.

Another serious limitation on the efficacy of TJC is the provision barring its use for rehires. Even if an individual qualifies as a member of a targeted group, the credit is not available if she or he previously worked for the same employer. In general, this limitation is understandable. If businesses were allowed to claim the TJC on behalf of people who had formerly worked for them, its purpose of encouraging employers to reach out to groups who might not otherwise be considered for hire could conceivably be frustrated. However logical this restriction may be for some of the targeted groups, its application to workers with disabilities makes little sense.

A person who leaves employment because of a disability, undergoes rehabilitation or retraining, and finally seeks to return to work one or more years later is in many respects a new worker. Job duties may be quite different, new technology or other accommodations may be required, established relationships may have undergone dramatic alteration, and the return to work may present a host of new issues for management, colleagues, and the returning worker. In many cases, the return to work may commence on a probationary or trial basis, notwithstanding the prior relationship. Accordingly, if a person has been out of work for a year or more because of a disability and qualifies for the credit at the time of returning to employment, the former employer should not necessarily be denied the use of the credit, especially when it could contribute to an ability and willingness to welcome the worker back. Since the situation itself is strange, there seems little justification for requiring that the parties also be strangers!

The disabled access credit is an innovative business incentive that encompasses public accommodations and employment. Due to problems in its drafting, a grave danger exists that its value in helping to achieve the goals of the ADA will be severely compromised.

The law needs to be amended to make several points absolutely clear. It needs to expressly state that the credit is available for those measures, activities, and purchases that constitute ADA compliance, whether or not the firm comes under the jurisdiction of the ADA. The law also needs to plainly state that when an activity is aimed at enhancing access by a person or people with disabilities, the credit will be available even if the measures taken are of a nature that would not be required by the ADA if that law were applicable.

A second problem with this credit relates to deliberate decisions that should be reconsidered. In drafting the provision, Congress was doing the usual and appropriate thing by vesting regulatory power in the IRS. No section of the law is self-executing or so self-evident as not to require the IRS to interpret and administer it. The problem in this case is that Congress followed the model that exists for the ATB in delegating this responsibility to the federal administrative agency. Whatever the merits of the approach, extension of the model to the DAC poses serious risks.

The approach taken under the ATB is for the IRS to draft detailed definitions of each of the barrier removal activities that qualify for the deduction. It is one thing for the law to define how wide a walkway must be in order to be considered accessible. It is quite another for the law to attempt to define in advance what equipment purchases, environmental modifications, provision of "auxiliary services," or other activities and procedures constitute "reasonable accommodations" within the meaning of the ADA. In every other sphere the law eschewed such an effort, recognizing that the ADA was uniquely open-ended, and preferring to leave it to the parties to determine on a case-by-case basis what specific actions would best meet the need. If the parties are granted this broad discretion, how can the IRS or any other agency hope to determine in advance what measures qualify for the credit and what do not?

Because of the central role accorded by Congress to the IRS in defining the scope of the credit, this provision's effectiveness and impact will hinge to an unusually high degree on how the federal agency chooses to interpret and apply the law. The IRS is charged with developing its access credit regulations (expected to be issued in early 1993) with the assistance of the Architectural and Transportation Barriers Compliance Board. While the Board's experience and ongoing research agenda represent a source of considerable expertise, neither the Board, the Treasury Department, nor anyone else can claim comprehensive knowledge in many of the most crucial areas.

In defining the barrier removals and the auxiliary aids and services that will be deemed eligible for the access credit, the IRS has two basic strategies available. It can, in the tradition of the barrier removal deduction, define eligible barriers, services, equipment, or procedures with great specificity. Taken to its extreme, such an approach could result in equipment being declared ineligible for the credit because it was not specifically designed for use by people with disabilities, or because it failed to meet certain design specifications deemed requisite to assuring its efficacy. With this approach, any compliance efforts undertaken in good faith and yielding positive results would fail to meet the criteria for credit eligibility.

The other basic approach the IRS could take would involve what might best be called an "intention and effect" standard, whereby access expenditures would generally be deemed eligible for the credit if they met three conditions: intention to enhance access; actual effect or reasonable likelihood of enhancing access; and avoiding creation of any new barriers or accommodation needs. With such an approach, prospects would be heightened for widespread use of the credit in meaningful ways, but tax expenditures would undoubtedly be greater and taxpayers would surely end up subsidizing a number of ADA compliance efforts that ultimately did not work.

Looking to the architectural barrier removal deduction as a precedent for administration of the ADA credit presents serious problems. When it came to deciding how wide a walkway or doorframe must be in order to safely and adequately accommodate a wheelchair or otherwise be *accessible,* the IRS and the Board were able to call upon a significant body of design research and established accessibility guidelines developed through an extensive consultative process. While such resources will continue to be available for many of the barrier removals contemplated under the ADA, no such standards or carefully developed guidelines exist for such other ADA compliance activities as equipment purchase or modification. For all its sincere desire to interpret the law in accordance with congressional intent, the IRS can claim little expertise on the subject of disability. Even the Board will be working largely in a vacuum in many of the most important areas.

Apart from the definitions that the IRS adopts, much of the credit's destiny will also depend on the flexibility accorded to small businesses in learning to use it. For example, many ADA compliance measures will arguably qualify either as a communications barrier removal or as an auxiliary service. Will firms claiming the credit be obliged to specify under which category they do so? In this connection, the definition given by IRS to the term *communications barriers* will also prove important. In its regulations implementing Title III of the ADA, the Department of Justice has essentially restricted this term, defining it to include only those barriers that are "structural" in nature. Presumably, this would mean that a metal screen or grillwork that inhibited verbal or visual communication between a customer and a clerk would constitute a communication barrier, but the failure of a store to post information in accessible forms would not.

If, as seems likely, the IRS follows the lead of federal agencies such as the Department of Justice in their interpretations of key ADA terms, tax planning for the credit may become all the more chancy. We do not suggest that the IRS can or should undertake an independent interpretation of Title III, but the implementing regulations can avoid many of the pitfalls by clearly recognizing that, for example, a bona fide barrier removal has occurred when a firm takes steps to enhance the exchange of relevant information between its staff and customers with sensory impairments, whether or not the obstacle to such communication it removed technically met the definition of a "communications barrier." In defining communications barriers the Justice Department was specifying when, at a minimum, a public accommodation would be required to take remedial action. In applying the term, the IRS is merely telling commercial facilities when they will be encouraged to do so.

The architectural and transportation barrier removal deduction could be much more effectively and widely used if several key problems were addressed. Some of these problems could be addressed by the IRS itself, others will require legislative revisiting of the provision.

Initially, the barrier removal guidelines, in effect now for nearly fifteen years, need revision. As discussed in Chapter 7(c), both our understanding of the nature of architectural and transportation barriers and our resources for their removal have expanded exponentially, including entering the electronic information age, since the existing guidelines were promulgated.

In this connection, a special emphasis must be given to the scope of the *transportation* barrier concept. Here legislation may be required to clarify that anything which hinders the autonomous and efficient movement of people with disabilities is properly includable under the transportation barrier rubric.

To the degree that the barrier removal deduction and the new access credit overlap in both covering removal of architectural and transportation barriers, the regulations implementing one provision or the other should specify any relevant interaction between them, including order of use or other factors. Again, to the degree that the deduction is complicated and the credit is new, we can readily expect that a number of small businesses will inadvertently use the wrong one. Even in an overlapping area such as architectural barriers, this could make a difference, since whereas the credit excludes from eligibility any modifications to facilities placed in service after November 5, 1990, the deduction appears to embody no comparable restriction.

In connection with both these provisions, measures to encourage consumer involvement could go a long way to ensuring against abuse or ineffectuality in their use by businesses. At the very least, the regulations implementing both provisions need to reflect the importance of consumer input to the barrier removal and reasonable accommodation processes. Within the scope of existing law, this can be done by treating evidence of consumer involvement in the identification and solution of access issues as tending to prove the validity of the measures undertaken. In the same way as the recommendation of a physician tends to prove the medical justification for a given purchase, so should the involvement of facility users and service consumers with a disability be accorded strong evidentiary weight in evaluating whether barrier removal and reasonable accommodation efforts meet the requirements of the law for tax subsidization.

Research and Development

However people may disagree about the causes of and remedies for our nation's economic problems, there is widespread agreement that the tax code provides inadequate incentives for research and development (R & D). The next year or two will almost certainly witness the enactment of a major new R & D credit aimed at stimulating basic research and heightened competitiveness on the part of American industry. How such a provision is implemented could have great significance for people with disabilities.

It is crucial that any such incentives incorporate support for research into what is called "universal" or "accessible" design. Put simply, accessible design is the principle that products should be designed to maximize their accessibility to and usability by all people. Everyone has difficulty using some consumer product, but for people who are elderly or have disabilities, the barriers posed by exclusionary product design are often particularly severe. For example, a household appliance is more or less accessible based on the size of the lettering on its controls, how the controls are operated, the availability of redundant sources of status information, its adjustability, and a host of other factors.

The related disciplines of industrial engineering, product design, and market research have devoted enormous amounts of time and energy to the question of how consumer products can be most effectively designed. Yet to a dismaying extent, indeed to a shocking degree, consumers with disabilities have remained out of the loop, their needs and preferences left to "special" products or services, their capacity to fully use and enjoy the product often marginal at best. Accessible design should be axiomatic, if for no other reason than that it represents good business. Life is not so simple, and accessible design is still in its infancy, as a discipline and as a commitment.

A discussion of what accessible design means and why it has not been more fully embraced by the manufacturing and retailing sectors of our economy is beyond the scope of this book. Suffice it to say, any R & D reforms that are added to the tax law must make clear that work on accessible design will qualify for whatever tax benefits are available. Whether as an element of basic research or in relation to the development of particular products, it must be made clear that accessible design is central, not peripheral, to mainstream R & D. The demographics of disability and the aging of our population make this imperative. Indeed, broad-based economic revitalization and reindustrialization may be impossible without the incorporation of accessible design principles into the structure of our economy. Indeed, any domestic firm wishing to build or recapture market share in communications, household electronics, consumer goods or other spheres would do well to recognize that a commitment to accessibility can increasingly become a source of positive identification and reliable market strength.

In the post-ADA world, the accessibility of products and services is more important than ever, for these are the tools with which legal equality is implemented. Moreover, incorporating accessibility into a building or product from the beginning costs far less than providing it retroactively or through add-ons. However the economic costs of legal equality are allocated—and these costs will be far less than those of dependency and separateness—they will be far smaller in a world of accessible design than in one where individuals must continuously reinvent the wheel in their struggle to achieve full use of society's technological and informational tools. From the standpoint of tax policies that would encourage the goals of the ADA, few provisions could be more highly leveraged or more beneficial than use of a forthcoming research and design or investment tax credit to encourage universal design.

Ongoing Monitoring

Throughout this chapter we have discussed provisions that need to be updated, that would have benefited from more careful drafting, or that reflect an unduly narrow sense of who people with disabilities are. In addressing the law from these perspectives, however, we are inevitably and eternally playing catch-up.

What would the content of our law be today if its existing provisions bearing on disability had been systematically reviewed periodically, and if all tax law amendments had been evaluated from the standpoint of their potential impact on this sector of the population? It is too late to do this for existing provisions, of course, but it is just the right time to apply this scrutiny to the host of reforms and structural changes in our tax system that are inevitable as we attempt to cope with our new postindustrial economy. No one suggests that the interests or needs of people with disabilities ought to take preference over other vital goals. Indeed, in a population as large and diverse as ours, defining such interests and needs, let alone organizing to advocate for them, is often impossible. Nevertheless, to the extent that tiny provisions of law cast long shadows, simple awareness of such implications would by itself go a long way toward ensuring that opportunities are not unwittingly missed and harm not inadvertently done.

For example, both major political parties now accept that some sort of capital gains tax cut is needed. As a result, some legislation in this area is likely. To what kinds of investments will it be targeted? What holding periods will be required? How large will the rate reduction ultimately be? These questions remain to be answered, but will anyone ask whether and how such a change in the law could impact the lives of people with disabilities? Should there be some provision included specifically to encourage private investment in the development or the successful marketing of assistive technology? Should investments in the capitalization of assistive technology loan funds be subject to the lowered capital gains rate? Should holding periods be shortened for investments in businesses owned and operated by people with severe disabilities?

We do not offer answers to these or the host of similar questions that might be posed. What we do propose is that these issues must be considered. They are not fringe issues or parochial concerns of tiny pressure groups or "special interest" lobbies. They represent increasingly important dimensions of the fundamental economic decisions our society must make. A mechanism must be established whereby consideration of the implications for people with disabilities of proposed tax legislation can be instituted and made a standard part of the legislative process. Properly implemented through the congressional committee system, this would pay large dividends in coherent and timely public policy.

Conclusion

The proposals made in this chapter are not written in stone. As important as their specifics is the discussion that we hope they will engender. For people with disabilities, tax advocacy may seem novel, yet such changes may be as instrumental to a variety of worthwhile goals as any of the traditional programs with which we are familiar.

It is literally true that the tax law changes every day. Short of the enactment into law of dramatic changes in the way our government levies or collects taxes, small changes over time can have great cumulative impact. It is unlikely that most of you will ever testify before the House Ways and Means Committee or the Senate Finance Committee about proposed tax legislation. But each of you is an advocate in the way you approach tax planning and problem solving, in your recognition of the importance of education and awareness, and in your understanding that all of us approach the subject of taxation in the dual role of taxpayer and citizen. In your role as taxpayer, use every legal and responsible means at your disposal to minimize your payment obligation and to maximize the effectiveness of those provisions that can reduce your burden. As a citizen, remember it is your moral and legal duty to pay your fair share; it is also your right to lobby for an equitable tax system that gives you the best opportunity to strive and to achieve.

Appendix
Notes
Index

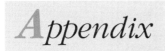

*A*ppendix

Explanation of Reference Sources

In these references, a number of different sources are utilized. In the interests of space, and in accordance with legal formatting rules, they have been abbreviated. The following list explains what these sources are and how they are used.

CFR

This is the Code of Federal Regulations. The number before CFR is the title, the number after is the section number. The section number in turn has two components. The digits before the decimal point indicate which Part of the particular Title the material is drawn from. Titles and Parts are the organizing tools that the CFR uses. The CFR contains the final text of all regulations implementing and interpreting federal law, and embodying the responsibilities, procedures, and objectives of all federal agencies. The income tax regulations are contained in Tit. 26 of the CFR, but they are usually cited in an abbreviated fashion (see Regs. below).

Comm'r.

This stands for Commissioner, specifically the Commissioner of the Internal Revenue Service, who is a named party to almost every tax law case.

F. 2d

This is the Federal Reporter, Second Series. It contains the decisions of the U.S. Court of Appeals. A typical citation begins with the volume number in which the case can be found, then identifies the reporter, then gives the page on which the case begins. If there is a second number following the word *at,* this refers to a specific page within the text of the decision on which the material of interest appears. The material in parentheses, such as (2d Cir. 1983) indicates which Court of Appeals decided the case and in what year. Divided geographically, there are eleven numbered Circuits, plus one for the District of Columbia.

IRC

This refers to the Internal Revenue Code. The Internal Revenue Code comprises Title 26 of the US Code (described below), but IRC is generally substituted for the complete citation, which would otherwise be 26 USC Sec. whatever.

Ltr. Rul.   These are letter rulings, or private letter rulings, issued by the Internal Revenue Service to taxpayers in response to specific questions. They have seven-digit numbers, the first two indicating the year of the decision, the second two the week, 01 through 52, within that year. References to years here are to federal fiscal years, not calendar years, so that a Ltr. Rul. beginning with the four digits 9301 would have been issued in the first week of October, 1992. Letter rulings do not have precedent value beyond the particular tax situation for which and the taxpayer to whom they are issued. Nevertheless they are cited because they often give a good indication what the law is, and because they frequently contain excellent summaries of the law that can be useful for orientation purposes.

Regs. Sec.   This is a reference to the Internal Revenue Service's income tax regulations. Tax regulations constitute the entirety of Title 26 of the CFR, with the income tax regulations representing Part 1 of these.

Rev. Rul.   These are revenue rulings. A revenue ruling is issued by the IRS, in connection with a particular case or to deal with matters of general interest, to explain the law on one or more points. Unlike private letter rulings, revenue rulings can be cited as authorities in subsequent cases where the facts make them applicable. In the citation to revenue rulings, the first two digits indicate the year of issuance, those after the hyphen the sequence number during that year. Strictly speaking, the citations should be longer, because some additional location material (such as 1967-1, C.B. 99) can also be used, but since this is not necessary for locating the Rev. Rul. these are omitted here.

P.L   This is public law. Apart from their codification in the U.S. Code, federal statutes are numbered consecutively as they are enacted. Thus, the number before the hyphen indicates in which Congress the law was adopted, the number after the hyphen the sequence number of the statute's adoption in that Congress. Since each Congress lasts for two years, you cannot necessarily tell from a P.L. number in which of the two years the statute became law.

TC   These are regular decisions of the U.S. Tax Court. A typical citation would consist of a volume number, the identifier of the reporter, the page on which the decision begins, and finally the year of decision in parentheses.

TC Memo — These are memorandum decisions of the Tax Court. Here the first four digits represent the year of decision, those after the hyphen are sequence numbers for the decisions of that year.

USC — This is the United States Code, the complete codification of federal statutes. It is organized by Title and Section, so that a citation to 42 USC Sec. 12101 would mean Tit. 42. Section 12101. Many libraries contain something called the US Code Annotated (USCA), which, although unofficial, is equally useful in looking up federal laws, and which also contains notes of decision listing court decisions involving each section.

Notes

1.1 IRS Publication 1200, Reference List of 1991 Federal Tax Forms and Publications, contains a list of forms and publications that taxpayers may need. As of this writing (September, 1992), the 1992 edition of this list is not yet available, but most of these entries are likely to remain unchanged. If past experience is any guide, a few new forms will be added. Of interest among current informational publications are: Pub. 1, Your Rights as a Taxpayer; Pub. 4, Student's Guide to Federal Income Tax; Pub. 15, Circular E, Employer's Tax Guide; Pub. 17, Your Federal Income Tax (this is the basic general publication); Pub. 54, Tax Guide for U.S. Citizens and Resident Aliens Abroad; Pub. 225, Farmer's Tax Guide; Pub. 334, Tax Guide for Small Business; Pub. 463, Travel, Entertainment and Gift Expenses; Pub. 501, Exemptions, Standard Deduction and Filing Information; Pub. 502, Medical and Dental Expenses; Pub. 503, Child and Dependent Care Credit; Pub. 504, Tax Information for Divorced or Separated Individuals; Pub. 505, Tax Withholding and Estimated Tax; Pub. 508, Educational Expenses; Pub. 519, U.S. Tax Guide for Aliens; Pub. 520, Scholarships and Fellowships; Pub. 521, Moving Expenses; Pub. 523, Tax Information on Selling Your Home; Pub. 524, Credit for the Elderly or the Disabled; Pub. 525, Taxable and Nontaxable Income; Pub. 526, Charitable Contributions; Pub. 529, Miscellaneous Deductions; Pub. 533, Self-Employment Tax; Pub. 538, Accounting Periods and Methods; Pub. 547, Nonbusiness Disasters, Casualties, and Thefts; Pub. 550, Investment Income and Expenses; Pub. 552, Recordkeeping for Individuals; Pub. 554, Tax Information for Older Americans; Pub. 555, Tax Information for Community Property; Pub. 556, Examination of Returns, Appeal Rights, and Claims for Refund; Pub. 557, Tax-exempt Status for Your Organization; Pub. 559, Tax Information for Survivors, Executors, and Administrators; Pub. 571, Tax Sheltered Annuity Programs for Employees of Public Schools and Certain Tax-exempt Organizations; Pub. 587, Business Use of Your Home; Pub. 589, Tax Information for S Corporations; Pub. 590, Individual Retirement Arrangements (IRAs); Pub. 596, Earned Income Credit; Pub. 721, Tax Guide to U.S. Civil Service Retirement Benefits; Pub. 907, Tax Information for Persons with Handicaps or Disabilities; Pub. 908, Bankruptcy and Other Debt Cancellation; Pub. 910, Guide to Free Tax Services; Pub. 915, Social Security Benefits and Equivalent Railroad Retirement Benefits; Pub. 926, Employment Taxes for Household Employers; Pub. 1192, Catalog of Reproducible Forms, Instructions, and Publications; Pub. 1345, Handbook for Electronic Filers of Individual Income Tax Returns; and Pub. 1388, Should You be Filing Information Returns?

1.2   42 USC Sec. 12101 (a)(1).
1.3   42 USC Sec. 12101 (a)(6). See also, "Willing and Able: Americans with Disabilities in the New Work Force," by K. Hopkins and S. Nestleroth, *Business Week* (Oct. 28, 1991), at pp. 64 and 70.
1.4   e.g., "Medical Expenses," by D. V. Burckel, Z. W. Daughtrey, and M. E. Bakke, 21 *Tax Adviser* 371 (June 1990).
2.1   IRC Sec. 1.
2.2   IRC Sec. 1 (f).
2.3   IRC Sec. 7703.
2.4   IRC Sec. 61.
2.5   IRC Sec. 86.
2.6   IRC Sec. 1 (i).
2.7   IRC Sec. 61 (a); Regs. Sec. 1.61-1 (a).
2.8   IRC Sec. 105.
2.9   e.g., Rev. Rul. 57-102 (payments under state blind pension fund excludable from income because provided under legislative program to promote the general welfare); Rev. Ruls. 70-341 and 79-173 (on Medicare); Rev. Rul. 75-246 (training payments under Comprehensive Employment and Training Act excludable if intended to facilitate training, but includable if provided as compensation for the performance of services). See also, Rev. Rul. 63-136 and Rev. Rul. 72-340. See generally, IRS Transmital 45-945-92 (7/29/92).
2.10   IRC Sec. 62 (a).
2.11   P.L. 99-514.
2.12   IRC Sec. 62 (a)(1 through 13).
2.13   IRC Sec. 162.
2.14   IRC Sec. 212.
2.15   IRC Sec. 67 (b).
2.16   IRC Sec. 62 (a)(9).
2.17   IRC Sec. 63 (c).
2.18   IRC Sec. 67 (d).
2.19   IRC Sec. 67 (b)(7); see also, IRS Publication 502 at p.12.
2.20   IRC Sec. 68 (c).
2.21   IRC Sec. 68 (a).
2.22   IRC Secs. 151-52.
2.23   IRC Sec. 151 (d)(3).
2.24   IRC Sec. 151.
2.25   IRC Sec. 44.
2.26   IRC Sec. 21.
2.27   IRC Sec. 22.
2.28   IRC Sec. 39; see also, IRC Sec. 38 (b)(2 and 7).
2.29   IRC Sec. 32.
2.30   IRC Sec. 86.
2.31   IRC Sec. 55.
2.32   Rev. Rul. 78-39; see also, IRS Pub. 502 at p. 2.
2.33   IRC Sec. 164.

2.34 Rev. Rul. 57-489; see also, IRS Pub. 502 at p. 11.

3.1   "The Demographics of Disability," by Mitchell P. Laplante, in *The Americans with Disabilities Act: From Policy to Practice,* edited by Jane West (New York: Milbank Memorial Fund, 1991), pp. 55–56.

3.2   P.L. 101-336, codified at 42 USC Sec. 12101 et seq.

3.3   42 USC Sec. 12102 (2)(A).

3.4   42 USC Sec. 12102 (2)(B and C).

3.5   42 USC Sec. 423 (d). See also, 42 USC Sec. 416 (i)(1).

3.6   29 USC Sec. 706 (8)(B).

3.7   29 USC Sec. 706 (8)(A). As of this writing (September, 1992), the Federal Rehabilitation Act is scheduled to expire on September 30. Legislation to reauthorize the Act for the period beginning October 1 is currently making its way through Congress. The reauthorization legislation is certain to be enacted, probably for a period of five years. However, the definitions and key terms used in the reauthorization may differ from those currently in effect. The organization of the statute may change as well.

3.8   P.L. 100-407, codified at 29 USC Sec. 2201 et seq.

3.9   29 USC Sec. 2202 (3).

3.10 IRC Sec. 21 (b).

3.11 IRC Sec. 22.

3.12 IRC Sec. 22 (e)(3).

3.13 IRC Sec. 72 (m)(7).

3.14 42 USC Sec. 423 (d)(4); 20 CFR Secss. 404.1510 and 404.1571-75).

3.15 42 USC Sec. 422 (c).

3.16 20 CFR Sec. 404.1576.

3.17 IRC Sec. 44, Added by P.L. 101-508, Sec. 11611(a).

3.18 IRC Sec. 190 (b)(3).

3.19 IRC Sec. 67 (d).

4.1   IRC Sec. 262.

4.2   29 USC Sec. 2202 (1). See also, 29 USC Sec. 2202 (2) for the definition of assistive technology services.

4.3   See generally, IRS Pub. 502 at pp. 4–13. This lengthy list of deductible items is not comprehensive. Some other deductible medical expenses include: Jso v. Comm'r., TC Memo 1980-399 (tribal medical healing ceremony); Crain v. Comm'r., TC Memo 1986-138 (deduction allowable for "holistic" care, but denied here because taxpayer failed to be specific as to the specific nature of care received); Beyers v. Comm'r., TC Memo 1979-353 (hand rails); Rev. Rul. 79-76 (lead paint removal to height that lead-poisoned child could reach, where recommended by physician and ordered by local authorities); Ltr. Rul. 8134069 (naturopathic herbal treatment for eye condition); and Rev. Rul. 64-267 (water fluoridation equipment when recommended by dentist).

4.4   Rev. Rul. 55-261; Rev. Rul. 68-295.

4.5   Rev. Rul. 71-48 and Rev. Rul. 73-53. See also, Ltr. Rul. 8250040 (medical deduction allowed for computerized visual alert system in home of deaf person).

4.6   Rev. Rul. 80-340.

4.7   Rev. Rul. 58-223.

4.8   Rev. Rul. 66-80; Rev. Rul. 70-606; Ltr. Rul. 8024169. Contrast, Robb v. Comm'r., TC Memo 1982-687 (deduction denied for installation of bed, sink, and toilet in van, where motivated by fact that taxpayer's wife found it difficult to travel in regular vehicle, and where no showing either that equipment was therapeutic or that van used primarily to facilitate obtaining medical care).

4.9   Ltr. Rul. 8033038.

4.10   CCH Standard Federal Tax Reporter Para. 12, 540.0122 (Chicago: Commerce Clearing House, 1992).

4.11   Rev. Rul. 75-318 (cost of braille books and magazines deductible to extent exceeding cost of print editions). Compare, Ltr. Rul. 8221118 (orthopedic shoes prescribed for individual with cerebral palsy deductible to extent cost exceeds that for normal shoes).

4.12   Rev. Rul. 62-189.

4.13   Rev. Rul. 58-155.

4.14   Womack v. Comm'r., TC Memo 1975-232.

4.15   Rev. Rul. 62-210.

4.16   Lepson v. Comm'r., TC Memo 1982-304.

4.17   Gerard v. Comm'r., 37 TC 826 (1962).

4.18   Lev. Rul. 55-261.

4.19   Riach v. Frank, 302 F. 2d 374, at 378 (9th Cir. 1962).

4.20   Pols v. Comm'r., TC Memo 1965-222.

4.21   Riach, note 4.19, supra. See also, Rev. Rul. 70-395 (installation of second bathroom allowed for individual who could not climb stairs).

4.22   Rev. Rul. 70-170.

4.23   Estate of Dodge v. Comm'r., TC Memo 1961-346; Bye v. Comm'r., TC Memo 1972-57. See also, IRS Pub. 502 at p. 10.

4.24   Kohen v. Comm'r., TC Memo 1982-625. Compare, Ltr. Rul. 8137085 (infant diapers normally not deductible since incident to care of healthy babies, but deduction for disposable diapers allowed where advanced age of incontinent child and need to avoid skin breakdown through use of absorbent material demonstrated medical need).

4.25   See generally, IRS Pub. 502 at p. 10.

4.26   See, Estate of Dodge v. Comm'r., TC Memo 1961-346 (payments to non-medically trained caregiver for taxpayer's wife who needed help in walking and in other tasks due to severe arthritis were deductible, where recommended by doctor on basis of risk of injury if wife attempted to move about alone); Ungar v. Comm'r., TC Memo 1963-159 (payments for care of taxpayer's mother who had suffered a stroke were deductible, though care provided in a private home rather than in an institution or hospital; and use of private home as substitute for nursing facility did not render the care a matter of family convenience but was permissible in light of resulting financial savings); Frier v. Comm'r., TC Memo 1971-84 (dressing, feeding, bathing, walking without a walker, and taking medication constituted nursing services for individual who had had a series of strokes); Rev. Rul. 75-317 (health care deduction allowed for costs of taking neighbor on out-of-town business trip to help with wheelchair, carrying bags, getting up and down stairs, and other tasks); Rev. Rul. 76-106 (medical deduction available for taxpayer who hired "attendant" for dressing, grooming, bathing, and postoperative care of ileostomy condition); and Estate of Marantz v. Comm'r., TC Memo 1979-463 (assistance in keeping clean, taking pills, moving about, and cooking amounted to more than companionship and qualified as medical expenses, but housework was not deductible). Contrast, McVicker v. U.S., 194 F. Supp. 607 (S.D.Calif. 1961) (though doctor recommended complete rest to prevent recurrence of tuberculosis, deduction for household services denied); Borgmann v. U.S., 438 F. 2d 1211 (9th Cir. 1971) (man who lived alone and on doctor's advice hired domestic servant after heart attack was not entitled to medical deduction, even though housekeeper had summoned emergency medical assistance on at least one occasion; services were not medical but for the comfort of the taxpayer); and Van Vechten v. Comm'r., TC Memo 1973-282 (medically documented need for complete rest did not justify deduction for domestic services; services were not provided directly to the sick person).

4.27   States with Medicaid home health care waiver programs would be particularly appropriate here. In cases where the family, though its income is low, is obliged to supplement the home services made available under the waiver program, such as by paying for more attendant time than the state authorizes, a plausible argument may be available that IRS should defer to the state's determination that these services are medical in nature.

4.28   Taylor v. Comm'r., TC Memo 1987-399. Compare, Ltr. Rul. 8112069 (deduction for one-time cost of replacing moldy shingles allowed where recommended by physician for treatment of nasal infections).

4.29   Ende v. Comm'r., TC Memo 1975-256.

4.30   Rev. Rul. 63-91. See also, Rev. Rul.82-111.

4.31   Rev. Rul. 58-66; Ross v. Comm'r., TC Memo 1972-122; Peveler v. Comm'r., TC Memo 1979-60.

4.32   Gerstacker v. Comm'r. of Internal Revenue, 414 F. 2d 548 (7th Cir. 1969). See also, Rev. Rul. 71-281. Compare, Levine v. Comm'r. of Internal Revenue, 695 F. 2d 57 (2d Cir. 1982), (attorney's fees for day-to-day management of taxpayer's son's affairs were not deductible, since lawyer's services were not required to obtain or legitimate the psychiatric care).

4.33   Rev. Rul. 57-489; Rev. Rul. 74-176. See also, Rev. Rul. 76-106 (for general allocation rules).

4.34   Rev. Rul. 76-106. See generally, IRS Pub. 502 at p. 10.

4.35   Ltr. Rul. 8034087. See also, Porter v. Comm'r., TC Memo 1986-70.

4.36   IRC Sec. 213 (d)(1)(B).

4.37   See e.g., Ltr. Rul. 8024155 (distinguishing deductible medical transportation from nondeductible medical travel).

4.38   IRC Sec. 213 (d)(2).

4.39   Regs. Sec. 170A-9 (b). See e.g., Ltr. Rul. 8321042.

4.40   The regulation defining hospitals has not been amended in well over a decade. When it was adopted, travel away from home for treatment in a facility other than a hospital was extremely difficult to justify. See, Ltr. Rul. 8335036. In light of the growth in outpatient facilities and outpatient procedures and services, the time may be right for efforts to secure a definition of the equivalent facility language that supports various nontraditional settings. Moreover, in-patient lodgings are typically more expensive than those in hotels, so requiring people to seek institutions with such facilities would drive the costs up for rehabilitative and other services. Finally, for someone learning new techniques and skills for living in the community, in-patient status may be medically contraindicated for a variety of reasons.

4.41   e.g., Rodgers v. Comm'r., 25 TC 254 (1955); Ltr. Ruls. 8024155 and 8335036.

4.42   Cohn v. Comm'r., 38 TC 387 (1963).

4.43   Rev. Rul. 78-39. See also, Rev. Rul. 78-173 and Granan v. Comm'r., 55 TC 753 (1971) (where taxpayer took out loan to pay medical expenses, deduction available only in near medical costs paid, even if loan repaid in subsequent year).

4.44   Ltr. Rul. 8102010.

4.45   Estes v. Comm'r., TC Memo 1984-636. See also, Cooper V. Comm'r., TC Memo 1987-334 (difficulty of determining amount reimbursed in light of interaction between multiple insurance policies with varying deductibles).

4.46   Strickland v. Comm'r., TC Memo 1984-301. On substantiation generally, see Regs. Sec. 1.213-1 (h). See also, DeSargent v. Comm'r., TC Memo 1986-393 (substitute documentation can be accepted); Teichner v. Comm'r. of Internal Revenue, 453 F. 2d 944 (2d Cir. 1972) (court can make its own estimate of costs).

4.47   e.g., Adler v. Comm'r. of Internal Revenue, 330 F. 2d 91 (9th Cir. 1964).

4.48   Cohan v. Comm'r. of Internal Revenue, 39 F. 2d 540 (2d Cir. 1930).

4.49   Friend v. Comm'r., TC Memo 1990-144.

4.50   IRC Sec. 151 (c).

5.1   P.L. 94-142.

5.2   20 USC Sec. 1400 et seq.

5.3   20 USC Sec. 1401 (a)(16).

5.4   20 USC Sec. 1401 (a)(17).

5.5   20 USC Sec. 1401 (a)(25).

5.6   Compare, e.g., Donovan v. Campbell, 61-1 USTC Para. 9357 (N.D.Tex. 1961) and Greisdorf v. Comm'r., 54 TC 1684 (1970) with Glaze v. Comm'r., TC Memo 1961-244 and Barnes v. Comm'r., TC Memo 1978-339. See also, Rev. Rul. 58-280.

5.7   e.g., Ripple v. Comm'r., 54 TC 1442 (1970); Ltr. Rul. 8401024; Ltr. Rul. 8445032.

5.8 Compare, Estate of Baer v. Comm'r., TC Memo 1967-34 with Grunwald v. Comm'r., 51 TC 108 (1968).

5.9 Compare, e.g., Fischer v. Comm'r., 50 TC 164 (1968) with Pascal v. Comm'r., TC Memo 1956-83.

5.10 Fay v. Comm'r., 76 TC 408 (1981) (language development); Sims v. Comm'r., TC Memo 1979-499 (psychological services); Rev. Rul. 69-607 (amounts paid for remedial reading training for child with dyslexia); Rev. Rul. 70-285 (transportation costs to regular school with special retardation curriculum); and Rev. Rul. 78-340 (amounts paid to teacher specially trained and qualified to deal with severe learning disabilities, if recommended by physician).

5.11 Fay, note 5.10, supra; Rev. Rul. 78-340.

5.12 Rev. Rul. 64-173.

5.13 For example, under the Pennsylvania Long-Term Loan Program, some 53% of equipment loans made during 1989-90 involved vocal output technology. See, VII(2) *Assistive Device News* at pp. 1–2 (Spring, 1991).

5.14 Baer, note 5.8, supra.

5.15 Compare, Reiff v. Comm'r., TC Memo 1974-20 with Rev. Rul. 69-607.

5.16 IRC Sec. 135. See also, IRS Notice 90-7, I.R.B. 1990-3 (for IRS guidance); and IRS Form 8815 (for calculation of exclusion).

5.17 IRC Sec. 163 (h)(3 and 5).

5.18 IRC Sec. 117.

5.19 Regs. Sec. 1.117-2 (b). This regulation lags behind the statute. Major statutory changes such as those enacted in 1986 have not been embodied in these regulations. As a result, there may be a number of statutory issues for nondegree-candidate students to consider before accepting the regulations at face value.

5.20 IRC Sec.127. Note that this section expired on June 30, 1992. See, P.L. 102-227, Sec. 103(a). Its reenactment is likely, but its provisions could be modified.

5.21 Regs. Sec. 1.162-5. Compare, Rev. Rul. 72-450 (bar review course not deductible because it prepared Marine Corps artillery officer to become legal officer, which would be a change of job) with Granger v. Comm'r., TC Memo 1980-60 (courses that enabled worker to progress in stages from personnel assistant to personnel administrator were deductible, since they did not qualify individual for a new trade or business). See also, Blair v. Comm'r., TC Memo 1980-488.

5.22 Regs. Sec. 1.162-5.

5.23 Ltr. Rul. 8950016. But see, Malek v Comm'r., TC Memo 1985-428 (fact that college degree was required by employer as a condition for job retention did not make costs deductible, where degree qualified individual to pursue various lines of work).

5.24 Regs. Sec. 1.162-5 (b); Ltr. Rul. 8747020.

5.25 IRC Sec. 67 (b).

5.26 IRC Sec. 67 (b)(7). See also, IRS Pub. 502 at p. 13; IRS Pub. 907 at pp. 23–24; House of Representatives Conference Report No. 99-841 (99th

Cong., Second Session, September 1986) at p. 2-34.

6.1   IRC Sec. 67 (d).

6.2   20 CFR Secs. 404.1576 (IRWEs under the SSDI program); 416.976 (IRWEs under the SSI program); and 416.984 (blind work expenses under SSI).

6.3   See, note 5.26, supra.

6.4   IRC Sec. 190 (b)(3).

6.5   Regs. Sec. 1.190-2 (a)(3).

6.6   IRS Pub. 907 at pp. 7–8.

6.7   By way of examples of costs that would qualify as IRWEs, it mentions reader costs, away from the office and outside of regular working hours, as an expense category that would meet the test. See, IRS Pub. 907 at p. 23.

6.8   See, House Conference Report, note 5.26, supra; House Rpt. 99-426 (99th Cong., First Session, December 1985); Senate Rpt. 99-313 (99th Cong., Second Session, May 1986).

6.9   IRC Sec. 162 (a); Regs. Sec. 1.162-5.

6.10   Regs. Sec. 1.162-7; see also, Regs. Sec. 1.62-2.

6.11   The IRS supports this interpretation by telling taxpayers to deduct IRWEs as business expenses if they are "for goods and services not required or used (other than incidentally) in your personal activities." See, Pub. 907 at p. 23.

6.12   IRC Sec. 67 (b).

6.13   IRC Sec. 280F (d)(3)(A).

6.14   Cadwallader v. Comm'r., TC Memo 1989-356, aff'd. 919 F. 2d 1273 (7th Cir. 1990).

6.15   IRC Sec. 162 (b).

6.16   IRC Secs. 167-68.

6.17   IRC Sec. 179 (b).

6.18   IRC Sec. 179 (b)(3)(A). To be eligible for expensing, the election to expense must also be made in the same tax year the item is placed in service. See, Sherwood v. Comm'r., TC Memo 1988-544.

6.19   IRC Sec. 179 (c); Prop. Regs. Sec. 1.179-2 (c)(5)(iv). See generally, Primuth v. Comm'r., 54 TC 374 (1970) (the leading case on the proposition that, for various purposes, employees can be considered as being in the business of being employed).

6.20   IRC Sec. 179 (b).

6.21   IRC Sec. 280F (d)(4)(A).

6.22   IRC Sec. 280F (b)(2); see also, IRC Sec. 179 (d)(10).

6.23   This is called the predominant use test. IRC Sec. 280F (b); e.g., Govier v. Comm'r., TC Memo 1990-611.

6.24   e.g., Minor v. Comm'r., TCM 1990-418 (business use of vehicle determined on yearly basis, not over life of car).

6.25   IRC Sec. 280F (d)(4)(A)(iv).

6.26   IRC Sec. 280F (d)(4)(B).

6.27   IRC Sec. 280F (d)(4)(B).

6.28   Rev. Rul. 75-316.

6.29   Rev. Rul. 58-382.

6.30   IRC Sec. 51.

6.31   IRC Sec. 51 (d)(1)(A and D).

6.32   IRC Sec. 51 (d)(2)(B).

6.33   P.L. 102-227, Sec. 105(a).

6.34   IRC Sec. 38.

6.35   IRC Sec. 44. A previous Sec. 44 having nothing to do with this subject was repealed in 1984.

6.36   The credit was part of a bill that became effective on November 5, 1990. The ADA was signed into law and became effective at a memorable White House ceremony on July 26.

6.37   IRC Sec. 44 (b).

6.38   IRC Sec. 44 (c)(2).

6.39   42 USC Sec. 12111 (5)(A) (25 employees until 1994).

6.40   42 USC Sec. 12111 (10).

6.41   29 CFR Sec. 1630.1 et seq.

6.42   IRC Sec. 190.

6.43   IRC Sec. 190 (b)(3).

6.44   IRC Sec. 21.

6.45   IRC Sec. 21 (c)(2). Compare, Rev. Rul. 83-1 (actual expenses eligible for the credit must be reduced by nontaxable childcare assistance from state social service agencies).

6.46   IRC Sec. 21 (b)(1)(B).

6.47   Webb v. Comm'r., TC Memo 1990-581.

6.48   Rev. Rul. 76-278.

6.49   See, IRC Sec. 280A (c)(1).

6.50   See, Solomon v. Comm'r. of Internal Revenue, 935 F. 2d 52 (4th Cir. 1991) (grant of home office deduction affirmed; Tax Court's use of a "facts and circumstances" of the case test approved). The IRS has appealed this case to the Supreme Court.

6.51   IRC Sec. 21 (d)(2).

6.52   IRC Sec. 21 (e)(7).

6.53   IRC Sec. 32.

6.54   IRC Sec. 32 (c)(3)(C)(iii).

6.55   See, IRC Sec. 125 (g)(2).

6.56   IRC Secs. 127 and 129.

6.57   IRC Sec. 125.

6.58   e.g., Ltr. Rul. 8919009 (joint request by employer and employee to determine eligibility under plan for childbirth classes). Remember, too, that many fringe benefit programs include "flexible spending" (or flex plans, as they are sometimes called) under which employees can set aside a certain number of pre-tax dollars for use in meeting costs not covered by insurance. With these funds, the employer's permission should not be required at all, but again, if the plan administrator is fearful, the fact that an expense would be medically deductible should serve to put all doubts at rest.

7.1   IRC Secs. 401 et seq.

7.2   IRC Sec. 72 (q)(1) (annuity contracts); (t)(1) (qualified retirement plans); and (v)(1) (modified endowment contracts).

7.3   IRC Sec. 72 (q)(2)(C), (t)(2)(A)(iii), and (v)(2)(B)

7.4   Unfortunately, elimination of regular tax does not result in waiver of the penalty. This 10 percent additional tax is due on the amount of the withdrawal that is includable in gross income, whatever one's taxable income ends up being.

7.5   e.g., Ltr. Rul. 9018047.

7.6   IRC Sec. 72 (q)(2)(D).

7.7   IRC Sec. 72 (t)(2)(B).

7.8   Of the seven exceptions to the additional tax, five appear not to apply to IRAs.

7.9   IRC Sec. 22 (b).

7.10   IRC Sec. 22 (b)(2).

7.11   IRC Sec. 22 (e)(3).

7.12   42 USC Sec. 12182 (b)(2).

7.13   So numerous have ADA resources and consultants become that obtaining information is now far less a problem than assuring its quality. Good starting points for those seeking information would include the ten Regional Disability and Business Technical Assistance Centers set up around the country under the auspices of the National Institute on Disability and Rehabilitation Research, and the ADA Communication Accommodations Project jointly established by the American Foundation for the Blind and the National Center for Law and the Deaf.

7.14   P.L. 101-508 Sec. 11611(a). See also, "Tax Incentives," by Daniel C. Schaffer in West, note 3.1, supra, at pp. 293–312.

7.15   Note 3.3, supra.

7.16   IRC Sec. 44 (c)(2).

7.17   42 USC Sec. 12102 (1).

7.18   IRC Sec. 44 (c)(4).

7.19   IRC Sec. 44 (c)(5) and (e). Compare, IRC Sec. 190 (b)(2) (same regulatory structure for the architectural and transportation barrier removal deduction).

7.20   IRC Sec. 38.

7.21   IRC Sec. 39. See also, Form 3800. The disabled access credit itself is claimed on Form 8826.

7.22   IRC Sec. 190 (b)(3).

7.23   Regs. Sec. 1.190-2 (a)(3).

7.24   Regs. Sec. 1.190-2 (b)(2 through 22). As an election on the tax return, the barrier removal deduction does not require any additional numbered form.

7.25   See, Regs. Sec. 1.190-3 (c).

7.26   Regs. Sec. 1.190-2 (a)(2).

7.27   ANSI Standard A117.1 (New York: American National Standards Institute, 1971).

7.28 Regs. Sec. 1.190-2 (b)(22).

7.29 TD7634 (7/19/79).

7.30 This Standard was last revised in 1986 but the Sec. 190 regulations do not reflect this updating. See, ANSI Standard A117.1 Buildings and Facilities - providing accessibility and usability for physically handicapped people (New York: American National Standards Institute, 1986). A further revision of this Standard (ANSI/CABO A117.1) is currently under review and is likely to be issued in the first half of 1993.

7.31 IRC Sec. 63 (f).

7.32 IRC Sec. 63 (f)(4).

7.33 See, Regs. Sec. 1.213-1 (c).

7.34 Rev. Rul. 70-395.

7.35 See, Regs. Sec. 1.213-1 (e).

7.36 Ltr. Rul. 8250040.

7.37 e.g., Rev. Rul. 83-33; Oliver v. Comm'r., 364 F. 2d 575 (8th Cir. 1966).

7.38 Rev. Rul. 87-106.

7.39 Rev. Rul. 83-33.

7.40 Compare, e.g., Cherry v. Comm'r., TC Memo 1983-470 (return of bronchial symptoms after several days nonuse of pool showed its therapeutic value); Polacsek v. Comm'r., TC Memo 1981-569 (fact that pool only four feet deep indicated its nonrecreational purpose); Evanoff v. Comm'r., TC Memo 1982-600 (lack of diving board or other amenities indicated therapeutic purpose); Haines v. Comm'r., 71 TC 644 (1979) (lack of special equipment factor in conclusion that pool lacked medical justification for treatment of broken leg).

7.41 42 USC Sec. 3601 et seq.

7.42 See, IRS Pub. 502 at p. 10.

7.43 IRC Sec. 121 (a)(2).

7.44 IRC Sec. 121 (d)(9)(A).

7.45 IRC Sec. 121 (d)(9)(B).

7.46 IRC Sec. 170.

7.47 IRC Sec. 170 (e)(3).

7.48 IRC Sec. 151 (c)(5).

7.49 IRC Sec. 22 (e)(3).

7.50 29 USC Sec. 795j.

7.51 29 USC Sec. 795.

7.52 Note 2.09, supra.

7.53 e.g., Rev. Rul. 57-102.

7.54 IRC Sec. 102.

7.55 IRC Sec. 217.

7.56 IRC Sec. 217 (c)(2) and (d)(1)(A).

7.57 IRC Sec. 217 (d)(1)(B).

8.1 "State Taxation and the Handicapped," by Russell V. Mobley (unpublished Master's thesis, University of Florida 1992) (analyzes in depth the tax laws of Alaska, Colorado, Connecticut, Florida, Georgia, Hawaii, Illinois, Louisiana, New York, and Texas). I am grateful to Mr. Mobley for the opportunity to share these research findings.

8.2   *State Sales Tax and Assistive Technology: Securing Exemptions for Sensory, Communication and Mobility Aids,* by Steven Mendelsohn (Washington: Electronic Industries Foundation/Rehabilitation Engineering Center 1990).), p. 190.

*I*ndex